INTENTIONAL MENTORING
MENTOR'S GUIDE

Dr. Kenneth D. Davis

INTENTIONAL MENTORING HANDBOOK

Copyright © 2022 Kenneth D. Davis
All rights reserved.

No part of this publication may be reproduced, transmitted, or stored in a retrieval system, in any form or by any means electronic, mechanical, photocopying, recording or otherwise, without the prior permission of the author. This book of curriculum is sole subject to the condition that it shall not, by way of trade or otherwise, be lent, re-sold, hired, or otherwise circulated without the auth's prior consent/permission in any form of binding other than that in which is published and without a similar condition including this condition being imposed on subsequent purchaser.

All scriptures quotations, unless otherwise noted, all scriptures are from the 21ST CENTURY KING JAMES VERSION of the Bible. Copyright© 1994 by Deuel Enterprises, Inc. Used by Permission. Scripture taken from the New King James Version®. Copyright © 1982 by Thomas Nelson. Used by permission. All rights reserved.

ISBN: 978-1-957551-04-3

Cover/Interior Design: Bledsoe Publishing Company LLC

Published by: Bledsoe Publishing Company LLC

Printed in the United States of America

TABLE OF CONTENTS

Note to the Reader v
Introduction vii
Pillar: Living 1
    Introduction/Living/Getting to Know You 6
    Reaching My Goals 23
    Developing Meaningful Relationships 44
    Legacy/Cultural EYE 52

Pillar: Loving 63
    Self-Love/Critical Thinking/Boundaries 68
    Love Begins in Me 87
    The Power of Giving 105
    The Community of Love 118

Pillar: Learning 131
    Career Vs. Job 137
    Social Media and Digital Responsibility 149
    Organization is Key 161
    Health and Well-being 174

Pillar: Laughing 187
    Laugh Therapy 191
    Anger Management 202
    Overcoming Stress and Anxiety 223
    Express Yourself 240

Pillar: Leading 257
    Leading Social Change 263
    Financial Literacy 280
    Character Development 298
    Lead by Example 308

Pillar: LEGACY 325
    Understanding Legacy 329
    Living your Legacy 338
    Creating a Legacy 351
    A Living Legacy 361

About the Author 375

Introduction

NOTE TO THE READER

Intentional Mentoring is one of those works that's close to my heart. I was mentored during several critical points in my life. My hope is that every child, young adult, and/or adult can learn, interact with, and experience a mentor-mentee relationship. Mentors are special people and are not paid for their passion (*I call it God's work*). This book provides the steps, the thinking, the planning, and the research to the effectiveness of mentoring, and shares what I learned while organizing, implementing, and overseeing the Mentoring Project. It provides you (the reader) with invaluable information and a snapshot of what it can do for your organization, if followed. It made a difference for me, and my hopes are… it will do the same for you.

LIVING life has been a challenge yet I'm LEARNING that LAUGHING and LOVING are free, easy, and provides opportunities that I could have missed. I've grown up in poverty, disadvantaged communities, and have had obstacles to overcome. Haven't we all! Yet if it had not been for my career in education, I would not have experienced being MENTORED as I continued my education while LEADING others. I've spent 31 years in education working to encourage, inspire, became a teacher and after many promotions eventually becoming an area superintendent. In my growth and aspirations, I'm working on LIVING THE LEGACY I want to leave and providing a blueprint of what a successful career can look like. Intentional Mentoring is the LIVING LEGACY I choose to leave you, my community, and the world as I strive to make life better for all mankind one mentor-mentee relationship at a time. It is the path I was created to take.

Dr. Kenneth D. Davis

The Pillars...

LIVING...
LOVING...
LEARNING...
LAUGHING...
LEADING...
LEGACY...

INTRODUCTION

Throughout the history of humanity, it has become apparent that humans learn better when they participate in peer-to-peer learning opportunities. Mentoring is another aspect of peer-to-peer learning that presents the mentee with the modeling of behavior that leads to successful outcomes and firsthand experiences by identifying the skills and tools exemplified in leaders. Mentoring has become a universal opportunity to build a sense of self, improve personal and/or professional development, create a supportive learning environment, open avenues for exposure to opportunities and possibilities previously unknown, and an emotional support system for both the mentor and the mentee. This is why schools, corporations and organizations have created mentoring programs where leadership mentor's frontline and subordinate employees and/or youth. In schools, it has become even more effective when mentees are paired with educators who share their same ethnic and cultural beliefs.

In every instance, a mentee – whether students in an educational setting or adults in the workplace – benefits from the guidance mentors offer to better understand their pathway when navigating life and gaining knowledge. This is an essential ingredient in their development of their sense of self and when moving towards their purpose as they prepare to make decisions regarding their long-term personal and professional goals. The trust relationship that is built between the mentor and mentee empowers mentees to create a ripple effect, where they become a mentor to a new class of mentees. They take what they learned and experienced as a mentee and create a relationship with their mentee that introduces the mentee to a whole new world of opportunities and possibilities. The effectiveness of mentoring is why 89% of those who were mentored give back and become mentors. (10 Compelling Facts About National Mentoring Month, July 7, 2021, https://halo.com/10-compelling-facts-about-national-mentoring-month/)

The need for mentoring programs has not diminished over time, but because of its benefits for both the mentor and mentee, it is in demand even more. Every mentoring relationship should be viewed as mutually beneficial to both the mentor and mentee as they both seek to become a better version of themselves. Their consistent and positive interactions give them the opportunity to view the world and situations through the other person's eyes. As we cover the six pillars, we will share how each can have a positive impact on the lives of the mentor and mentee, if used correctly to create a stable and sound foundation on which the mentoring relationship is built. Just like with everything else in life, a successful mentoring relationship will be designed with both the mentor's and mentee's individual and collective need to set boundaries, clarify expectations and participate in open communication. This opens the door for the mentee and mentor to take part in and benefit from a rewarding and highly effective mentoring experience.

Why does anyone need a mentor? Many have proclaimed it is because they need the guidance to see beyond their limitations to discover the opportunities and/or possibilities available to them that have the potential of changing their future for the better. Others have said it is because it gives mentees insight into a realm of knowledge that was unknown to them (the mentee) that they can now envision themselves doing and/or living. Tomorrow is not promised to anyone and by having a mentor, the mentee is provided with the needed information to develop a roadmap to live a better life than they believed was available to them especially in situations where the circumstances of their birth, and/or the cultural, racial and/or economic disparities dictates as their only options in life.

A mentor/mentee relationship has the potential of expounding the mentee's mindset from one of limitations, to one that is limitless. What was not considered available to him/her becomes a myriad of possibilities that springs from the mentee's belief that nothing is impossible to him/her. For the mentor, they can introduce the unexpected and the previously thought impossible to their mentee and are afforded the unique opportunity to view the world through their mentee's eyes.

To truly see and experience the mentee's life in a way that empowers them to offer hope where only despair and hopelessness existed, is the reality many mentors in youth-based programs experience. By preparing the mentee for what they may encounter and by training the mentor to introduce the human component into the following lessons, each mentor speaks to their mentee in a way that gives the mentee permission to take part in the conversations, learn the lessons, begin applying the lessons learned to their life, situation and/or circumstances and grow into who they now envision themselves as being. In turn, they become successful, contributing members of society who have learned the importance of reaching back into their community, company, or organization and sharing what they learned as a mentee as they begin their new adventure of being a mentor. Building upon what has been given, taught, and shared with them during their mentee experience.

Life is about living, loving, learning, laughing, leading, and leaving your legacy. Each mentor and mentee live a life that represents what is left behind that says I have lived, learned, shared, and touched lives to help them live their best life now, all while envisioning a world that offers opportunities and

Introduction

possibilities. The following lessons are structured to speak into both the heart, mind, and lives of the mentor and mentee to realize their greatest potential as they envision a life founded on hope and hard work. A life that gives them the permission to take the blinders off and release the scales from their eyes to see what's there openly and honestly, while being vulnerable to the experience so they both walk away with a greater understanding of self and the knowledge that nothing is impossible. One that says if I can believe and conceive it (visualize it) and will do the work, it can become my reality.

This mutually beneficial relationship will equip both the mentor and mentee for the next season in their lives which reminds them never to forget who they once were. To forget is to return to what was and to experience it again. However, growing and sharing the mentor's story of overcoming with others gives the mentees permission to experience the hope that helps others continue growing, living, learning, loving, leading, and living their legacy as well!

"Anyone can follow a strategy as they read about it but remembering to stick with it in the real world is tough." –James Clear

Pillar 1: Lesson Structure

1. Intro: Getting to Know You Activity
    1. Intro to Mentoring Program
        a. Mission Statement
        b. Review of 6 Pillars
    2. Social and Emotional Learning
        a. Self-Awareness
        b. Self-Management
        c. Mentor/Mentee Interactions

Activities:

1. Have mentees write down and repeat the mentoring program's mission statement. (Have mentors/mentees repeat it at the beginning of each session.) Find a way to make it relevant in the life of the mentor's and mentee's relationship.

2. Review the six pillars by using culturally, socially and/or professionally relevant examples

a. **Living**: Live every moment with a purpose (daily activities that are completed intentionally/purposefully, which are meant to help the mentee grow and have a better future).

b. **Loving**: Love beyond words (Love is an action word and is to be used to help people reach their greatest potential). No act of love is too big or too small.

c. **Learning**: Learning is a conscious decision to change a person's perspective, viewpoint of self, and their view of the world around them.

d. **Laughing**: Laughing finds amusement in a shared experience that connects humans in a profound way.

e. **Leading**: Leading is about serving others by utilizing their core values, personal and professional skills, and their genuine concern for people.

f. **Legacy**: Legacy is a living reflection of who you are, the legacy you desire to leave the world, and the greatest gift you give yourself, your family, the community, and the world.

To reiterate the point, have each mentor and mentee give an example of each pillar after learning what each one represents.

2. Social and Emotional Learning
    a) Self-Awareness:

    Self-Awareness is having a strong understanding of oneself. It includes understanding our thoughts, emotions, strengths, challenges, needs, and dreams for the future. Self-Awareness is important for children and youth because it sets the stage for success. It also means being aware of and/or able to reorganize how other people see you. (*Teaching Self Awareness, www.positiveaction.com*)

    SUGGESTED LESSONS:

    1. How to Identify Your Emotions

    Help the mentee identify the difference between frustration and anger through (role play). Help the mentee recognize the link between their feelings, thoughts, and actions. This helps them learn how to address their feelings and respond to them appropriately.

Introduction

Encourage mentees to respond to life happening moments and/or situations instead of reacting to them. "Responding is a spinoff from the word responsibility and is considerate and deliberate. Whereas reacting literally means to meet an action with another unplanned or thought-out action. It is immediate and rash. (A Simple Formula for Responding Not Reacting – The Growth Equation, https://thegrowtheq.com)

a. Reactions are instinctive.

b. Responses require thought and planning.

c. Discuss the Thought – Action – Feelings Circle. It is integral to our social and emotional curriculum, and in ensuring the mentee understands they can change the circumstances they experience based upon the choices/decisions they make. Dr. Phil said, *"when you choose the behavior, you also choose the consequence."* It has the capability of depicting how the mentee's thoughts lead to their words and their words lead to actions which lead to their feelings, which starts the process all over again. Ultimately showing their character and their available destiny.

- Describe situations the mentee might find themselves.
- Discuss how those situations might make them feel, how and what they might think, and how they might act based on those thoughts and feelings.

2. See yourself honestly.

Teaching your mentees to look at themselves honestly can help them respond to compliments, feedback, and criticism openly and earnestly. This sense of self will enable them to see and acknowledge both the positive and negative aspects of their character.

a. Create Goals and Steps to Complete them.

Completing/Attaining their goals gives the mentee successes to celebrate, thereby fortifying their belief in themselves.

- Have mentees create and write down 3-5 realistic goals and what steps they need to take to attain the goals. They will learn and understand that self-love and growth are positive activities that lead to healthy and happy people with a drive to achieve.

3. Recognize your Strengths and Weaknesses

   Your mentee's ability to see themselves, acknowledge their shortcomings, and embrace their strengths is a great confidence booster. It reiterates that it is okay to admit they are wrong or don't understand something, it sets them up for continued growth. Acknowledging aptitude also builds confidence.

   - Use your strengths. Go through the process of helping your mentee to identify their strengths. The act of identifying things that your mentee is good at reinforces a positive self-image. Keep in mind that working to improve their strengths builds self-confidence, setting them up for continued and future success.

b) Self-Management

This ties into some of what was discussed with self-awareness.

1. Self-Management is the ability to not only identify but regulate emotions, thoughts, and actions. It includes responsible decision-making that supports the ability to make positive choices about the mentor's and mentee's behavior.

2. Behavior Monitoring

   Behavior Monitoring occurs when both mentors and mentees observe and record their behaviors, redirecting themselves whenever necessary to ensure the consequence is positive.

   a.) Self-Reinforcement is the act of rewarding oneself after completing the desired behavior or meeting a goal. Rewarding positive behavior increases the likelihood the mentee will repeat that behavior. (*Teaching Self-Management Skills: 5 Strategies to Create an Effective Plan,* www.positiveaction.net (blog))
   - According to Psychology Today, 85% of people who don't learn self-reinforcement have trouble in other areas, like self-esteem. Rewards can be anything that is healthy and motivates the mentee to act positively and/or reinforce positive behaviors.

c) Mentor/Mentee Interactions

1. Identify ways mentors and mentees can communicate. Establish the modes of communication the mentor and mentee will use.

2. In positive conflict, ideally, you can verbalize your needs and wants and mutually work out mutually beneficial compromises. The rule that all individuals agree to and operate in during the course of the mentor-mentee relationship defines expectations (Rules of Engagement) that are important in your mentor-mentee relationship which creates a sense of safety. Rules of Engagement are the internal rules and procedures created to deal with unique circumstances and dedicate situations that require actions with significant consequences.

3. Mentors are encouraged to be innovative and creative when getting to know each other. The mentor should find ways to connect with their mentee to help build a trusting and respectful relationship. It is important they learn about each other. Especially those things that show their uniqueness.

4. Be reliable, consistent, and positive. Be present at each scheduled meeting in both mind and body. Pay attention to the mentee and their accomplishments and failures. Share constructive criticism and praise whenever necessary. Remember to always build the mentee up and allow them to recognize the good they have done, their wrongdoings, and seek to change any negative behavior. (*Ten tips for a Successful Mentor-Mentee Relationship*, www.amtamassage.org)

PILLAR:

LIVING

PILLAR: LIVING

I was listening to a daily meditation that said, *"Every problem is a gift! Without problems, we would not grow!"* That immediately made me think about mentoring. Why? Because mentoring is an answer to a societal, community, cultural and/or economic problem. It speaks to the lack that is represented in our world, and by implementing a viable mentoring program, the organizers can offer both hope and an answer to each participant's life's question.

Humanity is designed to be in relationship with and to interact with each other. To interact, live and/or experience life as a community and not alone. In this pillar, both the mentor and mentee will learn the importance of living and not merely existing. While implementing and overseeing the Mentoring Project, I witnessed firsthand how the mentor-mentee relationship gave the mentee permission to live and see life beyond the limitations that initially restricted their belief system, value their view of the world and recognize what was available to them.

The mentee was not only able to visualize a different future for themselves, but to begin speaking out loud the life they desire. Sometimes, they saw themselves as doctors, lawyers and/or educators instead of only athletes who uses sports to save them from a dying community and/or culture. Mentees will learn from their mentor that *"Your life is a physical manifestation of what is going on in your mind's eye"* – Unknown. Instead of dying in the streets of the community they were born or raised in, the mentee now can see the opportunities and possibilities available to them. In corporate America, the low-level employee could go from hating their job and struggling to barely put food on the table and barely pay their bills to preparing a roadmap for their future that equips and prepares them to follow their dreams or do something that makes their job exciting and beneficial. All while affording them the opportunity to make a salary conducive to their skills and abilities.

I know you are saying how can I have that component in my mentoring program. You begin with identifying the various limiting beliefs the mentees you will serve carry in their hearts and minds through group discussions, surveys and/or activities/exercises designed to get them to open up and share. Which showcases the need for the program administrator to train the mentors on how to be culturally sensitive and understand how to recognize their biases to ensure they do not negatively impact the mentor-mentee relationship. Train the mentors on the components of open communication and encourage him/her to have open and informative dialogue with their mentee to derive the information they need while the mentee feels safe sharing with the certainty they will be seen or heard.

In most cases, life looks significantly different in the mentor's life than that of the mentee! The differences may be seen in how they live their lives, culturally, economically, racially, etc. Statistically a Caucasian living in the same house design in a predominantly white/Caucasian community property value is 37% higher than one in a predominantly black or community of color. Which in turn, affects the amount of property taxes collected and money available to fund schools and other social services. Thereby, negatively impacting black communities and those of color ensuring there's a distinct difference in the resources and opportunities available to them.

Although these differences and disparities are a part of life, if both the mentor, and mentee are committed to building a strong and respectful mentoring relationship, together they can work through any biases that may be present in both of their lives and viewpoints on life. In 2020 – 2021, there were protests, rallies, and speeches to bring the necessary people to the table to begin the conversations that can impact the lives and lifestyles of many people culturally, racially, and economically. It is in these settings that plans can be made to make conditions better and that promise to bring some equity to the equation that has been in place and is a part of the fabric of America.

The mindset of each of these individuals must change to ensure the conversations become a plan that is implemented. I share that to say the same thing needs to occur during the development of your mentoring program and in designing the lessons that will be the tool you used to effect change and offer hope to both the mentor and mentee who participates in your program. By having the conversations with a cross section of the community you want to impact, you will have the information necessary to impact their lives.

This pillar on living humanizes and puts a face to all races, their lifestyles, and the conditions in which ALL people live. This lesson should help the participants to become more aware of the racial, economic, and cultural disparities people endure daily and become sensitive to them while determining the best way to offer hope and introduce opportunities and possibilities that may not have been considered because the mentee could not see past their current living conditions and personal limitations.

Pillar: Living

According to Sunshine Parenting, there are "*5 Ways to Teach Kids to Live Life Well,*" (www.Sunshine-Parenting.com):

1. ***Unplug for a while each day***. Whereas the article talked about unplugging from social media. I challenge you to take that a step further. Create activities and/or experiences where the mentee can unplug from their communities, daily limitations, homelife, etc. Provide them with time to experience something different and debrief. During your debriefing time, ask questions to understand how the experience or activity impacted the mentee. This will help to widen their knowledge base while exposing the mentee to experiences and activities they never saw themselves doing or participating in.

2. ***Interact with Others***. This step encourages the mentees to maintain, nurture and build relationships. The mentee is to make it a priority to regularly communicate with friends, family and/or loved ones. As well as participate in activities that will encourage them to build new relationships. According to "*Health Benefits of Social Interactions*" (www.mercycare.org), "*spending quality time with friends, loved ones and/or others can lighten their mood and disposition* (better mental health), *lower the risk of dementia* (encourage good brain health), *promote a sense of safety, belonging and security and/or provides you with resources to share confidences.*"

Let's take this a step forward and teach the mentee how to make new connections, how to handle themselves when meeting new people, and/or how to build relationships that will equip them with the tools, connections and/or relationships to rise out of their current situations that are steppingstones that have the potential of becoming lifelong friends.

Corporate America is moving away from the boardroom to closing business deals during dinner or when out having fun. With that in mind, teaching mentors and mentees how to conduct themselves and the proper dining etiquette during a business dinner may help relieve some of the nervousness and give them more confidence to secure the job or close the deal. By ensuring they have the skills that are needed when going after business ownership or corporate jobs is imperative, especially when those skills aren't used in their daily life and activities in their current community. Mentoring can expose the mentee to what is possible based upon what they aspire to be or do. Then create an opportunity to use what they have learned. The experience can be life changing.

3. ***Take Care of You*** (your mind, body, and soul). Today, more people are sitting and are isolated from working remotely while completing their daily duties on a computer or for students in the physical or virtual classroom. Your physical health is just as important to maintain as maintaining your mental health. Create an atmosphere where it is safe for the mentee and mentor to move through exercises, dance, etc. Something that will get them up and moving around. Find out what kind of dance your mentees are interested in and have someone to come in and teach them a routine. Then create an opportunity for them to perform it. This builds confidence, self-esteem, and encourages them to try new things. Even for those who have 2 left feet, help them find their spot in the production and/or planning. Whatever you decide, be sure and have them up and moving together, both the mentee and mentor. This will not only improve their health but release those much-needed endorphins to overcome obstacles they encounter in life.

4. ***Learn to manage your time and priorities***. As I mentioned previously, time is our most valuable asset, or commodity. Learning how to use it will help with eliminating anxiety and feelings of being overwhelmed. I challenge you to have exercises and/or activities that teach organizational and time management skills. As a part of the exercise or activity, teach the importance of taking breaks while studying and/or working. It gives the brain time to refresh. This is also a time to get up and move around to kick off those endorphins to help you remain focused and on task.

    This may also be a time to introduce meditation and/or visualization. Our thoughts form the life we lead and as such we need to show the mentee, the importance of visualizing themselves living the life they want, doing the job or having the career they want and/or running their business. The mind is the core engine that manifests the story each person tells themself. Through visualization, the person can change the narrative based upon the new information they have and visualize themselves being successful while living their best life. Teach them how to create their individual life and stay on track to manifest what they visualized into their reality.

5. ***Figure out what you like***. Seldomly do people have time to figure out what they want or like. We can more readily tell what we do not want rather than to state what we want. In school and on the job, we are told what to do and if we want this or that what we need or should be

doing. Following this process does not teach anyone how to identify those things they believe will bring them happiness and/or ignite the drive to live their best life now. Look for different scenarios, activities, or experiences to help the mentee discover what he/she is passionate about. Give them an opportunity to experience the various hobbies to determine which one they are good at or interested in. This will help them live "...*thriving, vibrant, happy lives.*" And helps them flourish in the moment, and everyday thereafter.

Give yourself permission to think outside of societal lines and norms. Introduce mentees to the beauty within their community and outside of their communities. If you find graffiti that inspires and that has brought their community together, even if it was because of tragedy. Take them on a field trip to a small art studio or museum that showcases art from today's up and coming artists. If possible, have the artist visit your group of mentees to share their story and their art. Give them an opportunity to see that everyone's story matters and how they tell it indicates where their passion lies.

This can spark conversations that divulge the mental and emotional story the mentee tells him/herself to give the mentor further insight into how to reach, communicate, and inspire their mentee. The greatest life lessons are taught and learned outside of the classroom. Once again, give yourself permission to be creative to show both the mentor and mentee the importance of living a life that empowers and enables them to show up in their own life!

Intentional Mentoring Mentor's Guide

LESSON TITLE:

Introduction/Living/Getting to Know You

LEVEL: Youth

WEEKS 1-2

PACING: 55 min

OBJECTIVE(S): What will participants know, understand, and be able to do?
- The mentee will learn about the mentoring program through program's mission/vision statement and the 6 pillars.
- Mentor will spend time getting to know their mentee.

KEY VOCABULARY: What key terms will my participants need to understand?

MENTORING Creed: 6 MENTORING Pillars:

Live- *every moment with a purpose*

Love- *beyond words*

Learn- *something new every day*

Laugh- *with no regrets*

Lead- *to inspire others*

Legacy- *live your legacy*

WEEK 1

LESSON CYCLE:

1. Engage and Connect **(15 min)**

The facilitator/mentor will introduce the mentoring program to the participants using the mentoring program presentation. (Note: Develop your own mentoring program presentation to be used to train mentors and mentees. Every program's presentation should be unique to their program.)

2. Lead Guided and Independent Practice **(25 min)**

Activity 1: The facilitator/mentor will facilitate *"Two Truths and a Lie"* with the mentees. Volunteers can attempt to stump the mentor and other MENTORING participants.

Activity 2: The facilitator/mentor and participants can interview the participants/volunteers from the provided list of questions. Allow participants the opportunity to ask their own questions.

3. Close the Lesson and Assess Mastery **(15 min)**

The facilitator/mentor will close out the lesson with MENTORING pillars and allow participants to ask questions about the Mentoring Program. The participants will list 1-2 things they are excited about during their mentoring experience. (Note: All lessons can be facilitated using any of the available conferencing platforms.)

LOGISTICS: What materials, resources, and technology will I need to prepare and engage?

MENTORING Participant PowerPoint
Computer/Projector
Participant Agreement Form/Journal Pages
"Two truths and a lie" Activity

WEEK 2

LESSON CYCLE:

1. Engage and Connect (15 min)

The facilitator/mentor will have the participants recite the MENTORING Creed as listed above. The facilitator/mentor will recite a quote from Dr. Seuss: *"Today you are you! That is truer than true! There is no one alive who is you-er than you!"*

Discussion Question: What does this quote mean to you? Allow the participants time to think and share.

2. Lead Guided and Independent Practice (25 min)

The facilitator/mentor will guide participants in a discussion on the importance of building healthy relationships. Facilitator/Mentor will explain to the participants the role of the mentor/mentees. The facilitator/mentor will provide examples of how a mentor has supported them in the past. Lead the *"Get to Know Me"* activity in the Mentee Workbook.

3. Close the Lesson and Assess Mastery (15 min)

The facilitator/mentee will complete the *"Get to Know Me"* graphic organizer activity. (Facilitator/Mentor is to verify the activity is completed and check the lesson off on the Mentor's tracker.) (Virtual option: Participants can show their completed activity to the facilitator/mentor via their camera.)

LOGISTICS: What materials, resources, and technology will I need to prepare and engage?

MENTORING Participant PowerPoint
Computer/Projector
"Get to Know Me" Graphic Organizer Activity
"Let me introduce myself…" Activity Sheet
Journal Pages

LESSON VOCABULARY WORDS

INSTRUCTIONS: Study the vocabulary words listed below for a good understanding of each one.

MENTORING Creed: 6 MENTORING Pillars:

1. *Live-* every moment with a purpose
2. *Love-* beyond words
3. *Learn-* something new every day
4. *Laugh-* with no regrets
5. *Lead-* to inspire others
6. *Legacy-* live your legacy

Discussion Topic: Quote from Dr. Seuss: *"Today you are you! That is truer than true! There is no one alive who is you-er than you!"*

Question: What does this quote mean to you?

_____

_____

_____

_____

_____

_____

_____

_____

_____

_____

Pillar: Living

ACTIVITY: TWO TRUTHS AND A LIE

In this activity, every person says three things about themselves, but two of the statements must be true and one must be a lie. The goal of the game is for the rest of the group to guess which statement is false. For example, you might say, "I play the guitar, I've never been on a plane, and I can't swim." The group must then guess which of those statements is a lie. The great thing about Two Truths and a Lie is that everyone gets to learn something new about each other while still having fun and building problem-solving skills.

Let me introduce myself...

Graphic Organizer Activity

Favorites

COLOR: ....
MOVIE: ....
FOOD: ....
CELEBRITY: ....
SUBJECT: ....
HOBBY: ....
SPORT: ....
MUSIC: ....

Favorite Summer Memory
....
....
....
....

SELF PORTRAIT

Birthday _____

Grade _____

Siblings _____
_____
_____
_____

the best book I read:
_____
_____
_____

Pets

What makes me unique?
_____
_____
_____

Biggest Accomplishment
_____
_____
_____
_____
_____
_____

What makes a good teacher?

My future plans are...
_____
_____
_____

3 Words that describe me...
1. _____
2. _____
3. _____

CREATIVE SOCIAL SKILLS ACTIVITIES FOR YOUTH

(https://teens.lovetoknow.com/creative-social-skills-activities-teens-tweens)

The following are social skills activities for youth. The best way for youth to learn social skills are from real-life experiences. Remain mindful and astute for ways to make the activities relevant for youth.

STRESS REDUCTION CIRCUIT

Youth are encouraged to explore different stress reduction techniques to find out which is most calming in this activity. Learning how to calm yourself down in stressful situations or conversations is a vital social skill. Use the happiness pyramid to measure your results.

1. Find five images of various stages of happiness or write those stages on a piece of paper.
2. Choose 3 to 5 calming techniques like drawing, listening to music, yoga, counting backward from 10, deep breathing exercises, running, or playing basketball.
3. Set up a "station" for each of your chosen calming techniques.
4. Write down something that stresses the youth out or makes them frustrated. Write down which stage of happiness from the pyramid this thing makes the youth feel.
5. Spend about five minutes doing one of the youth's chosen calming techniques. When time is up, use the happiness pyramid to write down what stage the youth is at.
6. Repeat Step 5 with each calming technique.
7. Which calming technique made them feel the happiest? How could the youth use this knowledge to help him/her deal with stressful interactions in real life?

Which one made you feel the happiest? How could you use this knowledge to help you deal with stressful interactions in real life?

NONVERBAL TELEPHONE

Middle schoolers can practice using and understanding nonverbal communication with this twist on the classic talking game Telephone. This also serves as a good activity for practicing being attentive. You'll need a small group to play this game, but you could adapt it for just two people to be more like Charades.

1. Write a bunch of emotions on slips of paper and put them in a bowl. Emotions include angry, excited, tired, and grumpy.
2. Stand everyone in a line so you're all facing the same direction. You should be facing the back of the person in front of you.
3. The person at the back of the line will secretly draw one emotion.
4. The person at the back of the line will tap the person in front of them. This person should turn around to face whoever tapped them.
5. The person who tapped will use 3 nonverbal clues to show their emotion, then the person they tapped will turn back around.

6. Each successive player repeats Steps 4 and 5. They must try to use the same or similar nonverbal cues the person before them used.
7. The last person will try to guess the emotion after they see the clues.

You can play as many rounds as you want, drawing a new emotion and starting with a new player each time.

EMAIL MADNESS

Help participants make quick decisions about personal versus professional communication with a quick email activity. Make sure the participants have your email address before the activity begins.

1. Each participant will need an electronic device capable of sending email in real time.
2. You should also have your email account open on a separate device.
3. Call out a recipient and subject such as "*Dr. Brown, homeopathic suggestions for a headache,*" or "*Grandma, planning Easter.*"
4. Give participants five minutes to craft and send you an email that fits the scenario you called out.
5. At the end of five minutes, call out another scenario. Ask participants to "*reply*" to the previous email they sent you for each round so all their answers are in one email thread.
6. Repeat this as many times as you want.
7. Together, look at the emails they sent. What major or minor changes were made based on the recipient and/or the subject?

TAKE A VIRTUAL ART TOUR

Some benefits of art activities include being assertive, sharing opinions, networking, seeing different perspectives, and networking. In this activity, you'll want a small group of people so everyone can critique and discuss works of art. The goal is to share real opinions and feelings while being respectful of each other's opinions.

1. Find a virtual tour (https://travel.lovetoknow.com/world-travel-destinations/50-free-virtual-tours-unique-famous-places) of an art museum on their website or YouTube.
2. Stop at each piece of art and share commentary on it. How does it make you feel? Do you like it? What does it look like to you?
3. Discuss the differences in your opinions and feelings on each work of art.

Pillar: Living

QUESTIONS THAT MENTORS CAN ASK THEIR MENTEES

1. Tell me the 5 best things about you?
2. If you could have the following superpower, which one would you pick? (The ability to fly, Super Strength, or can turn invisible)
3. If you were trapped on a deserted island and could pick on famous person to be with, who would it be?
4. If you could tell your parents to never serve two vegetables again, which would you choose?
5. Who do you think your mother would prefer you to become: An NBA ballplayer, the mayor, a famous explorer, or a movie star? Why? Which would you prefer?
6. Which of your friends do you like the most? Why?
7. If a genie could grant you any 3 wishes, what would they be?
8. What profession do you want to be when you're older?
9. Who was the best teacher you ever had? Tell me why?
10. What would the ideal teacher be like?
11. What college would you like to attend?
12. How much privacy would you like? What time of the day would like to be alone, and why?
13. If you are feeling sad, what meal would be the one that would cheer you up?
14. Do you believe men and women are equally smart? Why or why not?
15. Do you ever have a dream that comes back over and over? If so, what is it like?
16. Is there anything you pretend you understand, but you really don't? What is it?
17. Name the 3 movie stars you most admire
18. Have you ever imitated something you saw in a movie? What was it?
19. Are you afraid to fly?
20. Tell me who you think are the 3 greatest musicians in the world? Why? (Living or dead.)
21. If you could change 3 things about yourself, what would they be?
22. If you could keep your room anyway you wanted, how would it look?
23. If you could visit any place in the world, where would it be?
24. What is the most enjoyable thing your family has done together in the last three years?
25. What are the qualities that make a good friend?

(https://resources.finalsite.net/images/v1526099357/springbranchisdcom/nr4wqrwigifzmykvizot/80QuestionsMentorscanaskthierMentees.pdf)

QUESTIONS MENTEES CAN ASK THEIR MENTORS

1. Why did you decide to be a mentor?
2. What are your goals for the relationship?
3. I'm keen to get your input on my goals for this mentorship. Can we review them together?
4. How often do you want to meet?
5. What's your preferred method of communication?
6. How can I better prepare for our meetings?
7. What are your goals for this relationship?
8. Where do you see yourself in 3-5 years?
9. What are your greatest challenges right now?
10. What part of your job most excites you?
11. What motivates you?
12. How are you feeling?
13. What are you excited about right now?
14. What's new since we last spoke?
15. How are you staying motivated?
16. What's a goal you're currently working towards?
17. What's going on outside of work in your life?
18. If someone was writing the story of your career, what would you want it to be?
19. Do you have any advice on how I can approach discussions about a promotion?
20. I feel like I'm being pigeonholed at work right now and would like to try some new things. In your experience, what's the best way to approach this?
21. If you were me, how would you have approached X situation?
22. Do you think I should accept this new job offer?
23. My salary isn't in line with what my peers are making. How do I ask for more?
24. What skills would be beneficial for me to work on?
25. Where do you think I can improve?
26. What could I have done differently in this specific situation that may have improved the outcome?
27. Do you have any recommendations for professional development courses?

https://www.togetherplatform.com/blog/29-questions-to-ask-your-mentor-in-your-next-meeting

Pillar: Living

LESSON TITLE:

Introduction/Getting to Know You

OBJECTIVE(S): What will participants know, understand, and be able to do?

- The mentee will learn about the mentoring program through its mission/vision statement and 6 pillars.

- Mentor will spend time getting to know their mentee.

LEVEL: Employee or Community Citizen

WEEKS 1-2

PACING: 55 min

KEY VOCABULARY: What key terms will my participants need to understand?

MENTORING Creed: 6 MENTORING Pillars:

Live- every moment with a purpose

Love- beyond words

Learn- something new every day

Laugh- with no regrets

Lead- to inspire others

Legacy- live your legacy

WEEK 1

LESSON CYCLE:

1. Engage and Connect (15 min)

The facilitator/mentor will introduce the mentoring program to the participants using the mentoring program presentation. (Note: Develop your own mentoring program presentation to be used to train mentors and mentees. Every program's presentation should be unique to their program).

2. Lead Guided and Independent Practice (25 min)

Activity 1: The facilitator/mentor will facilitate the *"Skills"* Activity with the mentees. Facilitator/Mentor/Volunteer can ask each mentee what talent or skill they would like to improve or develop.

Activity 2: The facilitator/mentor will facilitate *"10 Things in Common"* Activity. Have each mentee pair up with another mentee and have each pair identify 10 things they have in common with one another.

3. Close the Lesson and Assess Mastery (15 min)

The facilitator will close out the lesson with MENTORING protocols and allow participants to ask questions about the Mentoring Program. The participants will list 1-2 things they are excited about during their mentoring experience. (Virtual option: Participants can type their responses in Microsoft Teams).

LOGISTICS: What materials, resources, and technology will I need to prepare and engage?

MENTORING Participant PowerPoint
Computer/Projector
"Skills" Activity

"10 Things in Common" Activity

WEEK 2

LESSON CYCLE:

1. Engage and Connect **(15 min)**

Have the participants recite the MENTORING Creed. The facilitator will recite a quote from Dr. Seuss: *"Today you are you! That is truer than true! There is no one alive who is you-er than you!"*

What does this quote mean to you? Allow the participants time to think and share.

2. Lead Guided and Independent Practice **(25 min)**

The mentee will complete the *"Get to Know Me"* graphic organizer activity. (Facilitator/Mentor is to verify the activity was completed and check the lesson off on the Mentor's tracker.) (Virtual option: Participants can show their completed activity to the facilitator/mentor via their camera.)

3. Close the Lesson and Assess Mastery **(15 min)**

The mentee will complete the *"Get to Know Me"* graphic organizer and submit to the Program Manager.

LOGISTICS: What materials, resources, and technology will I need to prepare and engage?

MENTORING Participant PowerPoint
Computer
Projector
"Get to Know Me" graphic organizer activity

Pillar: Living

LESSON VOCABULARY WORDS

INSTRUCTIONS: Review vocabulary words listed below with the participants to ensure they have a good understanding of each before starting any of the activities.

MENTORING Creed: 6 MENTORING Pillars:

1. **Live-** *every moment with a purpose*
2. **Love-** *beyond words*
3. **Learn-** *something new every day*
4. **Laugh-** *with no regrets*
5. **Lead-** *to inspire others*
6. **Legacy-** *live your legacy*

Discussion Topic: Quote from Dr. Seuss: *"Today you are you! That is truer than true! There is no one alive who is you-er than you!"*

Question: What does this quote mean to you?

_____

_____

_____

_____

_____

_____

_____

_____

_____

ACTIVITY: TWO TRUTHS AND A LIE

In this activity, every person says three things about themselves, but two of the statements must be true and one must be a lie. The goal of the game is for the rest of the group to guess which statement is false. For example, you might say, "I play the guitar, I've never been on a plane, and I can't swim." The group must then guess which of those statements is a lie. The great thing about Two Truths and a Lie is that everyone gets to learn something new about each other while still having fun and building problem-solving skills.

Pillar: Living

SUGGESTED QUESTIONS MENTORS CAN ASK THEIR MENTEES

1. What does success look like to you?
2. What obstacles do you see that might prevent you from achieving success?
3. Where do you see yourself in five years?
4. What do you hope to gain from our mentoring sessions?
5. What is an obstacle you're currently facing?
6. What are some things that you can control?
7. If you could learn any new professional skill, what would it be? Why?
8. Have you ever quit a job? If so, why?
9. Who do you talk to about challenges and successes at your job?
10. What are your short-term goals?
11. What are your long-term goals?
12. What's working in your career? What strides are you making? What accolades have you received?
13. What's not working in your life/career? Explain your answer.
14. What ideas have you developed to help you overcome challenges and meet your goals?
15. What areas do you feel comfortable addressing in your life/career on your own and what areas do you require more support?
16. Who are you? Who do people say you are?
17. What are your favorite things to do to relax or take a break?
18. Name the 3 movie stars you most admire?
19. Have you ever imitated something you saw in a movie? What was it?
20. Are you afraid to fly?
21. Tell me who you think are the 3 greatest musicians in the world? Why? (Living or dead.)
22. If you could change 3 things about yourself, what would they be?
23. If you could visit any place in the world, where would it be?
24. Who is your best friend? Why?
25. What are the qualities that make a good friend?

https://fairygodboss.com/career-topics/questions-to-ask-a-mentee

SUGGESTED QUESTIONS MENTEES CAN ASK THEIR MENTORS

1. Why did you decide to be a mentor?
2. What are your goals for the relationship?
3. I'm keen to get your input on my goals for this mentorship. Can we review them together?
4. How often do you want to meet?
5. What's your preferred method of communication?
6. How can I better prepare for our meetings?
7. What are your goals for this relationship?
8. Where do you see yourself in 3-5 years?
9. What are your greatest challenges right now?
10. What part of your job most excites you?
11. What motivates you?
12. How are you feeling?
13. What are you excited about right now?
14. What's new since we last spoke?
15. How are you staying motivated?
16. What's a goal you're currently working towards?
17. What's going on outside of work in your life?
18. If someone was writing the story of your career, what would you want it to be?
19. Do you have any advice on how I can approach discussions about a promotion?
20. I feel like I'm being pigeonholed at work right now and would like to try some new things. In your experience, what's the best way to approach this?
21. If you were me, how would you have approached X situation?
22. Do you think I should accept this new job offer?
23. My salary isn't in line with what my peers are making. How do I ask for more?
24. What skills would be beneficial for me to work on?
25. Where do you think I can improve?
26. What could I have done differently in this specific situation that may have improved the outcome?

28. Do you have any recommendations for professional development courses?
29. Are there any good books you can suggest that would help me improve X skill?

   https://www.togetherplatform.com/blog/29-questions-to-ask-your-mentor-in-your-next-meeting

Let me introduce myself...

Graphic Organizer Activity

SELF PORTRAIT

Favorites
COLOR: _____
MOVIE: _____
FOOD: _____
MUSIC: _____

Favorite Childhood Memory
_____
_____
_____

Your Funniest Memory
_____
_____
_____

Birthday
_____

Professional Role Model
_____

Personal Role Model
_____

The best book I read:
_____
_____
_____

Pets

What makes me unique?
_____
_____
_____

My Greatest Accomplishment
_____
_____
_____
_____
_____

3 Words that describe me...
1. _____
2. _____
3. _____

Pillar: Living

LESSON TITLE:

Reaching My Goals

LEVEL: Youth   **WEEKS 3-4**

PACING: 55 min

OBJECTIVE(S): What will participants know, understand, and be able to do?

- Mentee will learn what a goal is and how to set them.
- Enable Participants to establish realistic short-term and long-term goals.

KEY VOCABULARY: What key terms will my participants need to understand?

Goal: An aim or desired result.
Short-term: Relating to or extending over a limited period.
Long-term: Things that are so enduring that they're nearly permanent.

WEEK 3

LESSON CYCLE:

1. Engage and Connect **(15 min)**

Facilitator/Mentor will ask the participants what a goal is. Listen to the responses of the participants. Provide participants with a simple definition. The mentor will help participants distinguish between short-term and long-term goals.

Hand out to mentees the list of popular goals list and have participants partner together to look at them for ideas on what basic goals look like.

2. Lead Guided and Independent Practice **(30 min)**

Facilitator/Mentor will encourage mentees to get in touch with what they would like to accomplish in life. Using the "Understanding Goals Worksheet and *Reaching My Goals*" activity sheet, participants will set short-term and long-term goals. By listing the action steps, they visually see how they can execute their plans and that their aspirations are attainable. This also provides a bonding moment between mentor and mentee.

3. Close the Lesson and Assess Mastery **(10 min)**

Discuss with participants the importance of staying focused on their goals. Encourage the participants to post their goals in their binder, journal, or bedroom wall.

LOGISTICS: What materials, resources, and technology will I need to prepare and engage?

Computer/Projector
Understanding Goals
Reaching My Goals Activity Sheet
Mentor/Mentee Agreement Form

WEEK 4

LESSON CYCLE:

1. Engage and Connect **(10 min)**

"*What are you going to do today, tomorrow, and next week to get closer to your goal?*" Inform participants' goal setting activities are good ways for them and their mentors to develop plans and think about the future. Reflect with participants about goals set during the previous session.

2. Lead Guided and Independent Practice **(25 min)**

Complete the Participant Information Worksheet and the Mentor-Mentee Participant Agreement. This is a great way for mentors and mentees to reach a common understanding about what they want and expect from the mentoring relationship. These forms will also serve as a good self-discovery activity for both the mentor and the mentee.

3. Close the Lesson and Assess Mastery **(10 min)**

Close out the session with an open discussion on staying motivated and resources available to help the participants reach their goals.

LOGISTICS: What materials, resources, and technology will I need to prepare and engage?

Computer/Projector
Participant Information Form
Mentor/Mentee Agreement Form

Pillar: Living

LESSON VOCABULARY WORDS

INSTRUCTIONS: Review vocabulary words listed below with the participants to ensure they have a good understanding of each before starting any of the activities.

1. **Goal:** An aim or desired result.
2. **Short-term:** Relating to or extending over a limited period.
3. **Long-term:** Things that are so enduring that they're nearly permanent.

Discussion Question: What are you going to do today, tomorrow, and next week to get closer to your goal?"

PARTICIPANT INFORMATION WORKSHEET

Name: _____

Organization: _____ Date: _____

What name do you prefer to be called? _____

Do you have a nickname? _____

What are your three favorite subjects… why?

1. _____ because _____
2. _____ because _____
3. _____ because _____

What do you like to do in your spare time (LIST 3 THINGS)
Besides EAT and SLEEP

Favorite kind of music? _____
2 of your favorite songs right now? _____
_____

Do you or anyone in your family speak any languages besides English?
Yes (who) _____ No _____
If so, what languages? _____

Where is the farthest away from home you have ever been? _____

What activities are you involved in at the school? (Sports, music, clubs, etc.) _____

Tell me something interesting about you… _____

Is there anything else I should know about you? (Medical issues? Left-handed? Very shy? Good with computers?) _____

Have you been a part of a mentoring program before? Yes ___ No ___
If yes, which program and for how long? _____

What OBSTACLES do you see in your present life that might make it more difficult to REACH your goals? _____

If you had the opportunity to work with a mentor, what would be your objectives for that relationship? Circle all that apply.

- ☐ Career advice & development
- ☐ Improve Reading
- ☐ Improve Writing
- ☐ Learn Leadership Skills
- ☐ Learn About College
- ☐ Learn/Practice Another Language
- ☐ Work on Math Skills
- ☐ Help with Science
- ☐ Help with Social Studies
- ☐ Help with Health
- ☐ Have someone to talk to

Please circle all applicable options that describe you.

Considerate	Outgoing	Serious	Efficient	Friendly
Convincing	Organized	Independent	Agreeable	
Responsible	Authoritative	Helpful	Enthusiastic	Precise

Pillar: Living

MENTOR PROGRAM AGREEMENT

Mentor Expectations

1. To meet regularly with a participant (see Mentor-Mentee Contact Log)
2. To monitor mentee's progress and identified goals
3. To notify campus leadership if unable to keep to scheduled meeting
4. To engage in the relationship with an open mind
5. To collaborate with campus leaders in identifying critical mentee needs
6. To keep (non-safety) conversations with mentee confidential
7. To seek assistance and ask for clarification when help is needed
8. To establish contact and maintain ongoing communication with mentee's family or identified support network

Acknowledgement of Forms (Please initial by each line)

_____ I have read and understand the overall mission/vision of the _____ Mentoring Program Objectives.

_____ I understand my roles and responsibilities per the expectations identified above.

_____ I understand that I am a part of a larger team of social, emotional support leaders assigned to my scholar

_____ I have received a copy of the scholar expectations, Mentor-Mentee Questionnaire, and Contact Log

_____ I have completed the mentor profile and submitted to the _____

_____ I have read and understand the Mentor-Mentee Transition Outline

Mentor (Print Name) _____

Organization/Affiliation: _____

Signature: _____ Date: _____

MENTEE AGREEMENT

As a mentee with the _____ Mentoring Program, I agree to the following:

1. To meet regularly with my mentor
2. To be on time for scheduled meetings
3. To notify the mentor if I cannot keep my weekly meeting
4. To engage in the relationship with an open mind
5. To accept assistance from my mentor
6. To keep discussions with my mentor confidential
7. To practice skills and behaviors taught to me by my mentor

Acknowledgement of Program Expectations (Please initial by each line)

_____   I have read and understand the overall mission/vision of the _____ Mentoring Program Objectives.

_____   I understand what is expected of me as a mentee

_____   I understand I should put forth an effort to practice new skills and behaviors

_____   I am willing to continue working with my mentee after the scheduled program timeline

---

Mentee (Print Name) _____

Signature: _____   Date: _____

Pillar: Living

UNDERSTANDING GOALS

The main thing to remember is that today's youth's goals must be their own, not goals anyone else has set for them. Even extremely lofty goals should be respected, and you can show your mentee how to break down that goal into smaller steps on the way to reaching the goal. For example, a good education is an important first step in becoming president of a corporation. Perhaps more to the point, doing tonight's homework is the first step toward getting a good education.

CHARACTERISTICS GOALS SHOULD HAVE

- *Conceivable*: The mentee should be able to define his/her goal and see it clearly, so he/she can understand what the steps are to achieve it.
- *Believable*: The mentee must believe he/she can reach their goal.
- *Achievable*: The goals the mentee sets must be within his/her strengths and abilities. For example, someone who has never lifted weights before probably should not set a goal of a 300 lb. bench press by next week. (That could be an achievable long-term goal.)
- *Controllable*: To the extent possible, the mentee's ability to reach their goal should not depend on anyone else. For example, getting a job may depend on the job market and your mentee's parents' approval. However, talking to his/her parents about getting a job or developing a resume are things your mentee can control.
- *Measurable*: The goal should be measurable by a certain time or quantity. If the goal is to get an "A" in algebra, then the mentee should know what grades he/she needs to get on tests and assignments.
- *Desirable*: The goal should be something your mentee really wants to do, not something he/she feels they must do, or should do. For example, earning a living is something that we must do, while learning to play baseball may be something we would like to do.
- *Help you grow*: The goal should never be self-destructive or be destructive towards others, their community and/or society. Help your mentee to distinguish between constructive and destructive goals.

PLANNING FOR ACTION

After your mentee has finished identifying his/her goals, it's time to talk about an action plan. A good action plan will help your mentee recognize all the steps needed to meet his/her goals. It also helps your mentee prepare for the difficulties he/she might face. Use the following for further discussion:

- ☐ What actions are needed to reach the goal
- ☐ Who will take those actions (if someone besides the youth is involved)
- ☐ When will the actions be taken
- ☐ What resources are needed in support of the action
- ☐ What difficulties will your mentee face, and their possible solutions
- ☐ Encourage your mentee to talk to about his/her plans

https://ctb.ku.edu/en/table-of-contents/implement/youth-mentoring/youth-goal-setting/main

POPULAR GOALS YOUTH HAVE

Lose Weight	Learn to play an instrument
Set up a budget	Get more sleep
Start journaling	Do something I have never done
Drink More Water	Complete a driver's ed course
Graduate High School	Read more
Build good study habits	Join a school club organization
Learn a new language	Make 3 new friends
Apply to college	Exercise more
Save money	Practice gratitude

GOAL

Education

Career

Health

Financial

Family

Personal Pleasure

Pillar: Living

REACHING MY GOALS

What to do: Think of some of your personal goals. Try to think of 5. Write the goal. Beside the goal write what type of goal it is. Be prepared to discuss your goals with your mentor.

Goal #1: _____

                                        Type of goal: _____

Goal #2: _____

                                        Type of goal: _____

Goal #3: _____

                                        Type of goal: _____

Goal #4: _____

                                        Type of goal: _____

Goal #5: _____

                                        Type of goal: _____

LESSON TITLE:

Reaching My Goals

LEVEL: Employee or Community Citizen

WEEKS 3-4

PACING: 55 min

OBJECTIVE(S): What will Participants know, understand, and be able to do?
Mentee will learn what a goal is and how to set them.

KEY VOCABULARY: What key terms will my Participants need to understand?
Goal: An aim or desired result.

Short-term: Relating to or extending over a limited period.

Long-term: Things that are so enduring that they are nearly permanent.

WEEK 3

LESSON CYCLE:

1. Engage and Connect   **(10 min)**

Ask the participants what a goal is. Listen to the responses of participants. Provide participants with a simple definition. The mentor will help participants distinguish between short-term and long-term goals.

Hand out to mentees the list of popular goals list and have participants partner together to look at them for ideas on what basic goals look like.

2. Lead Guided and Independent Practice   **(25 min)**

Mentees are encouraged to truly get in touch with what they would like to accomplish in life. Using the "*Reaching My Goals*" activity sheet participants can set short-term and long-term goals. By listing the action steps, they can visually see how they to execute their plans and that their aspirations are attainable. This also provides a bonding moment between mentor and mentee. Mentors use the available forms as necessary.

3. Close the Lesson and Assess Mastery   **(20 min)**

Discuss with participants the importance of staying focused on their goals. Encourage the participants to post their goals in their binder, journal, or bedroom wall.

LOGISTICS: What materials, resources, and technology will I need to prepare and engage?

Computer/Projector
Reaching My Goals Activity Sheet

Pillar: Living

WEEK 4

LESSON CYCLE:

1. Engage and Connect (10 min)

"*What are you going to do today, tomorrow, and next week to get closer to your goal?*" Inform Participants goal setting activities are good ways for participants and mentors to develop plans and think about the future. Reflect with a participant about goals set during the previous session.

2. Lead Guided and Independent Practice (25 min)

Complete the Participant Information Worksheet and the Mentor-Mentee Participant Agreement. This is a great way for mentors and mentees to reach a common understanding about what they want and expect from the mentoring relationship. These forms will also serve as a good self-discovery activity for both the mentor and the mentee.

3. Close the Lesson and Assess Mastery (20 min)

Discuss with participants the importance of staying focused on their goals. Encourage the participants to post their goals in their binder, journal, or bedroom wall.

LOGISTICS: What materials, resources, and technology will I need to prepare and engage?

Computer/Projector
Participant Information Worksheet
Mentor/Mentee Program Agreement Form

LESSON VOCABULARY WORDS

INSTRUCTIONS: Review vocabulary words listed below with the participants to ensure they have a good understanding of each before starting any of the activities.

1. **Goal:** An aim or desired result.
2. **Short-term:** Relating to or extending over a limited period.
3. **Long-term:** Things that are so enduring that they're nearly permanent.

Discussion Question: What are you going to do today, tomorrow, and next week to get closer to your goal?"

Pillar: Living

PARTICIPANT INFORMATION WORKSHEET

Name: _____

Organization: _____ Date: _____

What name do you prefer to be called? _____

Do you have a nickname? _____

What are your three favorite subjects… why?

1. _____ because _____
2. _____ because _____
3. _____ because _____

What do you like to do in your spare time (LIST 3 THINGS) Besides EAT and SLEEP _____

Favorite kind of music? _____
2 of your favorite songs right now? _____

Do you or anyone in your family speak any languages besides **English**?
Yes (who) _____ No _____
If so, what languages? _____

Where is the farthest away from home you have ever been? _____

What activities are you involved in at the school? (Sports, music, clubs, etc.) _____

Tell me something interesting about you… _____

Is there anything else I should know about you? (Medical issues? Left-handed? Very shy? Good with computers?) _____

Have you been a part of a mentoring program before? Yes ___ No ___
If yes, which program and for how long? _____

What OBSTACLES do you see in your present life that might make it more difficult to REACH your goals? _____

If you had the opportunity to work with a mentor, what would be your objectives for that relationship? Circle all that apply.

☐ Career advice & development
☐ Improve Reading
☐ Improve Writing
☐ Learn Leadership Skills
☐ Learn About College
☐ Learn/Practice Another Language
☐ Work on Math Skills
☐ Help with Science
☐ Help with Social Studies
☐ Help with Health
☐ Have someone to talk to

Please circle all applicable options that describe you.

Considerate   Outgoing   Serious   Efficient   Friendly

Convincing   Organized   Independent   Agreeable

Responsible   Authoritative   Helpful   Enthusiastic   Precise

MENTOR PROGRAM AGREEMENT

Mentor Expectations

1. To meet regularly with a participant (see Mentor-Mentee Contact Log)
2. To monitor mentee's progress and identified goals
3. To notify campus leadership if unable to keep to scheduled meeting
4. To engage in the relationship with an open mind
5. To collaborate with campus leaders in identifying critical mentee needs
6. To keep (non-safety) conversations with mentee confidential
7. To seek assistance and ask for clarification when help is needed
8. To establish contact and maintain ongoing communication with mentee's family or identified support network

Acknowledgement of Forms (Please initial by each line)

_____ I have read and understand the overall mission/vision of the _____ Mentoring Program Objectives.

_____ I understand my roles and responsibilities per the expectations identified above.

_____ I understand that I am a part of a larger team of social, emotional support leaders assigned to my scholar

_____ I have received a copy of the scholar expectations, Mentor-Mentee Questionnaire, and Contact Log

_____ I have completed the mentor profile and submitted to the _____

_____ I have read and understand the Mentor-Mentee Transition Outline

Mentor (Print Name) _____

Organization/Affiliation: _____

Signature: _____ Date: _____

Pillar: Living

MENTEE AGREEMENT

As a mentee with the _____ Mentoring Program, I agree to the following:

1. To meet regularly with my mentor
2. To be on time for scheduled meetings
3. To notify the mentor if I cannot keep my weekly meeting
4. To engage in the relationship with an open mind
5. To accept assistance from my mentor
6. To keep discussions with my mentor confidential
7. To practice skills and behaviors taught to me by my mentor

Acknowledgement of Program Expectations (Please initial by each line)

_____ I have read and understand the overall mission/vision of the _____ Mentoring Program Objectives.

_____ I understand what is expected of me as a mentee

_____ I understand I should put forth an effort to practice new skills and behaviors

_____ I am willing to continue working with my mentee after the scheduled program timeline

Mentee (Print Name) _____

Signature: _____ Date: _____

Intentional Mentoring Mentor's Guide

SMART GOALS

Make it specific

In order for a goal to be effective, it needs to be specific. A specific goal answers questions like: What needs to be accomplished? Who's responsible for it? What steps need to be taken to achieve it? Thinking through these questions helps get to the heart of what you're aiming for.

Make it measurable

Specificity is a solid start, but quantifying your goals (that is, making sure they're measurable) makes it easier to track progress and know when you've reached the finish line. To make this SMART objective more impactful, Jane should incorporate measurable and trackable benchmarks.

Make it attainable

This is the point in the process when you give yourself a serious reality check. Goals should be realistic — not pedestals from which you inevitably tumble. Ask yourself: is your objective something you can reasonably accomplish?

Make it relatable

Here's where you need to think about the big picture. Why are you setting the goal that you're setting? Consider your objective.

Make it timely

To properly measure success, you need to on the goal and determine when it can be reached. What's your time horizon? When will you start creating and implementing the tasks you've identified? When will you finish? SMART goals should have time-related parameters built in, so you know how to stay on track within a designated time frame.

https://www.atlassian.com/blog/productivity/how-to-write-smart-goals

Pillar: Living

GOAL SETTING

WHAT IS YOUR GOAL?

_____

_____

_____

ACTION STEPS

01 _____

02 _____

03 _____

04 _____

START DATE: DEADLINE: MARK COMPLETE:

Intentional Mentoring Mentor's Guide

MONTHLY GOALS

MONTH :

FOCUS

GOAL

ACTIONS STEPS

GOAL

ACTIONS STEPS

GOAL

ACTIONS STEPS

TASK LIST

NOTES

Pillar: Living

Goal Setting

Goals	Action Steps

Problems	

Progress Tracker

Date	Progress

setting goals

MY PRIORITIES

1.

2.

3.

4.

5.

When I feel like giving up, I will tell myself...

GOAL: _____
Action Steps-
1.
2.
3.
DEADLINE: _____

GOAL: _____
Action Steps-
1.
2.
3.
DEADLINE: _____

GOAL: _____
Action Steps-
1.
2.
3.
DEADLINE: _____

GOAL: _____
Action Steps-
1.
2.
3.
DEADLINE: _____

GOAL: _____
Action Steps-
1.
2.
3.
DEADLINE: _____

Pillar: Living

Week at a Glance   PLAN DO REVIEW

TOP 3 GOALS OF THE _____
1.
2.
3.

APPOINTMENTS & EVENTS

TO DO
- [ ]
- [ ]
- [ ]
- [ ]
- [ ]
- [ ]
- [ ]

BOOK I'M READING

SKILL I'M PRACTICING

HABITS

	S	M	T	W	T	F	S

INCOME GOAL // SAVINGS GOAL

END OF WEEK REVIEW

WHAT WORKED?	WHAT DIDN'T WORK?
DO MORE:	**DO LESS:**
GRATITUDE:	**EPIPHANY:**

get the whole kit at: www.bit.ly/lifebinder

LESSON TITLE:

Developing Meaningful Relationships

LEVEL: Youth

WEEKS 5-6

PACING: 55 min

OBJECTIVE(S): What will Participants know, understand, and be able to do?

The participant will examine various attitudes, values, and behaviors to develop meaningful interpersonal relationships.

KEY VOCABULARY: What key terms will my Participants need to understand?

Relationships: The way in which two or more concepts, objects, or people are connected, or the state of being connected.

Development: Process of improvement and changes required for better living and existence.

Self-Awareness: become mindful; acknowledge what you need rather than what you want; set boundaries.

Relationship Skills: forgive; guiding love

Purpose: the reason for which something is done, created, or exists.

Week 5

LESSON CYCLE:

1. Engage and Connect (15 min)

1. The facilitator/mentor will ask participants to define the term **RELATIONSHIP**.
2. Allow the group to provide examples of different types of relationships (family, friends, teachers, church, sports, and coach).
3. Ask participants to list some of the benefits of having/developing relationships (examples: Someone is there for you, love and companionship, safety, sharing culture, religion, challenges, and/or someone to just have fun with.)

Healthy Relationships	Unhealthy Relationships
Happiness/Gratitude	No fun/depressed
Mutual Respect	No Respect
Good Communication	Unfair arguments/never feels heard
Honesty	Lies/Cheats
You can be yourself	Another person tries to control/change you

2. Lead Guided and Independent Practice (30 min)

Lead a discussion by asking:

- What does a healthy relationship look like?
- What does an unhealthy relationship look like?
- How do you know the difference?
- Why do some people stay in unhealthy relationships?

3. Close the Lesson and Assess Mastery (10 min)

Attitude of Gratitude: Remind participants of the positive relationships they currently have in their life. Facilitator/Mentor will encourage participants to tell the people they are in a healthy relationship with how grateful they are for the relationship. Have them share their gratitude in person, in a written message, or by using technology.

Logistics: What materials, resources, and technology will I need to prepare and engage?

Computer/Projector
Chart paper/Whiteboard
Markers

WEEK 6

LESSON CYCLE:

1. Engage and Connect   **(15 min)**

The facilitator/mentor will allow participants to share their experiences when they expressed their appreciation/gratitude to the positive relationships they identified.

Show the participants *"All-Star Athletes Share How their Own Mentors have Inspired Them"*

https://www.youtube.com/watch?v=96dVwzXE_A0&feature=youtu.be

2. Lead Guided and Independent Practice   **(25 min)**

Write down the word *'Mentor'* on the chart paper or white board. Ask participants to help you explain this term with words, ideas and/or examples. Show participants prepared examples of mentoring relationships.

Examples of Mentor/Mentee relationships:

- NBA-Phil Jackson and Kobe Bryant/Michael Jordan
- Maya Angelou and Oprah Winfrey
- Chloe and Halle Bailey and Beyonce
- Harry Potter – Harry and Dumbledore
- Avengers- Iron Man/Tony Stark and Spiderman
- Valerie Jarrett and Michelle Obama

Lead a discussion using a group discussion strategy by asking:

- Why can dealing with friends, family, and the people we work with sometimes be so difficult?
- What are the most effective ways to start talking about a difficult topic?
- What skills and elements were used to maintain these relationships?
- Can you suggest other ways the characters may have handled this situation?

3. Close the Lesson and Assess Mastery   **(15 min)**

Facilitator/Mentor will close out with the quote from the Alberta Mentoring Partnership, *"A mentor is a caring person who provides another person with support, advice, friendship, reinforcement, and constructive role modeling over time."*

Remind participants their mentors are there as a support to them in a positive relationship and here to assist them with challenging relationship situations they may face.

LOGISTICS: What materials, resources, and technology will I need to prepare and engage?

Computer
Projector
Chart paper/Whiteboard/Paper
Markers

Pillar: Living

LESSON VOCABULARY WORDS

INSTRUCTIONS: Review vocabulary words listed below with the participants to ensure they have a good understanding of each before starting any of the activities.

1. **Relationships:** The way in which two or more concepts, objects, or people are connected, or the state of being connected.
2. **Development:** Process of improvement and changes required for better living and existence.
3. **Self-Awareness:** become mindful; acknowledge what you need rather than what you want; set boundaries
4. **Relationship Skills:** forgive; guiding love
5. **Purpose:** the reason for which something is done, created, or exists

Discussion Questions: Be prepared to answer these questions during the open discussion time with the group.

1. What does a healthy relationship look like?

   _____
   _____

2. What does an unhealthy relationship look like?

   _____
   _____
   _____

3. How do you know the difference?

   _____
   _____
   _____

4. Why do some people stay in unhealthy relationships?

   _____
   _____
   _____

ATTITUDE OF GRATITUDE: The positive relationships you currently have in your life impact how you see life and interact with the world around you. Tell the people you are in a healthy relationship with how grateful you are for the relationship. Take the opportunity to share your gratitude for a person, in a written message, and/or by using technology.

LESSON TITLE:	LEVEL: Employee or Community Citizen	WEEKS 5-6

Developing Meaningful Relationships

PACING: 55 min

OBJECTIVE(S): What will Participants know, understand, and be able to do?

The participant will examine various attitudes, values, and behaviors to develop meaningful interpersonal relationships.

KEY VOCABULARY: What key terms will my Participants need to understand?

Relationships: The way in which two or more concepts, objects, or people are connected, or the state of being connected.

Development: Process of improvement and changes required for better living and existence.

Self-Awareness: become mindful; acknowledge what you need rather than what you want; set boundaries

Relationship Skills: forgive; guiding love

Purpose: the reason for which something is done, created, or exists

WEEK 5

LESSON CYCLE:

1. *Engage and Connect* **(15 min)**

    a. The facilitator/mentor will ask participants to define the term relationship.

    b. Allow the group to provide examples of different types of relationships (family, friends, teachers, church members, sports teammates, and coach).

    c. Facilitator/Mentor will ask participants to list some of the benefits of relationships (examples: Someone is there for you, love and companionship, safety, sharing culture, religion, challenges, or someone to just have fun with).

Healthy Relationships	Unhealthy Relationships
Happiness/Gratitude	No fun/depressed
Mutual Respect	No Respect
Good Communication	Unfair arguments/never feels heard
Honesty	Lies/Cheats
You can be yourself	Another person tries to control/change you

Pillar: Living

2. Lead Guided and Independent Practice **(25 min)**

Lead a discussion by asking:

- What does a healthy relationship look like?
- What does an unhealthy relationship look like?
- How do you know the difference?
- Why do some people stay in unhealthy relationships?

3. Close the Lesson and Assess Mastery **(15 min)**

Facilitator/Mentor will close out with the quote from the Alberta Mentoring Partnership, *"A mentor is a caring person who provides another person with support, advice, friendship, reinforcement and constructive role modelling over time."* Remind participants you are there as a support to them as a positive relationship and here to assist them with challenging relationship situations they may face.

LOGISTICS: What materials, resources, and technology will I need to prepare and engage?

Computer/Projector
Chart paper/Whiteboard
Markers

WEEK 6

LESSON CYCLE:

1. Engage and Connect **(10 min)**

The facilitator/mentor will allow participants to share their experience when they expressed their appreciation to the positive relationships they identified.

Show the participants *"All-Star Athletes Share How their Own Mentors have Inspired Them"* https://www.youtube.com/watch?v=96dVwzXE_A0&feature=youtu.be

2. Lead Guided and Independent Practice **(25 min)**

Write down the word '*Mentor*' on the chart paper or white board. Ask participants to help you explain this term with words, ideas and examples. Show participants prepared examples of mentoring relationships.

Examples of Mentor/Mentee relationships:

- NBA-Phil Jackson and Kobe Bryant/Michael Jordan
- Karate Kid – Mr. Miyagi and Daniel
- Star Wars – Yoda and Luke Skywalker
- Harry Potter – Harry and Dumbledore
- Avengers- Iron Man/Tony Stark and Spiderman

Lead a discussion using a group discussion strategy by asking:

- Why can dealing with friends, family, and the people we work with sometimes be so difficult?
- What are the most effective ways to start talking about a difficult topic?
- What skills and elements were used to maintain these relationships?
- Can you suggest other ways the characters may have handled this situation?

3. Close the Lesson and Assess Mastery **(10 min)**

Facilitator/Mentor will close out with the quote from the Alberta Mentoring Partnership, *"A mentor is a caring person who provides another person with support, advice, friendship, reinforcement, and constructive role-modeling over time."* Remind participants you are there as a support to them in a positive relationship and here to assist them with challenging relationship situations they may face.

LOGISTICS: What materials, resources, and technology will I need to prepare and engage?

Computer
Projector
Chart paper/Whiteboard
Markers

Pillar: Living

LESSON VOCABULARY WORDS

INSTRUCTIONS: Review vocabulary words listed below with the participants to ensure they have a good understanding of each before starting any of the activities.

1. **Relationships:** The way in which two or more concepts, objects, or people are connected, or the state of being connected.
2. **Development:** Process of improvement and changes required for better living and existence.
3. **Self-Awareness:** become mindful; acknowledge what you need rather than what you want; set boundaries
4. **Relationship Skills:** forgive; guiding love
5. **Purpose:** the reason for which something is done, created, or exists

Discussion Questions: Be prepared to answer these questions during the open discussion time with the group.

1. What does a healthy relationship look like?

   _____
   _____

2. What does an unhealthy relationship look like?

   _____
   _____

3. How do you know the difference?

   _____
   _____
   _____

4. Why do some people stay in unhealthy relationships?

   _____
   _____
   _____

ATTITUDE OF GRATITUDE: The positive relationships you currently have in your life impact how you see life and interact with the world around you. Tell the people you are in a healthy relationship with how grateful you are for the relationship. Take the opportunity to share your gratitude for a person, in a written message, and/or by using technology.

LESSON TITLE:

Legacy/Cultural EYE

LEVEL: Youth

WEEKS 7-8

PACING: 55 min

OBJECTIVE(S): What will Participants know, understand, and be able to do?

The participants will define character and bias.

The participants will define culture; and find evidence of culture in their lives and all around; create a culture wheel project depicting culture in their lives.

KEY VOCABULARY: What key terms will my Participants need to understand?

Culture: The customary beliefs, social forms, and material traits of a racial, religious, or social group.

Ethnicity: The fact or state of belonging to a social group that has a common national or cultural tradition.

Race: Each of the major groupings into which humankind is considered (in various theories or contexts) to be divided on the basis of physical characteristics or shared ancestry.

Stereotype: A widely held but fixed and oversimplified image or idea of a particular type of person or thing.

Discrimination: The unjust or prejudicial treatment of different categories of people or things, especially on the grounds of race, age, or sex.

Bias: a disproportionate weight in favor of or against an idea or thing, usually in a way that is closed-minded, prejudicial, or unfair.

WEEK 7

LESSON CYCLE:

1. Engage and Connect   **(15 min)**

Facilitator/Mentor will ask the following questions but tell participants to hold off on their responses. You will come back and get their answers later in the session.

Guiding Questions for participants: (write the questions on the board or have the Participants write them down.)

a. What is culture?
b. What is bias?
c. How does culture and bias play out in the school or in the community?

Participants will then watch a short video, "What is culture?" https://www.youtube.com/watch?v=hTxKv6n6M2Y

Pillar: Living

2. Lead Guided and Independent Practice **(25 min)**

    a. Set up the space for the presentation of various cultural representations. If you have a map, it is helpful to post the map where it is visible as a reference.

    b. Call participants one at a time to present their cultural traditions to the group. Remind the group to be supportive of each other!

Questions facilitator can ask the Participants:

    a. What did you find to share?
    b. What culture is it representing?
    c. What does this cultural tradition mean to you?
    d. Direct participants to locate where their cultural tradition is from and place a marker on the map for each region or area represented.

After the participant presents, allow others to ask questions of the presenter.

3. Facilitator/Mentor will c*lose the Lesson and Assess Mastery* **(15 min)**

Close out the lesson facilitating an activity with the participants using the following guided questions:

    a. What is culture?
    b. What does culture look like?
    c. What is the purpose of culture?

Facilitator/Mentor will ask participants to find examples of diverse cultural traditions in their community, or even within their families, and report back to the group.

LOGISTICS: What materials, resources, and technology will I need to prepare and engage?

Computer
Projector
Chart paper/Whiteboard
Markers

WEEK 8

LESSON CYCLE:

1. Engage and Connect **(10 min)**

Facilitator/Mentor will ask the participants, *"If you were to invent a cultural tradition or ritual, what would it be? A language? A food? A dance? Describe your new tradition and why you would have people practice it."* (Note: With larger groups, th[e] activity can be broken up into groups of participants asking each other the questions).

2. Lead Guided and Independent Practice **(30 min)**

   a. Facilitator/Mentor will write down the various nationalities/race that may be represented in their scho[ol] and/or community before the mentoring session. Turn 3x5 cards face down on the table.

   b. Have each participant to pick a 3x5 card and share what they know about their selection. Once everyon[e] has had a turn, open the discussion up for others to share what they know about each nationality/ra[ce] covered. <u>Remind the group to be supportive of each other!</u> (Purpose: bring awareness and insp[ire] acceptance /inclusion.)

Questions facilitator can ask the participants after their discussion:

   a. What did you learn?
   b. Did the information shared, change your viewpoint of the nationalities/races discussed?

Additional activity: Discuss what food dishes are specific to the nationalities/races discussed.

3. Close the Lesson and Assess Mastery **(15 min)**

Facilitator/Mentor will close out the lesson facilitating an activity with the Participants using the following guide[d] questions:

   a. What is culture?
   b. What does culture look like?
   c. What does acceptance and inclusion mean?

Facilitator/Mentor will ask participants to identify examples of diverse cultural traditions in their community, [or] even within their families. Ask participants to share the cultural traditions they celebrate within their family and/[or] community using symbols, food items/dishes, language, etc.

Lesson source: http://www.sdcda.org/office/girlsonlytoolkit/toolkit/got-12-culture.pdf

LOGISTICS: What materials, resources, and technology will I need to prepare and engage?

Computer/Projector
Index Cards/Post-it Notes
Paper/Writing Utensils

Pillar: Living

LESSON VOCABULARY WORDS

INSTRUCTIONS: Review vocabulary words listed below with the participants to ensure they have a good understanding of each before starting any of the activities.

1. **Culture:** The customary beliefs, social forms, and material traits of a racial, religious, or social group.
2. **Ethnicity:** The fact or state of belonging to a social group that has a common national or cultural tradition.
3. **Race:** Each of the major groupings into which humankind is considered (in various theories or contexts) to be divided on the basis of physical characteristics or shared ancestry.
4. **Stereotype:** A widely held but fixed and oversimplified image or idea of a particular type of person or thing.
5. **Discrimination:** The unjust or prejudicial treatment of different categories of people or things, especially on the grounds of race, age, or sex.

Discussion Questions: Be prepared to answer these questions during the group's discussion period.

1. What is culture?

2. What is bias?

3. How does culture and bias play out in the workplace or in the community?

4. What does acceptance and inclusion mean?

5. What is bias?

During the Cultural Representations Presentation answer the following questions:

a. What is being shared?

b. What culture is being representing?

c. What dis you take away from this cultural tradition?

d. Where did the cultural tradition originate? Place a marker on the map for each region or area represented.

e. Write down two examples of diverse cultural traditions in your community, or within your family.

Pillar: Living

LESSON TITLE:

Cultural EYE

LEVEL: Employee or Community Citizen

WEEKS 7-8

PACING: 55 min

OBJECTIVE(S): What will Participants know, understand, and be able to do?

- The participants will define character and bias.

- The participants will define culture; and find evidence of culture in their lives and all around; create a culture wheel project depicting culture in their lives.

KEY VOCABULARY: What key terms will my Participants need to understand?

Culture: The customary beliefs, social forms, and material traits of a racial, religious, or social group.

Ethnicity: The fact or state of belonging to a social group that has a common national or cultural tradition.

Race: Each of the major groupings into which humankind is considered (in various theories or contexts) to be divided on the basis of physical characteristics or shared ancestry.

Stereotype: A widely held but fixed and oversimplified image or idea of a particular type of person or thing.

Discrimination: The unjust or prejudicial treatment of different categories of people or things, especially on the grounds of race, age, or sex.

Bias: a disproportionate weight in favor of or against an idea or thing, usually in a way that is closed-minded, prejudicial, or unfair.

WEEK 7

LESSON CYCLE:

1. Engage and Connect (10 min)

Facilitator/Mentor will ask the following questions but tell participants to hold off on their responses. You will come back and get their answers later in the session.

Guiding Questions for participants: (write the questions on the board or have the Participants write them down.)

1. What is culture/cultural bias?
2. What does culture look like?
3. What does acceptance and inclusion mean?
4. What is legacy?
5. What part does culture play in legacy?

Facilitator/Mentor will have participants watch a short video, *"What is culture?"* https://www.youtube.com/watch?v=E_dbaugeRh8

2. Lead Guided and Independent Practice **(30 min)**

1. Begin by explaining culture is a shared set of practices and traditions that characterize a society or group of people. Culture can include clothing, food, traditions, rituals, ceremonies, spiritual practices and beliefs, language, family structure, and communication styles. Explain that culture influences who we are, just like our parents and personalities.

2. Have participants brainstorm a few examples of culture (ex: speaking English, speaking Spanish, wearing a blue and white school uniform, saying "please" and "thank you," giving a teacher a hug at the end of the day, wearing your hair in braids, using American money, wearing flip flop shoes). Record their ideas on a board or on large paper.

3. Explain that today they will be having a cultural scavenger hunt. They will identify evidence of culture in their lives and all around. Participants can write 3-6 of on a note card or small sheet of paper.

Examples:

a. "Eating Ethnic food"
b. "Celebrating Hanukkah"
c. "Going to church on Sunday
d. "Watching a Futbol game on television"
e. "Someone wearing a Hijab"
f. "Shopping at Supermercado La Frontera"

Suggested activity: When participants have finished at least 3 cards, punch two holes on the top of each card and string them together.

3. Close the Lesson and Assess Mastery **(15 min)**

Close out the lesson facilitating an activity with the Participants using the following guided questions:
a. What is culture?
b. What does culture look like?
c. What does acceptance and inclusion mean?
d. What is legacy?
e. What part does culture play in legacy?

Ask participants to find examples of diverse cultural traditions in their community, or even within their families, and report back to the group.

LOGISTICS: What materials, resources, and technology will I need to prepare and engage?

Computer/Projector
Index Cards/Post-it Notes
Paper/Pen/Pencil

Pillar: Living

WEEK 8

LESSON CYCLE:

1. Engage and Connect **(10 min)**

Facilitator/Mentor will ask the participants, *"If you were to invent a cultural tradition or ritual, what would it be? A language? A food? A dance? Describe your new tradition and why you would have people practice it."* (Note: With larger groups, this activity can be broken up into groups of participants asking each other the questions).

2. Lead Guided and Independent Practice **(25 Min)**

a. Facilitator to write down the various nationalities/race that may be represented in their workplace and/or community before the mentoring session. Turn 3x5 cards face down on the table.
b. Have each participant pick a 3x5 card and share what they know about their selection. Once everyone has had a turn, open the discussion up for others to share what they know about each nationality/race covered. <u>Remind the group to be supportive of each other!</u> (Purpose: bring awareness and inspire acceptance/inclusion.)

Questions facilitator can ask the participants after their discussion:

1. What did you learn?
2. Did the information shared, change your viewpoint of the nationalities/races discussed?

Additional activity: Discuss what food dishes are specific to the nationalities/races discussed

3. Close the Lesson and Assess Mastery **(10 min)**

The facilitator will close out the lesson with final remarks. *"Culture is a shared set of practices and traditions that characterize a society or group of people. Culture can include clothing, food, traditions, rituals, ceremonies, spiritual practices, and beliefs, language, family structure, and communication styles. Celebrating a diversity of cultural traditions promotes tolerance and understanding. Cultural beliefs/values impact the legacy you desire to leave the world because they are infused in your core values and beliefs."*

Lesson source: http://www.sdcda.org/office/girlsonlytoolkit/toolkit/got-12-culture.pdf

LOGISTICS: What materials, resources, and technology will I need to prepare and engage?

Computer/Projector
Index Cards/Post-it Notes
Paper
Writing Utensils

LESSON VOCABULARY WORDS

INSTRUCTIONS: Review vocabulary words listed below with the participants to ensure they have a good understanding of each before starting any of the activities.

1. **Culture:** The customary beliefs, social forms, and material traits of a racial, religious, or social group.
2. **Ethnicity:** The fact or state of belonging to a social group that has a common national or cultural tradition.
3. **Race:** Each of the major groupings into which humankind is considered (in various theories or contexts) to be divided on the basis of physical characteristics or shared ancestry.
4. **Stereotype:** A widely held but fixed and oversimplified image or idea of a particular type of person or thing.
5. **Discrimination:** The unjust or prejudicial treatment of different categories of people or things, especially on the grounds of race, age, or sex.

Discussion Questions: Be prepared to answer these questions during the group's discussion period.

1. What is culture?

2. What is bias?

3. How does culture and bias play out in the workplace or in the community?

4. What does acceptance and inclusion mean?

5. What is legacy?

6. What part does culture play in legacy?

_____

_____

PILLAR: LOVING

PILLAR: LOVING

Merriam's Dictionary defines love as a strong affection for another arising out of kinship or personal ties; attention based on affection and tenderness; affection based on admiration, benevolence, or common interest. As we understand love, we must first begin with the most important aspect of love: self-love, before moving to loving entities outside of ourselves. According to *"Self-Love and What it Means,"* (www.bbrfoundation.org, February 12, 2020), self-love is a state of appreciation for oneself that grows from actions that support our physical, psychological, and spiritual growth. Self-love means having a high regard for your own well-being and happiness (above that of others). Self-love means taking care of your own needs and not sacrificing your happiness and/or wellbeing to please others. Knowing your value and worth is what self-love is all about. Self-love means not settling for less than you deserve.

In the *"A Seven Step Prescription for Self-love"* article (www.psychologytoday.com, by Deborah Khoshaba, PsyD., 3/27/2012), there are seven steps to cultivate self-love:

1. *Become Mindful*. Take a minute and take the pulse of your self-love. Be mindful of who you believe yourself to be and act on this knowledge rather than focusing more on what others want for you. This connects with the mentee's lesson on living (discovering what he/she is passionate about) while learning how to make themselves the most important person in their life. It is easier for him/her to discover their passions when they become mindful of who they are and are respecting and loving of themselves.

2. *Acknowledge what you need rather than what you want*. When a person learns to practice self-love, they can turn away from things that don't serve them, even if it looks and feel good or are emotionally gratifying. The person can focus on those things that are needed *"...to stay strong, centered, and moving forward in their life..."* By staying focused on what you need, you turn away from automatic behavior patterns that get you into trouble, stuck in the past, connected to things designed to destroy you and/or encourages self-destructive behaviors/actions.

3. *Set Boundaries to Protect Yourself*. In the article it states that a person who practices setting personal and professional boundaries will set limits on activities that deplete or harm them physically, emotionally, professionally, and spiritually or that poorly expressed who he/she is publicly and/or privately. It will help them correctly select and bring the right people into their

life, especially those who are invited in to be a part of their inner circle. Having and building solid self-love enables and empowers him/her to remove those individuals who find pleasure in his/her pain and loss rather than their success and happiness even if the person is a family member. Learning how to love from a distance will give him/her the space they need to focus on themself and their needs.

4. **FORGIVE**. It seems like one of the hardest things to do in life is to forgive oneself for those things they have done or taken part in that have not serviced them and/or improved their view of themself. As humans, we seem to punish ourselves instead of accepting responsibility and forgiving ourselves. When practicing self-love, he/she must accept their humanness and their propensity to mess up every now and then. Learning to offer themself some forgiveness for not being perfect but cognizant of who they are. Remember there are no failures if he/she has learned and grown from their mistakes; they are only lessons learned.

5. *Live Intentionally and Purposefully*. Live your life with purpose, and intentionally. While discovering your purpose, live a meaningful and healthy life. The decisions and choices you make will support this intention and help you see yourself in a positive light. It will help you learn how to love yourself even more when you see yourself accomplishing your goals and building a better life for yourself.

Helping both the mentor and mentee understand and begin practicing self-love will help them envision the life they want because now they see themselves as being worthy of having it. This is where setting personal goals, mapping them out, and celebrating their attainment is essential to their continued growth and development. Because it speaks to the love, they display or show themselves daily. When they learn the importance of loving themselves, it impacts how they talk to themselves and the mental dialogue they have with themselves. I once heard that "*…when you speak, I AM the unconscious mind says, 'you are so!'*" (*The I Am Principe*, by Charles Ogada, Published 2011) and moves behind the scenes to make what you have spoken to manifest itself in your reality. One important aspect of learning how to love ourselves empowers us to become kinder to ourselves and begin to speak about the future we desire in love and lovingly.

As the person learns how to love themselves, they can love and respect others in a manner that enables them to accept them where they are without it having a negative impact on them. The greatest gift one human can give another is love. As we take a deeper dive into loving as it relates to the relationships we nurture through love and respect, it is important that our personal definition represents the love we experienced early in life. The love that was shown within the family and village/community that helped to raise you or the lack thereof. However, it isn't the same, but it is the foundation on which we build self-love and the guiding love and respect that is developed in the mentor-mentee relationship and is being nurtured. The greatest gift a human can give another is LOVE.

As we take a deeper dive into loving as it relates to relationships, we nurture through love and respect. It is important that our personal definition is impacted by the love we experienced early in life. The love that was shown within the family and village/community that helped raise you or the lack thereof. This lesson rebuilds or renovates the foundation on which self-love, guiding love and respect are built as the mentor/mentee relationship is being nurtured.

GUIDING LOVE

Guiding love offers guidance from a mentor to the mentee and from mentee to mentor in the sharing of different aspects of their life, sharing their likes and dislikes, skills, abilities and/or areas of expertise and/or knowledge that exposes the mentee to opportunities and possibilities they otherwise would not have known is available to him/her. For the mentor, it gives him/her insight into how to best communicate and interact with their mentee. As well as giving the mentor the opportunity to realize the influences, hinderances and/or mindset of their mentee.

This type of love is founded on respect and a genuine desire for both parties to grow and succeed in life. The guiding-love shown from a mentor to a mentee opens them up to recognizes the need in their life to build a structured relationship through which the mentee benefits from receiving advice, wisdom, and instruction from a seasoned, caring, and engaging individual (mentor). All while gaining the awareness, respect and care when building the mentor-mentee relationship and interacting with people.

While researching guiding-love I discovered it is an aspect of agape love, an aspect of the five love languages kept showing up, and integral when building and nurturing any kind of relationship. Yes, even the guiding-love we have been discussing. The following is how it would be conceptualized in the mentor-mentee relationship: words of affirmation, quality time, acts of service, receiving gifts, and physical contact.

Scott Aoki says, *"I believe the love languages have a place in all human relationships and should play an active role in how we communicate as mentors and mentees."* He also states, *"...the connection between a mentor and mentee can be a multifaceted mix of other personal and professional interactions... therefore it follows its own rules regarding personal interactions and open communication."*

1. **WORDS OF AFFIRMATION**

    Words of affirmation include celebratory compliments that are shared after the mentor and/or mentee has accomplished an achievement or goal. It also includes moments when encouragement is needed, and/or when using a salutation and/or sharing one's opinion.

2. **QUALITY TIME**

    One of the most valuable assets a person has is time. Spending quality time when building the mentor/mentee relationship is paramount. What makes it quality time? When both the mentor and mentee attempt to make the time productive. It helps build confidence individually and collectively. Sometimes a kind or encouraging word said during a scheduled or impromptu interaction can be the difference between life and death.

3. **ACTS OF SERVICE**

    Throughout the mentoring relationship, there will be opportunities where the mentor may expose the mentee or vice versa to something that inspire, empower and/or enables them to see life differently. It is found when they take part in community service projects and/or do something unexpected yet encouraging that builds another person's self-esteem. Keep in mind, acts of service within the mentoring relationship builds trust and respect. The act of service can be something small yet impactful or big, and thoughtful. Whichever it is, it speaks of the reverence and respect being developed between the mentor and mentee, and others.

4. **PHYSICAL TOUCH**

    This type of love language can be seen as too much for some, however, it is necessary even when building a supportive and respectful mentoring relationship. I am talking about something kind and innocent: a part on the back, high-five, a handshake, an encouraging smile and/or eye contact during a conversation. These all can offer a level of communication between two people that encourages them to be and do better.

5. **RECEIVING GIFTS**

    At first glance, most people would say this love language is inappropriate in a mentoring program. I challenge that thought! Merriam-Webster's dictionary defines a gift or present as an item given to someone without the expectation of payment or anything in return. Giving the gift of knowledge, understanding, acceptance, skills, tools, examples to right living, and/or being seen are invaluable to the person receiving it. It isn't about the gift itself or the person receiving it, as much as it is about the recipient (mentee) receiving it, opening it, and using it. Under this guise, giving gifts from mentor to mentee is not only necessary but required to ensure the mentee receives the pertinent information that fosters their mentor-mentee relationship, and equips the mentee with the information, tools, and/or skills to make wise choices and/or decisions in their life during the various stages of their growth and/or development personally and professionally.

The interpretation and use of these five love languages ensures both the mentor and mentee are benefiting from the mentoring relationship. It helps to shape their lives by going forward while encouraging them to show the best version of themselves each day. Love is an essential ingredient in human development and is essential when developing/building a mentoring relationship.

LESSON TITLE:

Self-Love/Critical Thinking/Boundaries

LEVEL: Youth

WEEKS 9-10

PACING: 55 min

OBJECTIVE(S): What will Participants know, understand, and be able to do?

- Participants will think critically, make meaningful personal connections, and learn how to build healthy relationships.
- Participants will learn how to create healthy boundaries.
- Participants will learn the five love languages associated with building mentoring and other relationships.

KEY VOCABULARY: What key terms will my Participants need to understand?

Love: a strong affection for another arising out of kinship or personal ties; attention based on affection and tenderness; affection based on admiration, benevolence, or common interests.

Personal Boundaries: are the limits and rules we set for ourselves within relationships.

Forgiveness: a conscious, deliberate decision to release feelings of resentment or vengeance toward a person or group who has harmed you, regardless of whether they actually deserve your forgiveness.

Critical Thinking: making reasoned judgments that are logical and well-thought out.

(Merriam-Webster)

WEEK 9

LESSON CYCLE:

1. Engage and Connect (15 min)

Facilitator/Mentor will open by showing the: *"What is Critical Thinking?"* Youth Video: https://www.youtube.com/watch?v=HnJ1bqXUnIM

    a. Facilitator/Mentor will share the definition of **Critical Thinking.** Critical Thinking helps people make good decisions, understand the consequences of our actions, and solve problems.

Pillar: Loving

2. Lead Guided and Independent Practice (25 min)

a. Facilitator/Mentor will discuss the components of critical thinking: step back to see the full picture; ask open-ended questions; use decision-making skills; and build confidence.

b. *"How Many Can You Think Of?"* Activity: This game challenges children to think of words that fit into a theme or category.
   1. Choose a category, such as colors, vegetable, fruit, cars, etc. and put a timer on for one minute. Ask each participant to write down as many words as they can think of that are in the chosen category.
   2. Have each participant to write down the total number of correct answers on the top of their paper.
   3. Complete this activity as many times as time permits.

3. Close the Lesson and Assess Mastery (15 min)

Facilitator/Mentor will discuss how critical thinking is one of the most essential life skills used in our everyday life. It helps youth to think independently, form their own opinions and trust their own thinking when challenged to do things.

LOGISTICS: What materials, resources, and technology will I need to prepare and engage?

Computer/Projector
Index Cards/Post-it Notes/Paper
Writing Utensils

WEEK 10

LESSON CYCLE:

1. Engage and Connect **(15 min)**

Facilitator/Mentor will open by defining the words **Love** and **Boundary**. Discuss how self-love is an integral part of every person's life. Share that self-love shows the love a person displays or shows themselves daily through their internal/mental dialogue and when setting personal boundaries.

  a. **Boundaries** are limits youth set to protect themselves from being hurt, manipulated, or taken advantage of. As an expression of self-worth, boundaries let other people know who your teen is, what they value, and how they want to be treated.
  b. **Love** is an intense feeling of deep affection; **Self-love** regards one's own well-being and happiness.

2. Lead Guided and Independent Practice **(25 min)**

  a. Facilitator/Mentor will take the participants through the *"What are Boundaries?"* lesson and activity.
   1. **Activity 1**: Explain that personal boundaries are like a fence around a house; the fence keeps the house protected.
      i. Have each participant draw a picture of a house (the house represents them) and draw a fence around it.
      ii. On the outside of the fence, write down words that describe behaviors that make them feel uncomfortable.
      iii. On the inside of the fence, list words that describe how they want to be treated, and how they will treat others.
   2. **Activity 2**: Instruct the participants to make a list of their personal boundaries and explain why they have chosen their personal boundaries.

Examples of Personal Boundary	Participants top 5 Boundaries
1. Saying No and sticking with it.	1.
2. Expecting and giving respect.	2.
3. The right to ask for help when needed.	3.

3. Close the Lesson and Assess Mastery **(15 min)**

Facilitator/Mentor will share *"love is an essential ingredient in human development and is essential when developing/building relationships. Discuss how setting healthy boundaries shows an individual's love of self. Review the various ways a person can show love to them self and to others. Share your list with the participants and have a few to share theirs as well. "*

Pillar: Loving

Discussion Questions:

1. Who will you go to for help if your boundaries are not being respected at home, school, church, etc.?
2. What will you say to an adult/friend who does not respect your boundaries?
3. How can you tell what someone's personal boundaries are regarding personal space and/or touch?
4. How will you respect another person's boundaries?

(https://educateempowerkids.org/wp-content/uploads/2019/09/Boundaries-2.pdf)

LOGISTICS: What materials, resources, and technology will I need to prepare and engage?

Computer
Projector
Paper/Pencil/Pen
Boundaries Lesson/Activity

LESSON VOCABULARY WORDS

INSTRUCTIONS: Review vocabulary words listed below with the participants to ensure they have a good understanding of each before starting any of the activities.

1. **Love:** a strong affection for another arising out of kinship or personal ties; attention based on affection and tenderness; affection based on admiration, benevolence, or common interests.
2. **Personal Boundaries:** are the limits and rules we set for ourselves within relationships.
3. **Forgiveness:** a conscious, deliberate decision to release feelings of resentment or vengeance toward a person or group who has harmed you, regardless of whether they actually deserve your forgiveness.

Discussion Questions: Be prepared to answer the following questions during the group's discussion time.

1. What is Critical Thinking?

   _____
   _____

2. What are the components of critical thinking?

   _____
   _____

3. Who will you go to for help if your boundaries are not being respected at home, school, church, etc.?

   _____
   _____

4. What will you say to an adult/friend who does not respect your boundaries?

   _____
   _____

5. How can you tell what someone's personal boundaries are regarding personal space and/or touch?

   _____
   _____

6. How will you respect another person's boundaries?

   _____
   _____

Pillar: Loving

Activity: *"How Many Can You Think Of?"* Facilitator/Mentor will think of 1-2 words that fits into a theme or category during the group's discussion period to write down as many words that are related to the theme or category the word belongs to.

BOUNDARIES WORKSHEET – EMOTIONAL BOUNDARIES

OBJECTIVES: To enable an individual to explore his/her emotional boundaries and pre-plan healthy ways of dealing with the situation where somebody violates his/her boundaries.

INSTRUCTIONS: Emotional boundaries of an individual are his thoughts, feelings, and cognitions that separate him from the thoughts, feelings, and cognitions of others. In the table given below, state some of your emotional boundaries and how they differ from those of others. Brainstorm and write down the healthy ways in which you would react if somebody tried to cross your emotional boundaries.

Emotional Boundaries	Difference from Other's Emotional Boundaries	My Reaction if Someone Violates my Emotional Boundaries

https://optimistminds.com/boundaries-worksheets/

Pillar: Loving

BOUNDARIES WORKSHEET – PERSONAL BOUNDARIES

Objectives: To help an individual identify healthy and unhealthy boundaries in their relationship and work on them.

Instructions: In the table given below, write down some of the healthy boundaries in your relationship and think of ways in which you can improve them further. In the next table, recall and write down the unhealthy boundaries to your relationship. Mention the ways in which you can replace them with healthy boundaries.

Healthy Boundaries in My Relationships	Ways to Improve Them

Unhealthy Boundaries in My Relationship	Ways to Replace Them with Healthy Ones

https://optimistminds.com/boundaries-worksheets/

BOUNDARIES WORKSHEET – PERSONAL BOUNDARIES

Objectives: To enable an individual to set his/her personal boundaries and pre-plan his reaction if someone violates his boundaries.

Instructions: Personal boundaries of an individual define his/her likes and dislikes, personal beliefs, emotions, etc. In the table given below write down your personal boundaries and the way, you would tell others about these. Also, mention the ways your boundaries can be violated and your reaction in that case.

Personal Boundaries	How do I communicate these Others	How Someone Can Violate my Personal Boundaries	My Reaction When Someone Violates my Boundaries

https://optimistminds.com/boundaries-worksheets/

Pillar: Loving

LESSON TITLE:

Self-Love/Critical Thinking/Boundaries

LEVEL: Employee or Community Citizen

WEEKS 9-10

PACING: 45 min

OBJECTIVE(S): What will Participants know, understand, and be able to do?

- Participants will think critically, make meaningful personal connections, and learn how to build healthy relationships.
- Participants will learn how to create, communicate, and maintain healthy boundaries.
- Participants will learn the difference between facts and opinions.

KEY VOCABULARY: What key terms will my Participants need to understand?

Critical Thinking: helps people make good decisions, understand the consequences of their actions, and solve problems.

Facts: statements that can be verified.

Opinions: statements that express a person's feelings, attitudes, or beliefs.

Boundaries: limits people set to protect themselves from being hurt, manipulated, or taken advantage of; personal limits.

Love: an intense feeling of deep affection.

(Merriam-Webster)

WEEK 9

LESSON CYCLE:

1. Engage and Connect (15 min)

Open by sharing the definition of **Critical Thinking**. Critical Thinking helps people make good decisions, understand the consequences of their actions, and solve problems. Show the "*What is Critical Thinking?*" video: https://www.youtube.com/watch?v=-eEBuqwY-nE

2. Lead Guided and Independent Practice (25 min)

a. Discuss the difference between fact vs. opinion.

1. **Facts** are statements that can be verified. They can be proven true or false. Statements of fact are objective – they contain information but do not tell what the writer thinks or believes about the topic/subject. (i.e. My car payment is $250 per month.) Questions to Identify Facts:

    i. Can the statement be proved or demonstrated to be true?
    ii. Can the statement be observed in practice or operation? Can you see it happen?
    iii. Can the statement be verified by witnesses, manuscripts, or documents?

2. **Opinions** are statements that express a writer's feelings, attitudes, or beliefs. They are neither true nor false. They are one person's view about a topic or issue. (i.e. My car payments are too expensive.) ***Types of Opinions***: positions on controversial issues; predictions about things in the future; and evaluations of people, places, and things.

Words to Identify Opinions: Biased Words (bad, worse, worst, good, better, best, worthwhile, worthless, etc.); Qualifiers (all, always, likely, never, might, seem, possibly, probably, should, etc.) Questions to identify opinion/informed opinions:

  i. Does the speaker have a current and relevant background to the topic under discussion?
  ii. Is the speaker generally respected within the field or with the topic being discussed?
  iii. Is the speak using judgment words, to identify when presenting opinions vs. facts?

b. "***Fact vs Opinion***" Activity: This activity causes people to think of words that fit into a theme or category.
  1. Activity One: **Locating Judgment Words**. (*Underline or circle the bias or qualifying words.*):
      i. Purchasing a brand-new car is a terrible waste of money.
      ii. I hate or love my job and the company I work for.
      iii. Marvel Comics are better than DC Comics, especially Luke Cage and the Black Panther.
      iv. The new iPhone I purchased came with a set of ear-buds.
      v. Volunteers for Habitat for Humanity are engaged in a worthwhile activity.

  2. Activity Two: **Distinguishing Between Fact and Opinion in a Paragraph**.
  [1] Flowering plants that are native to the South include purple coneflower and rose verbena. [2] In the view of many longtime gardeners, these two plants are an essential part of the Southern landscape. [3] Trees that are native to the South include a variety of oaks, as well as flowering dogwoods and redbuds. [4] Dogwoods are especially lovely, with their white, pink, or coral blossoms announcing the arrival of spring. [5] For fall color, the deep red of the Virginia willow makes a spectacular show in the native Southern Garden.

  1. _____   2. _____   3. _____
  4. _____   5. _____

  (https://www.montgomerycollege.edu/_documents/academics/support/learning-centers/writing-reading-learning-ctr-rockville/Participant-resources-tech/fact-vs-opinion.pdf)

3. *Close the Lesson and Assess Mastery*   **(15 min)**

Discuss how critical thinking was used during the activities when determining the difference between fact and opinion.

LOGISTICS: What materials, resources, and technology will I need to prepare and engage?

Computer
Projector
Paper
Pencil/Pen

Pillar: Loving

WEEK 10

LESSON CYCLE:

1. Engage and Connect **(15 min)**

Open by defining the words **Love** and **Boundary**. Discuss how self-love is an integral part of every person's life. Share that self-love shows the love a person displays or shows themselves daily through their internal/mental dialogue and when setting personal boundaries.

    a. ***Boundaries*** are limits people set to protect themselves from being hurt, manipulated, or taken advantage of. Boundaries are personal limits, and no two sets of boundaries are the same that is where your values, beliefs, and emotions meet (and sometime clash). As an expression of self-worth, boundaries let other people know who you are, what you value, and how you want to be treated.

    b. ***Love*** is an intense feeling of deep affection; *Self-love* regards one's own well-being and happiness.

2. Lead Guided and Independent Practice **(30 min)**

    a. Share that setting healthy boundaries help you establish what is acceptable and what is unacceptable to you, as well as where your responsibilities begin and end. Take the participants through the "*Find Your Core Values*" Activity. Everyone has different personal values that are the foundation of their boundaries. Therefore, it is essential they are clear on what their values are.

        1. ***Find Your Core Values*** Activity: In your relationship, your values may include having shared interests or working towards common goals. At work, your values may include having a healthy work-life balance or a strong company culture. Your family values may include spending quality time together or even limiting the amount of time spent together.

            i. Write down your ten most important values, then narrow them down to 3 or 4 core values. These will help you determine what you can accept or tolerate and what you will not accept in any given situation.

            ii. For each core value, ask yourself the following 3 questions and write down your answers:
                a. What will I allow given this value?
                b. What will I tolerate given this value?
                c. What will I not allow given this value?

            iii. Learn how to clearly communicate your boundaries. It allows others to know what your expectations of them are. Since we all have different boundaries, we will sometimes unintentionally cross the line with one another.
                a. Do not approach the conversation from a place of blame to avoid provoking conflict.
                b. Use the following non-violent communication to communicate your boundaries. Take a problem-solving approach.
                c. Share how the other person's actions impact you and explain how this relates to your core values. This will help them understand what your boundaries are without becoming defensive — which means they will be much more

receptive to taking your message on board. For example, you could say your boss: *"One of my core values is having a healthy work-life balance so that I can spend time with my family. When you ask me to work overtime without warning, I feel that crosses a boundary and comprises my core value."*

    iv. Consistently maintain your boundaries
        a. When dealing with crossed boundaries, keep your core values at the forefront of your mind and refer to them during the conversation.
        b. Use a constructive approach that will lead to less conflict and greater harmony and understanding.

(https://www.coaching-online.org/files/5-Best-Boundaries-Setting-Exercises.pdf)

3. Close the Lesson and Assess Mastery **(10 min)**

Love is an essential ingredient in human development and is essential when developing/building relationships. Discuss how knowing, communicating, and maintaining your boundaries helps to set healthy boundaries. It shows an individual's love of self. Review the various ways a person can show love to them self and to others.

Discussion Questions:
1. How will you maintain your boundaries when they are not being respected at home, school, church, etc.?
2. What will you say to an adult/friend/family-member who does not respect your boundaries?
3. How can you tell when you have unintentionally crossed someone's personal boundaries?

LOGISTICS: What materials, resources, and technology will I need to prepare and engage?

Computer
Projector
Paper
Pencil/Pen

Pillar: Loving

LESSON VOCABULARY WORDS

INSTRUCTIONS: Review vocabulary words listed below with the participants to ensure they have a good understanding of each before starting any of the activities.

1. **Critical Thinking:** helps people make good decisions, understand the consequences of their actions, and solve problems.
2. **Facts:** statements that can be verified.
3. **Opinions:** statements that express a person's feelings, attitudes, or beliefs.
4. **Boundaries:** limits people set to protect themselves from being hurt, manipulated, or taken advantage of; personal limits.
5. **Love:** an intense feeling of deep affection.

Discussion Question:

1. What is Critical Thinking?

2. What are the components of critical thinking?

3. What is the difference between facts and opinions?

4. What are boundaries?

5. What are core values?

6. In what way can facts and opinions impact your core values?

Activity: Write down your ten most important values and answer the questions for each value.

1. _____

   a. What will I allow given this value: _____

   b. What will I tolerate given this value: _____

   c. What will I NOT allow given this value: _____

2. _____

   a. What will I allow given this value: _____

   b. What will I tolerate given this value: _____

   c. What will I NOT allow given this value: _____

3. _____

   a. What will I allow given this value: _____

   b. What will I tolerate given this value: _____

   c. What will I NOT allow given this value: _____

4. _____

   a. What will I allow given this value: _____

   b. What will I tolerate given this value: _____

   c. What will I NOT allow given this value: _____

Pillar: Loving

5. _____

   a. What will I allow given this value: _____

   b. What will I tolerate given this value: _____

   c. What will I NOT allow given this value: _____

6. _____

   a. What will I allow given this value: _____

   b. What will I tolerate given this value: _____

   c. What will I NOT allow given this value: _____

7. _____

   a. What will I allow given this value: _____

   b. What will I tolerate given this value: _____

   c. What will I NOT allow given this value: _____

8. _____

   a. What will I allow given this value: _____

   b. What will I tolerate given this value: _____

   c. What will I NOT allow given this value: _____

9. _____

   a. What will I allow given this value: _____
   _____

   b. What will I tolerate given this value: _____
   _____

   c. What will I NOT allow given this value: _____
   _____

10. _____

    a. What will I allow given this value: _____
    _____

    b. What will I tolerate given this value: _____
    _____

    c. What will I NOT allow given this value: _____
    _____

Pillar: Loving

BOUNDARIES WORKSHEET – PERSONAL BOUNDARIES

Objectives: To help an individual identify healthy and unhealthy boundaries in their relationship and work on them.

Instructions: In the table given below, write down some of the healthy boundaries in your relationship and think of ways in which you can improve them further. In the next table, recall and write down the unhealthy boundaries to your relationship. Mention the ways in which you can replace them with healthy boundaries.

Healthy Boundaries in My Relationships	Ways to Improve Them

Unhealthy Boundaries in My Relationship	Ways to Replace Them with Healthy Ones

https://optimistminds.com/boundaries-worksheets/

BOUNDARIES WORKSHEET – PERSONAL BOUNDARIES

Objectives: To enable an individual to set his/her personal boundaries and pre-plan his reaction if someone violates his boundaries.

Instructions: Personal boundaries of an individual define his/her likes and dislikes, personal beliefs, emotions, etc. in the table given below write down your personal boundaries and the way, you would tell others about these. Also, mention the ways your boundaries can be violated and your reaction in that case.

Personal Boundaries	How do I communicate these Others	How Someone Can Violate my Personal Boundaries	My Reaction When Someone Violates my Boundaries

https://optimistminds.com/boundaries-worksheets/

Pillar: Loving

LESSON TITLE:

Love Begins in Me

LEVEL: Youth **WEEKS 11-12**

PACING: 55 min

OBJECTIVE(S): What will Participants know, understand, and be able to do?

Participants will learn how to self-care by:

- Enhancing health and wellbeing
- Managing stress
- Maintaining professionalism as a Participant
- Identifying healthy activities and practices
- Sustaining positive self-care in the long-term

KEY VOCABULARY: What key terms will my Participants need to understand?

Self-care: The practice of taking action to preserve or improve one's health.

Stress: A state of mental or emotional strain.

Meditation: Continued or extended thought; reflection; contemplation.

Prevention: The act of preventing or hindering.

(Merriam-Webster)

WEEK 11

LESSON CYCLE:

1. Engage and Connect   **(15 min)**

Self-care is anything you enjoy doing that helps make you happy and maintains your physical, mental, or emotional health. Ask the Participants, why it is important to take care of themselves? Should females/males just *"get over it"* when they are stressed?

2. Lead Guided and Independent Practice   **(30 min)**

Facilitator/Mentor will ask participants what stress do they experience daily? What stresses him/her out at home or school? Are these things he/she can control? Are they overreacting?

This will be used as a safe space for venting to release any built-up stress (school, home, sports, society). Let the participants know what they are experiencing are normal emotions, and that everyone experiences them (children/youth/adults).

Facilitator/Mentor will ask how is this stress impacting them in school and personal life?

3. Close the Lesson and Assess Mastery   **(10 min)**

Have the Participants keep track of their stress-induced events over the next few days.

LOGISTICS: What materials, resources, and technology will I need to prepare and engage?
Computer
Projector
Paper

Pencil/Pen

WEEK 12

LESSON CYCLE:

1. Engage and Connect (15 min)

Self-care only works when you intentionally take the time needed for yourself. It can be as simple as every day listening to music, reading a book and/or an article, or playing outside or a video game.

Or

Bigger events like having a meal with friends, doing a hobby, or playing sport.

Facilitator/Mentor will ask each participant to share how you know when you need to dedicate time to self-care, and how it helps when it's time for you to mentor?

2. Lead Guided and Independent Practice (25 min)

Have the Participants draft a list of their self-care routines. Allow them to share to get a few additional ideas. Below is a list to share with the Participants to give them more ideas as well. Have them commit to 3.

| 1. Listen to music
2. Talk to a friend
3. Watch a movie
4. Talk it out with a family member
5. Read a book
6. Go for a walk
7. Ride your bike
8. Exercise
9. Watch motivational YouTube videos | 10. Sketch
11. Play with your pet
12. Stretch your muscles
13. Eat your favorite snack
14. Play video games
15. Meditate or pray
16. Talk to a friend on the phone
17. Go to the park with a friend | 18. Paint
19. Get a haircut
20. Take a nap
21. Go to a friend's house
22. Do something nice for someone
23. Contact your mentor
24. Write in a journal
25. Write a song/poem |

3. Close the Lesson and Assess Mastery (15 min)

Have the Participants share which practices they will commit to in the future.

LOGISTICS: What materials, resources, and technology will I need to prepare and engage?

Computer
Projector
Paper
Pencil/Pen
Feelings Handout

Pillar: Loving

Stress Relief Activities

LESSON VOCABULARY WORDS

INSTRUCTIONS: Review vocabulary words listed below with the participants to ensure they have a good understanding of each before starting any of the activities.

1. **Self-care:** The practice of taking action to preserve or improve one's health.
2. **Stress:** A state of mental or emotional strain.
3. **Meditation:** Continued or extended thought; reflection; contemplation.
4. **Prevention:** The act of preventing or hindering.

SELF-CARE: Self-care is anything you enjoy doing that helps make you happy and maintains your physical, mental, or emotional health.

1. Why is it important to take care of ourselves?

___

2. Should females/males just *"get over it"* when they are stressed?

___

Discussion Questions:

1. Have you ever experienced stress at home or in school?

___

2. Do you have a safe place and person to share your concerns and/or stressors?

___

3. How much time do you dedicate to self-care?

4. List your self-care routines below:

   a. _____

   b. _____

   c. _____

   d. _____

   e. _____

   f. _____

   g. _____

   h. _____

   i. _____

   j. _____

   k. _____

   l. _____

   m. _____

Pillar: Loving

The following are activities the participant can participate in as a self-care activity. Before and after each activity identify how you are feeling by using the "*How Do I Feel Right Now*" Chart above.

Anchor Breathing

Anchor breathing can be quickly learned and helps a child to focus their mind on one point. Such mental training offers a valuable method for gaining perceived self-control and reducing stress.

Step Sounds

1. Imagine being on a boat, feeling calm and safe.
2. Attached to the boat is an anchor. It keeps you there, where you want to be, and happy.
3. Our bodies, like the boat, also have anchors, and they can help us focus. Our belly, our nose and mouth, and our chest and lungs can help us feel grounded.
4. With your hands on your chest, breathe in deeply.
5. Breathe out slowly.
6. Feel your ribs rise and fall.
7. As your mind wanders, gently bring it back to the anchor point.

The Anchor Breathing method also works with hands placed gently on the belly or in front of the nose.

Nature Play

Senses, often underused, such as sound, can heighten a sense of awareness and promote mindfulness. This can be especially true in an unfamiliar environment, including walking through the countryside with family.

Step Sounds

1. Pause and listen
2. What can you hear that is nearby?
3. What can you hear that is far away?
4. What is the loudest sound?
5. What is the quietest sound?
6. Can you walk without making a noise?

Meditation on the Soles of the Feet

Using mindfulness or meditation to regulate emotional responses can be a challenging task. Especially when emotions are strong, being able to observe the emotion while resisting the impulse to act upon that emotion is often more easily said than done. In some cases, using mindfulness and meditation with individuals with lower mental abilities becomes difficult. This tool was designed for individuals with lower mental abilities to enhance their ability to cope with aggressive responses.

Pillar: Loving

It must be noted that most studies on the effects of this meditation on aggression have used small numbers of participants (1-18 participants). However, the results of 13 studies have been reviewed and suggest that mindfulness practices, like this exercise, can help reduce anger and aggressive responding (see Fix & Fix, 2013).

Goal: This exercise aims to help clients effectively regulate the urge to be physically or verbally aggressive.

INSTRUCTIONS:

1. If you are standing, assume a natural rather than an aggressive posture, with the soles of your feet flat on the floor. If sitting, relax with the soles of your feet flat on the floor.
2. Think about a time when something caused you to experience strong anger. Try to reconnect to that experience. Try to relive the experience that caused anger.
3. You are feeling anger, and angry thoughts may arise. Let the thoughts flow naturally without pushing them away. Stay with anger. You may have physical reactions that display anger, including an increased heart rate, increased breathing rate, and tension in the jaw, neck, and/or shoulders.
4. Shift the focus of your attention to the soles of your feet.
5. Slowly, move your toes, feel your shoes covering your feet, the texture of your socks or hose, the curve of your arch, and the heels of your feet against the back of your shoes. If you do not have shoes on, feel the floor or carpet with the soles of your feet.
6. Keep breathing naturally and focus on the soles of your feet until you feel calm.
7. Practice this exercise until you can use it wherever you are and whenever an incident occurs that may cause you to feel the urge to be verbally or physically aggressive.
8. Remember that once you are calm, you can walk away from the incident or situation with a smile on your face because you regulated your anger. Alternatively, if you need to, you can respond to the incident or situation with a calm and clear mind and without verbal threats or physical aggression.

Daily Journaling

A journal can be a fruitful way to track life's ups and downs. By capturing what went well, it is possible to identify and record the skills and talents for reuse in other areas of your life. Journaling allows people to clarify their thoughts and feelings, thereby gaining valuable self-knowledge. It's also a good problem-solving tool; oftentimes, one can hash out a problem and come up with solutions more easily on paper. Journaling about traumatic events helps one process them by fully exploring and releasing the emotions involved, and by engaging both hemispheres of the brain in the process, allowing the experience to become fully integrated within one's mind. Journaling can also help you to focus on areas of your life that you like to focus on more often, as is the case with gratitude journaling or even coincidence journaling.

Journaling doesn't release tension from your body like progressive muscle relaxation, guided imagery, and/or other physical and meditative techniques, however, it is a great practice for overall stress reduction as well as self-knowledge and emotional healing.

LESSON TITLE:

Love Begins in Me

LEVEL: Employee or Community Citizen

WEEKS 11-12

PACING: 55 min

OBJECTIVE(S): What will Participants know, understand, and be able to do?

Participants will learn how to use self-care as a representation of your self-love:

- Enhance health and wellbeing
- Manage stress
- Maintain professionalism as a Participant
- Identify healthy activities and practices
- Sustain positive self-care in the long-term

KEY VOCABULARY: What key terms will my Participants need to understand?

Self-care: The practice of taking action to preserve or improve one's health.

Self-love: is the practice of understanding, embracing, and showing compassion for yourself. It is adoration of your strengths and acceptance of your weaknesses.

Stress: A state of mental or emotional strain.

Meditation: Continued or extended thought; reflection; contemplation.

Prevention: The act of preventing or hindering.

(Merriam-Webster)

WEEK 11

LESSON CYCLE:

1. Engage and Connect **(20 min)**

Share that **self-care** means taking steps to look after yourself and your physical, emotional, mental, and spiritual needs. Self-care starts with the acknowledgment that you are responsible for your wellbeing. Once you take responsibility for yourself, you'll be able to function in a more relaxed and grounded way. All areas of your life will improve once you take time to nurture your needs. **Self-care** is an integral part of *self-love* which is the practice of being kind and compassionate towards yourself. Here are 5 ways to begin practicing self-love:

   a. ***Identify your subpersonalities.*** Within all of us, there are subtle and incessant voices that sabotage and paralyze us – these are the voices of our subpersonalities. Awareness is the key to overcoming the negative self-talk. To quiet these voices, practice self-compassionate mindfulness.
   b. ***Identify toxic people in your life.*** Learn to distance yourself (or flat out remove from your life) those who hinder your self-growth is a difficult, but necessary. A toxic person is often judgmental, manipulative, clingy, backstabbing, ruthless, aggressive, controlling, deceptive, self-pitying, and/or self-destructive.
   c. ***Seek supportive community.*** Supportive people encourage, uplift, and inspire us they have obtained a certain level of self-love. Because of their ability to respect themselves, they can easily respect and love others. Invite these individuals into your life and build lasting relationships with them. They can also act as accountability partners as you continue your professional and personal journey.

Pillar: Loving

    d. ***Make time to explore your passions***. What drives you? Fires you up? Fills you with joy and a sense of accomplishment. Sit down with these questions and ponder them deeply. Remember, passions are not static – they evolve with us. Whether painting, writing, dancing, designing, building or whatever excites you – pursue it – even if on the sidelines!

    e. ***Do a digital detox (aka. stop spending so much time on social media!)***. To practice self-love, we need to regularly practice digital detoxes. A digital detox involves voluntarily refusing to use any form of social media for a period of a few days to a month or more. Uninstall the apps on your phone. Go outside. Plan to do something more nourishing with your time. Journal about your progress. The benefits can often be felt within a day!

    (https://lonerwolf.com/self-love/)

2. Lead Guided and Independent Practice   **(25 min)**

Discuss how everyone desires to feel loved and receive love. Most people find it easy to love others but difficult to love them self. By practicing self-love (being empathetic and understanding of their flaws, and appreciation of their good), you accept who you are on your own terms and begin making necessary changes to ensure you grow into who you have the potential of being. Self-love is necessary for positive emotional health and various facets of success.

    a. **My Love Letter to Myself**. Instruct the participants to write a love letter to them self that emphasizes their most valued attributes. When writing the love letter have the participants to:
      1. Identify the top eight qualities they love most about them self.
      2. Lists eight ways in which these attributes have benefited them in life.
      3. Note several ways to honor the above qualities.

    b. **Self-Compassion Pause**. This exercise provides a way for individuals to discover more self-compassionate ways to approach/overcome stressful experiences. Instruct participants to use the following three steps during stressful encounters:
      1. Pause. Take special notice of your breath. Notice what you feel.
      2. Use the power of touch. Hug yourself or put your hand on your chest.
      3. When applicable, remind yourself, "This is a difficult moment for me. I am experiencing suffering. Suffering is a part of life. I accept myself as I am."

    (https://positivepsychology.com/self-love-exercises-worksheets/)

3. Close the Lesson and Assess Mastery   **(10 min)**

Ask participants to share what they learned about them self from this week's lesson.

LOGISTICS: What materials, resources, and technology will I need to prepare and engage?

Computer/Projector
Paper
Pencil/Pen
Feelings Handout
Self-Compassion Pause Worksheet
My Love Letter to Myself Worksheet

WEEK 12

LESSON CYCLE:

1. Engage and Connect **(20 min)**

Discuss how sometimes focusing on your personal and professional needs shows self-love. Loving ourselves is one of the most important things a person can do to achieve a satisfying, meaningful and joy-filled life. Loving yourself is the foundation for a flourishing future. Go over the following ideas of ways you can achieve this:

a. **Make Yourself Your Number 1 Priority**. Many people fall into the trap of putting their children, spouse, friends, etc. needs first. If you keep this up, you'll soon drain your own tank and once it's drained, you'll have nothing left to give. That's why it's so important to recharge, take a breather and put yourself first. If you don't, it's a recipe for disaster. Remember, to love others and be loved, you need to first love yourself.

b. **Take Care of Your Emotional/Mental Well-being**. Respect and nurture your body by eating a healthy, well-balanced diet, exercising on a regular basis, brushing your teeth, keeping yourself clean and well-groomed and getting enough sleep. Taking care of your body will improve your emotional, mental, and physical health.

c. **Be Your Own Best Friend**. Who better to be your best friend than you? Show yourself the same compassion and empathy you would your best friend. Learn to enjoy your own company. You know yourself better than anyone else.
(https://www.activebeat.com/your-health/women/lets-talk-about-loving-yourself/6/)

2. Lead Guided and Independent Practice **(25 min)**

Facilitator/Mentor will instruct the participants to draft a list of their self-care routines. Allow them to share to get a few ideas with each other. Below is a list to share with the participants to give them some more ideas as well. Have them commit to 6.

1. Listen to music	10. Sketch	19. Paint
2. Visit a loving friend/family member	11. Play with your pet	20. Get a haircut
3. Watch a movie	12. Stretch your muscles	21. Take a nap
4. Talk it out with a family member	13. Eat your favorite snack	22. Go to a friend's house
5. Read a book	14. Play video games	23. Do something nice for someone
6. Go for a walk/Take a hike	15. Meditate or pray	24. Contact your mentor
7. Ride your bike	16. Talk to a friend on the phone	25. Write in a journal
8. Exercise	17. Go to the park with a friend	26. Write a song/poem/book
9. Watch motivational YouTube videos	18. Take a long hot bath	27. Take a drive in the country/along a mountain road

Pillar: Loving

3. Close the Lesson and Assess Mastery **(10 min)**

Have the participants share the practices they will commit to in the future.

LOGISTICS: What materials, resources, and technology will I need to prepare and engage?

Computer/Projector
Paper
Pencil/Pen
Self-Care Routines List

LESSON VOCABULARY WORDS

INSTRUCTIONS: Review vocabulary words listed below with the participants to ensure they have a good understanding of each before starting any of the activities.

1. **Self-care:** The practice of taking action to preserve or improve one's health.
2. **Self-love:** is the practice of understanding, embracing, and showing compassion for yourself. It is adoration of your strengths and acceptance of your weaknesses.
3. **Stress:** A state of mental or emotional strain.
4. **Meditation:** Continued or extended thought; reflection; contemplation.
5. **Prevention:** The act of preventing or hindering.

Discussion Questions:

1. Have you ever experienced stress at home or in business?
   _____
   _____

2. Do you have a safe place and person to share your concerns and/or stressors?
   _____
   _____

3. How much time do you dedicate to self-care?
   _____
   _____

4. List your self-care routines below:
   a. _____
   b. _____
   c. _____
   d. _____
   e. _____
   f. _____
   g. _____
   h. _____
   i. _____

Pillar: Loving

DATE: _____

SELF-CARE ACTIVITIES

AFFIRMATION

- _____
- _____
- _____
- _____

TODAY'S MOOD

☹ 🙁 😐 🙂 😃

I'M GRATEFUL FOR:

_____

_____

INSPIRATION: ....

....

....

MY 'LOVE LETTER' TO MYSELF

The purpose of this exercise is for you to identify your many great qualities and how they benefit you. You also, will come up with ways to practice your strengths in daily life. This self-love exercise will help you to focus on your best traits, abilities, and talents. In doing so, you are on your way to becoming a more self-confident and resilient individual.

Step 1: Think about the things you love most about yourself. Focus on qualities of your personality that make you unique, strong, or lovable. For example:

♥ I am: *Honest*

♥ I am: *Brave*

♥ I am: *Creative*

Now list your positive qualities below:

♥ I am:

♥ I am:

♥ I am:

♥ I am:

♥ I am:

♥ I am:

♥ I am:

♥ I am:

Pillar: Loving

Step 2: Consider the ways in which these qualities have benefited you or someone else in your life. For example:

♥ The quality of honesty has benefited me because my boss trusts me to work on important projects independently.

♥ The quality of bravery has benefited me because I got through a very painful situation in my life and became stronger because of it.

♥ The quality of creativity has benefited me because I have created artwork that I am proud to display in my home.

Now list the benefits of your positive qualities below:

♥ The quality of _____ has benefited

me because: _____.

♥ The quality of _____ has benefited

me because: _____.

♥ The quality of _____ has benefited

me because: _____.

♥ The quality of _____ has benefited

me because: _____.

♥ The quality of _____ has benefited

me because:

_____.

♥ The quality of _____ has benefited

me because: _____.

♥ The quality of _____ has benefited

me because: _____.

♥ The quality of _____ has benefited

me because: _____.

Step 3: Next come up with ways to honor these qualities in ways that are personally meaningful to you. For example:

♥ *I will remind myself that I am a good and honest person each day.*

♥ *When faced with challenges, I will remember the times I have overcome adversity in my life.*

♥ *I will continue to create because doing so makes me feel more fulfilled and content.*

Now list the ways you will honor your positive qualities below:

♥ I am:

♥ I am:

♥ I am:

♥ I am:

♥ I am:

♥ I am:

♥ I am:

♥ I am:

Now that you have completed your "letter," keep it handy and feel free to add to it when you learn more wonderful things about yourself!

https://positive.b-cdn.net/wp-content/uploads/Self-love_My-Love-Letter-to-Myself-1.pdf

Pillar: Loving

SELF-CARE ROUTINES LIST

Self-Care Activities	Date Completed
1.	
2.	
3.	
4.	
5.	
6.	
7.	
8.	
9.	
10.	
11.	
12.	
13.	
14.	
15.	
16.	
17.	
18.	
19.	
20.	
21.	
22.	
23.	
24.	
25.	
26.	

SELF-COMPASSION PAUSE. Use the following three steps during stressful encounters:

1. **Pause.** Take special notice of your breath. Notice what you feel.

2. **Use the power of touch.** Hug yourself or put your hand on your chest.

3. **Say to yourself.** "This is a difficult moment for me. I am experiencing suffering. Suffering is a part of life. I accept myself as I am."

Pillar: Loving

LESSON TITLE:

The Power of Giving

LEVEL: Youth **WEEKS 13-14**

PACING: 55 min

OBJECTIVE(S): What will Participants know, understand, and be able to do?

- Participants will learn to think beyond themselves.
- Participants will learn leadership skills by learning how to give time and resources.
- Participants will learn about random acts of kindness.
- Participants will create a Community Service Plan.

KEY VOCABULARY: What key terms will my Participants need to understand?

Encourage: To inspire with courage, spirit, or hope.
Impact: to have a direct effect.
Recognition: Formal acknowledgment.
Volunteer: A person who voluntarily undertakes a service.
Giving: To make a present.
Kindness: Courtesy, mercy, service.
Community Service: non-paying job performed by one person or a group of people for the benefit of their community or its institutions.

(Merriam-Webster)

WEEK 13

LESSON CYCLE:

1. Engage and Connect (15 min)

Discuss the meaning of the following words:

"**community service**" voluntary work intended to help people
"**giving**" providing love or other emotional support, caring
"**volunteer**" is a person who performs a service for someone else

2. Lead Guided and Independent Practice (25 min)

Small acts of kindness can help someone who is having an unpleasant day see the positive in the world. Have each participant make a list of 2 people they know could use a bit of positivity and why. Example:

The person that could use some positivity	Why?
My best friend	He is sad because he must move to a different school.
The principal	She is doing the best she can to keep everyone at school safe and might be stressed.

Encourage the Participants to reach out to these people soon with something that can brighten their day.

3. *Close the Lesson and Assess Mastery* (15 min)

Allow a few Participants to share and develop ideas.

LOGISTICS: What materials, resources, and technology will I need to prepare and engage?

Paper
Pencil/Pen
Random Acts of Kindness Journal

Pillar: Loving

WEEK 14

LESSON CYCLE:

1. Engage and Connect (20 min)

Community Service projects or Random Acts of Kindness broadens your horizons by helping you understand the needs of the society and the population you are trying to help through the project. Instruct participants to make a list of possible community service projects.

2. Lead Guided and Independent Practice (25 min)

Instruct participants to pick 1 or 2 projects from their list and describe in detail how the community service project would be performed, who would benefit and the anticipated outcome. Help the participants to develop a community service project that they can complete during the mentoring program. Begin mapping out the Community Service project and create plan of action in the space below:

Community Service Project	Steps needed to complete the Community Service Project
Name:	1.
	2.
Date:	3.
Who will benefit:	4.
	5.

3. Close the Lesson and Assess Mastery (10 min)

Close the lesson by sharing the following message:

Kindness promotes empathy and compassion, which in turn, leads to a sense of interconnectedness with others. When we practice random acts of kindness, it releases energy. We feel better and the recipients of our acts feel better, which then makes them more likely to be kind to other people. Have participants share the random acts of kindness and/or community service projects they have been involved in, seen on social media, experienced firsthand, etc.

LOGISTICS: What materials, resources, and technology will I need to prepare and engage?

Paper
Community Service Project Planner
Pencil/Pen
Community Service Planner

LESSON VOCABULARY WORDS

INSTRUCTIONS: Review vocabulary words listed below with the participants to ensure they have a good understanding of each before starting any of the activities.

1. **Encourage:** To inspire with courage, spirit, or hope.
2. **Impact:** to have a direct effect.
3. **Recognition:** Formal acknowledgment.
4. **Volunteer:** A person who voluntarily undertakes a service.
5. **Giving:** To make a present.
6. **Kindness:** Courtesy, mercy, service.
7. **Community Service**: non-paying job performed by one person or a group of people for the benefit of their community or its institutions.

Pillar: Loving

Random Acts of Kindness
Journal

S M T W T F S

DATE | PLANNED ACT

be kind and grateful

WHAT DID I LEARN ABOUT MYSELF...

HOW WERE MY ACTS RECEIVED...

WHO DID I INSPIRE FROM MY RANDOM ACTS...

NOTES:

Intentional Mentoring Mentor's Guide

Project Planner
COMMUNITY SERVICE

MONTH: _____

COMMUNITY SERVICE PROJECT TITLE

ANTICIPATED START DATE

ANTICIPATED DEADLINE

IDEAS

to-do list

notes

Pillar: Loving

LESSON TITLE:

The Power of Giving

OBJECTIVE(S): What will Participants know, understand, and be able to do?

- Participants will learn to think beyond themselves.
- Participants will learn leadership skills by learning how to give time and resources.
- Participants will learn about random acts of kindness.

LEVEL: Employee or Community Citizen

WEEKS 13-14

PACING: 55 min

KEY VOCABULARY: What key terms will my Participants need to understand?

Encourage: To inspire with courage, spirit, or hope.

Impact: to have a direct effect.

Recognition: Formal acknowledgment.

Volunteer: A person who voluntarily undertakes a service.

Giving: To make a present.

Kindness: Courtesy, mercy, service.

Community Service: non-paying job performed by one person or a group of people for the benefit of their community or its institutions.

(Merriam-Webster)

WEEK 13

LESSON CYCLE:

1. Engage and Connect (15 min)

Discuss the meaning of the following words:

"**community service**" voluntary work intended to help people
"**giving**" providing love or other emotional support, caring
"**volunteer**" is a person who performs a service for someone else

2. Lead Guided and Independent Practice (30 min)

Small acts of kindness can help someone who is having an unpleasant day see the positives in the world. Have each participant list 3 people they know who could use a bit of positivity now and why. Develop a plan of action to aid them with an act of kindness? Example:

The person that could use some positivity	Why?	What can I do?
My friend/family member	They are experiencing trauma/loss. The anniversary of a loss is approaching.	Help them manage their trauma/loss. Come up with a doable way to remember their loved one. Share with them the contact information for a grief therapist.
A Stranger	They are experiencing hard times	Share a meal with them; do something to bring a smile to their face and allow them to feel included/accepted.

Encourage the participants to reach out to these people soon with an act of kindness.

3. Close the Lesson and Assess Mastery **(10 min)**

Allow a few participants to share and develop ideas. Give a date of when the participants of Acts of Kindness will be performed.

LOGISTICS: What materials, resources, and technology will I need to prepare and engage?

Random Acts of Kindness Planner
Journal Pages
Pencil/Pen

Pillar: Loving

WEEK 14

LESSON CYCLE:

1. Engage and Connect **(10 min)**

Community Service projects or Random Acts of Kindness broadens your horizons by helping you understand the needs of the society and the population you are trying to help through the project. Instruct participants to make a list possible community service project. Pick 1 or 2 from their list and describe in detail how the community service project would be performed, who would benefit and the anticipated outcome. Below are three benefits of Community Service:

  a. **Curbs biases and judgments**. Community service opens you to a door of multi-cultural diversity. It's a chance to forget about the judgments, biases, and stigma you may have. Open your mind, and show that despite the differences, everyone deserves a better life and equal opportunities.
  b. **Increases self-efficacy**. Self-efficacy is a person's belief in their ability to succeed in a particular situation. It allows people to gauge their own competence and build their confidence. It inspires them to continuously grow and become more efficient when dealing with day-to-day decision-making.

2. Lead Guided and Independent Practice **(25 min)**

  a. **Activity One**: Instruct participants to make a list possible community service project. Pick 1 or 2 from their list and share who will benefit from the Community Service idea and describe in detail how the community service project would be performed.

Community Service Idea	Who will benefit from the Community Service Idea
1.	
2.	
3.	
4.	
5.	

  b. **Activity Two**: Work with the Charitable branch of your organization/company/corporation and complete a sponsored community service project and share the plan of action and outcome(s) with your mentor/mentoring group.

3. Close the Lesson and Assess Mastery **(10 min)**

Close the lesson by sharing the following message: *"Kindness promotes empathy and compassion, which in turn, leads to a sense of interconnectedness with others. When we practice random acts of kindness, it releases energy. We feel better and the recipients of our acts feel better, which then makes them more likely to be kind to other people."* Have participants share the random acts of kindness and/or community service projects they have been involved in, seen on social media, experienced firsthand, etc.

LOGISTICS: What materials, resources, and technology will I need to prepare and engage?

Paper
Pencil/Pen
Community Service Planner

Pillar: Loving

LESSON VOCABULARY WORDS

INSTRUCTIONS: Review vocabulary words listed below with the participants to ensure they have a good understanding of each before starting any of the activities.

1. **Encourage:** To inspire with courage, spirit, or hope.
2. **Impact:** to have a direct effect.
3. **Recognition:** Formal acknowledgment.
4. **Volunteer:** A person who voluntarily undertakes a service.
5. **Giving:** To make a present.
6. **Kindness:** Courtesy, mercy, service.
7. **Community Service**: non-paying job performed by one person or a group of people for the benefit of their community or its institutions.

Random Acts of Kindness
Journal

be kind and grateful

S M T W T F S

DATE — PLANNED ACT

WHAT DID I LEARN ABOUT MYSELF...

HOW WERE MY ACTS RECEIVED...

WHO DID I INSPIRE FROM MY RANDOM ACTS...

NOTES:

Pillar: Loving

Project Planner
COMMUNITY SERVICE

MONTH: _____

COMMUNITY SERVICE PROJECT TITLE

ANTICIPATED START DATE

ANTICIPATED DEADLINE

IDEAS

_____
_____
_____
_____
_____
_____
_____
_____
_____

to-do list

_____
_____
_____
_____
_____
_____
_____
_____
_____

notes

_____
_____
_____
_____
_____
_____
_____
_____
_____

LESSON TITLE:

The Community of Love

LEVEL: Youth

WEEKS 15-16

PACING: 55 min

OBJECTIVE(S): What will Participants know, understand, and be able to do?

To develop an understanding of the benefits when a person belongs to a community and to experience the action of sharing strengths to improve a community.

KEY VOCABULARY: What key terms will my Participants need to understand?

Community: A group of people living in the same place or having a particular characteristic in common. a feeling of fellowship with others, as a result of sharing common attitudes, interests, and goals.

Vision: The ability to think about or plan the future with imagination or wisdom.

Strength: A good or beneficial quality or attribute of a person or thing.

WEEK 15

LESSON CYCLE:

1. Engage and Connect   **(10 min)**

Ask Participants about their understanding of community. Provide context on how we will be using community for this lesson. Do you think it's important for you to have a community?

Ask if they have heard the phrase, *"it takes a village,"* and who did they hear it from? How was it used? What does it mean to them?

The facilitator is to share *"It takes a village to raise a child"* is an African proverb that means an entire community of people must interact with children for those children to grow in a safe and healthy environment. It also became a popular saying in American culture several decades back.

2. Lead Guided and Independent Practice   **(25 min)**

Explain what having a community means to you.

This exercise will assist the participants with defining their specific community. Have them make a list of 3 people that are key to their community. These are individuals will hold them accountable and push them to excellence and being successful. This list can include friends, mentors, partners, teachers, and family- it must be someone the Participant has a relationship with. Example:

                (Participant's Name)
- John Doe
- Jane Doe
- Johnny Doe

Pillar: Loving

Have the participants share something about a least 1 of the people on their list.

3. Close the Lesson and Assess Mastery **(20 min)**

Activity: Have the participants play the Building a Community Bingo Game. Participants will mingle and talk with other participants until they find a person who matches the facts listed on a bingo-style sheet. The participant will write down the person's name. The first participant to get five in a row — or fill out their whole board — wins.

LOGISTICS: What materials, resources, and technology will I need to prepare and engage?

Building a Community Bingo Game/Activity
Paper
Pencil/Pen

WEEK 16

LESSON CYCLE:

1. Engage and Connect **(20 min)**

Start by asking if they see Mentoring as a community? Get the participants to share what the mentoring program means to them. What has each participant learned about themselves since being in the mentoring program? How have they grown as an individual? If asked, what would you tell someone about the mentoring program?

2. Lead Guided and Independent Practice **(25 min)**

This will be the time for the PM to communicate the community aspect of the program. Here are some things to think about:

- What led you to the Mentoring Program?
- Were you initially excited about participating in the Mentoring Program? Why or why not?
- Explain how the mentors and staff are a part of their community, and they can't serve the participants without them.

Allow the participants to share their thoughts on your view of their Mentoring Community.

3. Close the Lesson and Assess Mastery **(10 min)**

Ask the participants to share experiences they have had that has helped them to grow and do better at home and/or school since becoming a part of the mentoring program/community?

LOGISTICS: What materials, resources, and technology will I need to prepare and engage?

Paper
Pencil/Pen
Journal Pages
Building a Community Bingo Form & Questionnaire

Pillar: Loving

LESSON VOCABULARY WORDS

INSTRUCTIONS: Review vocabulary words listed below with the participants to ensure they have a good understanding of each before starting any of the activities.

1. **Community:** A group of people living in the same place or having a particular characteristic in common. a feeling of fellowship with others, as a result of sharing common attitudes, interests, and goals.

2. **Vision:** The ability to think about or plan the future with imagination or wisdom.

3. **Strength:** A good or beneficial quality or attribute of a person or thing.

Discussion Questions:

1. Do you think it's important for you to have a community?

   _____
   _____
   _____

2. Have you ever heard the phrase, "it takes a village?" Who did you hear it from? How was it used? What does it mean to you?

   _____
   _____
   _____

3. Who makes up your community?

   _____
   _____
   _____

4. What led you to the Mentoring Program? Is this now a part of your community?

   _____
   _____
   _____

Building a Community Bingo Questionnaire

INSTRUCTIONS: Answer the following questions in preparation for playing the Bingo Game and find others who match your answers.

1. Who is your hero? _____
2. I have a puppy and his/her name is? _____
3. What is your biggest fear? _____
4. What is your favorite family vacation? _____
5. My favorite hiding or quiet space is? _____
6. What makes you angry? _____
7. What motivates you to work hard? _____
8. What is your favorite subject in school? _____
9. What is your biggest complaint about school or home? _____
10. What is your proudest accomplishment? _____
11. What do you do best? _____
12. What is your favorite book to read? _____
13. What makes you laugh? _____
14. What was the last movie you went to see? What did you think? _____
15. What did you want to do when you grow up? _____
16. Have you ever had a nickname? What is it? _____
17. Do you like or dislike surprises? Why or why not? _____
18. What's your favorite zoo animal? _____
19. Who is your favorite comic strip character? _____
20. What's your favorite movie? _____
21. Who is your favorite Disney character? _____
22. Are you the oldest, middle, or youngest child in your family? _____
23. I love video games and I am really good at: _____
24. My favorite movie is: _____

Pillar: Loving

Building a Community
BINGO

B	I	N	G	O
1	17	5	11	3
10	13	19	15	24
7	16	FREE	22	8
21	9	23	14	20
4	12	6	18	2

LESSON TITLE:

The Community of Love

LEVEL: Employee or Community Citizen

WEEKS 15-16

PACING: 55 min

OBJECTIVE(S): What will Participants know, understand, and be able to do?

To develop an understanding of the benefits when a person belongs to a community and to experience the action of sharing strengths to improve a community.

KEY VOCABULARY: What key terms will my Participants need to understand?

Community: A group of people living in the same place or having a particular characteristic in common. a feeling of fellowship with others, as a result of sharing common attitudes, interests, and goals.

Vision: The ability to think about or plan the future with imagination or wisdom.

Strength: A good or beneficial quality or attribute of a person or thing.

WEEK 15

LESSON CYCLE:

1. Engage and Connect   **(20 min)**

Ask Participants about their understanding of community. Provide context on how we will be using community for this lesson. Do you think it's important for you to have a community?

Ask if they have heard the phrase, *"it takes a village,"* and who did they hear it from? How was it used? What does it mean to them?

The facilitator is to share *"It takes a village to raise a child"* is an African proverb that means an entire community of people must interact with children for those children to grow in a safe and healthy environment. It also became a popular saying in American culture several decades back.

2. Lead Guided and Independent Practice   **(25 min)**

One of the most important aspects of healthy human functioning is having a strong, reliable support system. They say it takes a village to raise a child, but a village is important even in adulthood. For some, their support system does in fact start in childhood. They have parents, grandparents, siblings, teachers, teammates that all help them find their place in life, give them advice when things become challenging, teach them right from wrong. But for others, building their tribe is a much more intentional process in adulthood. Have participants think about their supportive community, who they are and what makes them a part of their supportive community. Have the Participants share something about at least 2 of the people on their list.

Pillar: Loving

Members of Supportive Community	What's their role and what makes them a part of your community.
1.	
2.	
3.	
4.	
5.	

3. Close the Lesson and Assess Mastery **(10 min)**

Close the lesson by sharing the following message:

A good community is a cohesive, safe, confident, protective, and stable place/atmosphere. It is free of drama and chaos and provides a protective and somewhat insulated community where everyone feels seen, accepted, and included. It values and promotes open, participative development, opportunity for people to share personal experiences and feelings, goals, successes, and failures, and/or coping strategies who also acts as an accountability partner who challenges and interjects whenever necessary to help each member of the community to grow into the best version of them self personally and professionally. The positive benefits are a higher level of well-being, better coping skills, and a longer and healthier life. Studies have also shown that social support can reduce stress, depression, and anxiety.

LOGISTICS: What materials, resources, and technology will I need to prepare and engage?

Accountability Partner Form
Building a Community Form/Activity
Paper
Pencil/Pen

WEEK 16

LESSON CYCLE:

1. Engage and Connect   **(15 min)**

Start by asking if they see Mentoring as a community? Get the participants to share what the mentoring program means to them. What has each participant learned about themselves since being in the mentoring program? How have they grown as an individual? If asked, what would you tell someone about the mentoring program?

2. Lead Guided and Independent Practice   **(20 min)**

This will be the time for the PM to communicate the purpose of the program. Here are some things to think about:

- What led you to your career/community organization?
- What led you to MENTORING?
- Have you built professional and personal contacts that you respect and include in your community?
- Explain how the mentors and staff are a part of your Mentoring community.

Allow the Participants to share their thoughts on your view of the MENTORING Community and its benefits.

3. Close the Lesson and Assess Mastery   **(20 min)**

Ask the participants to share experiences they have had that has helped them to grow and do better in their personal and professional relationships since becoming a part of the mentoring program/community? Share that community/company sponsored mentoring programs assist people in attaining their personal and professional goals. Having someone who has already traveled the path they are attempting to travel is invaluable and necessary to their personal and professional growth and development.

LOGISTICS: What materials, resources, and technology will I need to prepare and engage?

Accountability Partner Tracker
Paper
Pencil/Pen
Journal Pages

Pillar: Loving

LESSON VOCABULARY WORDS

INSTRUCTIONS: Review vocabulary words listed below with the participants to ensure they have a good understanding of each before starting any of the activities.

1. **Community:** A group of people living in the same place or having a particular characteristic in common. a feeling of fellowship with others, as a result of sharing common attitudes, interests, and goals.

2. **Vision:** The ability to think about or plan the future with imagination or wisdom.

3. **Strength:** A good or beneficial quality or attribute of a person or thing.

Discussion Questions:

1. Do you think it's important for you to have a community?

   _____
   _____
   _____

2. Have you ever heard the phrase, "*it takes a village*?" Who did you hear it from? How was it used? What does it mean to you?

   _____
   _____
   _____

3. Who makes up your community?

   _____
   _____
   _____

4. What led you to the Mentoring Program? Is this now a part of your community?

   _____
   _____
   _____

WHO IS YOUR SUPPORTIVE COMMUNITY?

One of the most important aspects of healthy human functioning is having a strong, reliable support system. They say it takes a village to raise a child, but a village is important even in adulthood. For some, their support system does in fact start in childhood. They have parents, grandparents, siblings, teachers, teammates that all help them find their place in life, give them advice when things become challenging, teach them right from wrong. But for others, building their tribe is a much more intentional process in adulthood. Have participants think about their supportive community, who they are and what makes them a part of their supportive community. Have the Participants share something about at least 2 of the people on their list.

Members of Supportive Community	What's their role and what makes them a part of your community?
1.	
2.	
3.	
4.	
5.	

Pillar: Loving

Accountability Partner Tracker

ACCOUNTABILITY PARTNER'S NAME:

	Add your goal to the following worksheet, then use the Accountability Tracker to ensure your goals/objectives are being met.
GOAL	
ACTION STEP	
ACTION STEP	
ACTION STEP	
GOAL	
ACTION STEP	
ACTION STEP	
ACTION STEP	
GOAL	
ACTION STEP	
ACTION STEP	
ACTION STEP	
GOAL	
ACTION STEP	
ACTION STEP	
ACTION STEP	

PILLAR: LEARNING

PILLAR: LEARNING

Merriam-Webster dictionary defines learning as the acquisition of knowledge or skills through experience, study, or by being taught. In psychology, learning is defined as the relatively permanent change in behavior because of an experience. I sat in this space writing and rewriting this pillar concerned that the information being disseminated will be relevant, usable, and inspiring. So, I went back to the drawing board to determine why I chose education as a career. Like many others, I chose a career in education to help mold the minds and lives of the next generation. To help them navigate their educational career with the support, opportunities, and information that does more than just have students rotely memorize the information and regurgitated on a test, term paper, and/or during a class discussion. I wanted the lessons I taught to be seen as the living and exciting aspects of life, development, and growth they truly are. If I am being truthful, that is part of my motivation that energized and empowered me to begin the Mentoring Project. Take a minute and truly consider why you are considering starting a mentoring program and what you hope the mentor and mentee will take away from the experience. Initially, I was going to inundate you with the statistical data that proves the cultural, economic, and financial disparities that are woven into the fabric of America. Instead, I thought about the benefits of this pillar, as a level in the foundation both the mentor and mentee are building and securing, will be the place in which they spring forth to live the life of their choosing. So many times, people are judged by their last poor choice, bad act, circumstance surrounding their birth, and/or the communities they live in. I purposefully left out their race because that is a horse of a different color and is something that cannot be changed or taught. Everyone must come into the realization of self that is spoken about in the pillar on LIVING.

LEARNING is a choice, a conscious decision that is intentionally acted upon. It isn't something that happens by accident or unwillingly. Learning, if done correctly and received intentionally, has the power to change the person's perspective, viewpoint of themselves and their view of the world around them. It also influences how they allow the world to impact them and how they impact the world around them. I mentioned this before and find it relevant here as well. Doctor Phil said, "*…you cannot choose the behavior without also choosing the circumstance.*" That is also true in education. You cannot choose to be present and participate in the learning as it takes place and not receive the information shared to impact your life in some way, shape, or form. Nor can you walk away from the responsibility you now have to what you have learned. Which shines a light on what Maya Angelou said, "*…when you know better, do better.*" I know you are wondering why I ventured away from the style and playbook of the other pillars. The truth of the matter is this is one of the most important pillars the mentor will share with and teach to the mentee.

The mentor must allow him/herself to learn the pillars on LIVING and LOVING to ensure they present the lesson on LEARNING in a way that encourages, empowers, and enables the mentee to accept responsibility for the information they receive and the courage to activate it in their life. In a way that gives them permission to envision a life outside of the confines of their community, home, and/or societal limitations.

Let's revisit the definition of learning. The key components of the definition are (1) acquisition, (2) knowledge, (3) skills, and (4) experience. Follow me here because I am going somewhere. Acquisition is defined as an asset or object bought or obtained; the learning or developing of a skill, habit, or quality. Knowledge is the facts, information, and skills gained by a person through experience or education; and awareness or familiarity gained by experience of a fact or situation. Skill is the ability to do something well or with expertise, the ability to use one's knowledge effectively and readily. An experience is the process of doing and seeing things and of having things happen to you, an encounter, event, or occurrence. Each of the words defined above are components of learning and are relative only to the individual who is experiencing the episode of learning that is occurring at that moment. Learning does not happen without each aspect that is previously mentioned happening simultaneously. All while empowering and enabling the learner to show up and take part in their own life to activate, cultivate, and give themselves permission to use the information in the season of life, it is most needed and effective.

LEARNING only happens when we see the value in acquiring or getting the information for internal or external use. Sometimes the information is only valuable to you because of your own personal values and the accomplishments you desire for your life. The value is determined based upon how the information can be used and how the learner will use it to change their perspectives, attitude, and altitude. I was watching a movie and there was a scene where the character was holding on for dear life because they did not know how far down the ground was beneath their feet. Another character came along to help them and didn't stop quick enough and ended up falling into the limitless and smoke covered bottom. Their landing resounded with a loud thud and when they stood up, their nose was at the same level as the other characters' waist. Once the character realized the floor was closer than they initially thought, they released what they were holding onto and dropped to the floor. The lack of information left character #1 uncertain and afraid to act or even move. However, once the character had the information they initially lacked, they received it and acted upon it. In that moment, character #1 had the freedom to make a decision that changed their perspective and made the decision that was the right one for them at that moment.

Pillar: Learning

According to *4 Types of Learning Styles*, there are four learning styles: visual, auditory, reading and writing, and kinesthetic.

1. Visual learners are better able to retain information when it is presented to them in a graphic depiction.
2. Auditory learners prefer listening to information that is being presented vocally.
3. Reading and writing learners focus on the written word, reading and writing, and other text-heavy resources.
4. Kinesthetic learners are hands-on thrive when engaging all their senses during coursework and/or learning opportunities.

For the mentee to benefit and find value in this pillar, the mentor must identify their unique learning style and present the information in a manner that catches the mentee's attention. Do not assume your mentee learns in the same way you do. Ask! Pay attention to him/her and see how he/she responds to the information. It will give you the insight you need to determine their particular learning style.

In mentoring, LEARNING is the component or the result that happens from each mentor-mentee interaction. Do not leave these experiences to chance. Plan them out with your mentee's style of learning and personal interests in mind. For the purposes of this book, LEARNING comprises the various ways information can be shared and/or introduced to the mentee during group sessions and/or individual mentor-mentee interactions. I have found that using open discussion after a lesson or an opportunity to experience the information learned in real time is more effective than just listening. For example, if the lesson is being taught on life skills, the mentor can offer real-life scenarios where the mentee applies the information, he/she has learned. This will provide the mentee with a reference point that helps them process and remember the information. Another example is if the lesson is about discipline and organization. The mentor can take their mentee to a ballet or interpretive dance program, and afterwards have a question-and-answer session with the dancers. During the session, the mentor and mentee can ask questions about what they did to reach their current level of success and/or how they've organized their lives to become successful dancers. The same scenario can be used with any profession. Once they finish the question-and-answer session, ask the mentees what they learned and to give an example of how they can incorporate the learned life lessons into their everyday life!

As mentioned before, learning is an experience and it presents itself differently based upon who is sharing or teaching the information, and who receives, interprets, and uses the information. Not to mention how they decide to activate or use the information. The mentor may look at the information being shared as common-sense information, while the mentee is receiving new information that expands their awareness and their view of themselves, their community, and even the world. Which affords the mentor a rare yet rewarding opportunity to experience the occurrence through the wonderment and excitement as the mentee experiences it. It changes them both in that moment. The mentor develops a new point of reference that teaches him/her how to view, process, and/or share information going forward. The mentor realizes another aspect of who they are and how they can affect change in the world, one mentee at a time. The mentee receives the information and sees themselves in a larger picture or on a world stage. Whereas previously, they could not see themselves outside of the confines of their community and/or their cultural and/or economic limitations. They have the chance to envision a life that is limitless. Regardless of the setting, the opportunity to learn, grow, and evolve helps both the mentor and the mentee to develop and experience life differently going forward. During the mentor-mentee interactions, they both develop the role each will play in the other person's life, and in what their mentoring relationship needs to look like for them to continue growing forward. What most people cannot recognize or realize is that every experience and/or information received changes who each of them are especially when the impact of the experience/information has left an indelible mark on their heart and/or mind. A fact of life that cannot be disputed in any way is that while the mentor and mentee have breath in their body, they will be in a constant state of learning.

GUIDANCE

Throughout the history of mankind, it has become apparent that humans learn better when they take part in peer-to-peer learning opportunities. Mentoring is another aspect of peer-to-peer learning that presents the mentee with the modeling of behavior that leads or guides them to experiencing successful outcomes and first-hand experiences with identifying the skills and tools exemplified in leaders. Mentoring has become a universal opportunity to build a sense of self, improve personal and/or professional development, create a supportive learning environment, open up avenues for exposure to opportunities and possibilities previously unknown to them, and an emotional support system for both the mentor and mentee during critical moments in each of their lives. Which is why schools, corporations, and organizations have created mentoring programs where leadership mentor's frontline and subordinate employees, teachers and/or community leaders mentor students/youth, and youth centers and/or youth organizations create programming where mentoring occurs in group settings. In schools, it has become even more effective when mentees are paired with educators who share their same ethnic and cultural

Pillar: Learning

beliefs. In corporations and/or organizations, it has become even more effective when mentees are paired with executive level personnel or community leaders who have attained the level of success they desire, but don't have access to.

In every instance, mentees, whether students in an educational setting, adults/youth in a community setting, or adults in the workplace, benefit from the guidance mentoring offers to better understand their pathway when navigating life, and when gaining knowledge. This is an essential ingredient in their development of their sense of self and when moving towards their purpose, they plan their long-term personal and/or professional goals. The trust relationship that is built between the mentor and mentee empowers the mentee to create a ripple effect, where they become a mentor to those coming up behind him/her. They take what they have learned and experienced as a mentee to create a relationship with a mentee that opens the mentee up to a whole new world of opportunities and possibilities.

Alan Bruce said, "*Even learning include strong elements of guidance... these elements of guidance are to enable the mentee to reflect, consider options, and in the end make choices based on the information... Guidance can point out the consequences of choices made by the mentee...*" All of which are necessary for the mentee to grow and mature while developing the confidence that the choices/decisions they face may be the right one for them to make. While actively considering if it is the right choice/decision for him/her to make during this time in their life. This is the case regardless if the mentee is a youth or an employee in a Fortune 500 company. Learning involves the introduction and retention of information that opens his/her eyes to see a world that is more accessible to them and has the potential of opening doors they may have never known were available to them. Doors that offer him/her entrance, access and/or the lenses to see a world outside of the confines of the one they have become comfortable and content living within.

According to *The Master's Voice: Learning Through Mentoring*, "*Mentoring plays a valuable role in imparting skills, attitudes, and experience-based lessons to develop relationships of trust and interactive communication in a paradigm of shared goals. It is a neutral space... that plays a vital role in developing the critical judgement, analytical skills and decision-making skills necessary for continued growth and development throughout the various phases of life.*" As the mentees have new experiences and take in more information, he/she understands and recognizes the choices they make today have the power to open or lock doors to the future currently available to him/her.

In every instance in my life, I have found anything worth having is worth working for, being committed to, and organizing my life to make it a reality. There is no greater feeling in the world than attaining your goals and respecting the hard work you put into it. That feeling of satisfaction can only be felt/experienced. Attempting to express those feelings in words does not do it justice! Which shines a light on the need for mentoring programs in schools, corporations and/or organizations and the benefits enjoyed by both the mentor and mentee.

Pillar: Learning

LESSON TITLE:

Career Vs. Job

LEVEL: Youth

WEEKS 17-18

PACING: 55 minutes

OBJECTIVE(S): What will Participants know, understand, and be able to do?

Mentee will learn the difference between a career and a job and understand that both options are necessary depending on where you are in life.

KEY VOCABULARY: What key terms will my Participants need to understand?

Career: One or more jobs in the same area of interest.

Job: Work that one does for pay.

Salary: A fixed amount of pay for a certain period.

Wages: A fixed amount of money paid for each hour worked.

Communication: the imparting or exchanging of information or news.

Guidance: the act or process of guiding; advice on vocational or educational goals

WEEK 17

LESSON CYCLE:

1. Engage and Connect (15 min)

Facilitator/Mentor will ask mentee(s) the question if anyone knows the difference between a career and a job?

Mentor will mention 10 occupations and ask the participants whether they think it's a career or a job.

Mentor will share their first job and how they ended up in their current role.

2. Lead Guided and Independent Practice (25 min)

Conduct a group or mentor/mentee discussion using some or all the following language as a guide:
- How Important is it to have a plan for your life?
- Is it important to just earn a paycheck?
- Does education alone help people move up in their careers?

3. Close the Lesson and Assess Mastery (15 min)

Think of it this way: If life were a video game, a job would be just one level. Having a career means that you are committed to playing the game to get better over time and advance to higher levels.

The real difference between a job and a career is your attitude:

- People who want a career are always thinking about their long-term goals. They are thinking about what they can do now to make those goals happen in the future and they make wise and informed decision and/or choices to ensure they attain their desired goals.
- Beginning job seekers often must work hard for little money. It might take a few years to earn bigger paychecks and have more interesting job duties, but these lower-level jobs can lead to great opportunities and give them the experience to secure jobs where education may be lacking.

LOGISTICS: What materials, resources, and technology will I need to prepare and engage?

Computer
Pen and paper
Career vs Job Worksheets

Pillar: Learning

WEEK 18

LESSON CYCLE:

1. Engage and Connect (15 min)

Watch this video on the difference between a career and a job
https://www.youtube.com/watch?v=YLrvnt3QxXw

2. Lead Guided and Independent Practice (25 min)

Facilitator/Mentor will review last week's lesson on "the real difference between a job and a career is your attitude." During the discussion, the facilitator/mentor will define **Attitude**: a set of emotions, beliefs, and behaviors toward a particular object, person, thing, or event.

The facilitator/mentor will initiate a conversation with mentees about the importance of having a positive attitude in life. It is a strong predictor of improved performance. Especially when it comes to their future goals and plans. Mentor will comprise 6 situations where attitude can either help or hurt an employee in the future. For example: *"Fighting on the playground everyday"* or *"getting smart or being disrespectful to authority figures/adults"*.

3. Close the Lesson and Assess Mastery (15 min)

Facilitator/Mentor will provoke critical thinking by asking the mentees what is one thing that they need to do or focus on to attain their personal and/or professional goals?

LOGISTICS: What materials, resources, and technology will I need to prepare and engage?

Computer
Microsoft Teams
Pen and paper

LESSON VOCABULARY WORDS

INSTRUCTIONS: Review vocabulary words listed below with the participants to ensure they have a good understanding of each before starting any of the activities.

1. **Career**: One or more jobs in the same area of interest.
2. **Job**: Work that one does for pay.
3. **Salary**: A fixed amount of pay for a certain period.
4. **Wages**: A fixed amount of money paid for each hour worked.
5. **Communication:** the imparting or exchanging of information or news.
6. **Guidance:** the act or process of guiding; advice on vocational or educational goals.

Discussion Questions:

1. Have you ever considered how Important is it to have a plan for your life?

   _____
   _____
   _____

2. Do you believe education alone helps people move up in their careers?

   _____
   _____
   _____

List of Careers and Jobs

Dentist	Cashier
Registered Nurse	Cook
Pharmacist	Automotive Technician
Information Security Analyst	Bartender
Software Developer	Office Assistant
Lawyer	Janitor
Physician	Assembly Line Technician
Veterinarian	Mailroom Clerk
Anesthesiologists	Front Desk Attendant
Occupational Therapist	Receptionist

Pillar: Learning

Career vs. Job
How They're Different and Why It Matters

What is the difference between a career and job? Though these two terms are often used to describe the same thing, they do have different meanings. The main purpose for obtaining a job is to earn money. With a job, people have a short-term goal of doing the work at their job. Most plan to be at a job for a year or two. They don't plan to be doing the same job for life. They plan to be at a job until they decide on a career or start a career. Also, most jobs don't require specialized skills, training, or a higher education. Though a job can be full-time, many jobs are part-time, and temporary work. When we are younger, we often have a job to earn some money or gain some work experience before starting our career. What is a career? A career is a profession. It is an occupation in a specific field of work. Some examples of

---

1. What is often the main purpose of a job? _____

True or False

2. _____ People typically plan to have the same job for the long-term.

3. _____ Most people have a job until they decide or start a career.

4. _____ Most jobs don't require specialized skills, training, or higher education.

---

careers are a carpenter, nurse, fire fighter, or a lawyer. With a career, we specialize in a field of work. We plan to stay working in a selected career for the long-term. With a career, the person plans to grow and develop their skills and advance in their field or profession. Also, careers often require obtaining specialized training, a set of skills, and/or a higher education. Unlike a job, motivation for a career is not mainly money. Instead, we are often motivated to obtain a certain career because of the desire for personal satisfaction, advancement, and eventually higher earning ability. What are the benefits of a job? Though the main motivation for obtaining a job is often money, there are many other benefits to having a job. A job gives you the

Directions: Answer each question.

1. What is a career?

2. Are careers long-term or short-term?

3. What do careers often require?

4. What are often the motivations to obtain a career?

opportunity to learn and improve key soft skills. Soft skills are those behaviors and social skills used in all workplaces. Some examples of key soft skills are teamwork, communication, dependability, and a strong work-ethic. Developing your soft skills improves your future job and career opportunities. When employers are looking for job candidates, they desire those candidates who possess a set of strong soft skills. Hence, when you have a job, it is important to take it seriously. Remember, it is not just a job, but an opportunity. You will learn valuable soft skills that will make you highly desired by employers. Also, a job can be a good testing ground to see if you like a certain type of work or career. You never know, because what might have begun as a job can turn into a great career. What are the benefits of a career?

Fill-in the blanks with the best word from the right-side.

1. A job gives you an opportunity to develop the _____.

2. Soft skills are those _____ and social skills used in the workplace.

3. Examples of key soft skills are communication, dependability, and _____.

4. _____ desire job candidate with a set of strong soft skills.

The benefits of choosing a career far outweigh the benefits of having a job. Choosing a career increases your job security, especially if you select a career that is in high demand. Because careers take a unique set of skills and/or education, a career tends to be more stable than a job. Careers cannot be easily replaced by machines, replaced by others, or impacted by social-economic changes. You also have a higher earning ability and a greater opportunity for advancement with a career. Also, those who have careers experience greater job satisfaction because they are doing what they like. They also feel a sense of purpose and accomplishment. Though a career takes planning, commitment, and sacrifice, it is well worth the effort. In fact, having a rewarding future will typically depend upon having a career.

True or False

1. _____ A job has more benefits than a career.

2. _____ Careers have more job security than a job.

3. _____ With a career, you will have a higher earning ability.

4. _____ A career gives you greater job satisfaction and purpose.

Teamwork ♦ Behaviors ♦ Employers ♦ Soft Skills

Career vs. a Job
Identify How They Are Different

· Short-term pursuit
  Long-term pursuit
· Earning money is the main motivation
  Motivated by personal satisfaction and advancement
· Often done before starting a career
· Higher earning potential
· Nurse
· Hostess at a restaurant
· Carpenter
	· A profession
	· Often requires a set of skills, education, or specialized training
	· Takes planning and commitment
	· Often doesn't require unique skills or education
	· Has more job security
	· Supports learning and developing soft skills
	· Police officer
	· Cashier

Directions: Place the terms from above in the correct box below.

A Job =	A Career =

Career vs. a Job

Vocabulary Practice

Career	Job
Soft skills	Profession
Employer	Job security
Part-time	Advancement

Directions: Select the best term for each sentence.

1. A/An _____ is the company that employs or puts a person to work.

2. A/An _____ is a profession or occupation in a specific field of work that requires a set of skills.

3. _____ is when a job is more secure and is unlikely to be dismissed.

4. A/An _____ is work that is primarily motivated by earning money and is usually short-term.

5. A/An _____ job position is when a person works only part of the day or week.

6. A/An _____ is the promotion of a person at work to a higher position.

7. A/An _____ is considered a career or occupation in a specific field of work.

Pillar: Learning

LESSON TITLE:

Career Vs. Job

LEVEL: Employee or Community Citizen

WEEKS 17-18

PACING: 55 minutes

OBJECTIVE(S): What will Participants know, understand, and be able to do?

Mentee will learn the difference between a career and a job and understand that both options are necessary depending on where you are in life.

KEY VOCABULARY: What key terms will my Participants need to understand?

Career: One or more jobs in the same area of interest.
Job: Work that one does for pay.
Salary: A fixed amount of pay for a certain period.
Wages: A fixed amount of money paid for each hour worked.
Communication: the imparting or exchanging of information or news.
Guidance: the act or process of guiding; advice on vocational or educational goals

WEEK 17

LESSON CYCLE:

1. Engage and Connect **(10 min)**

Facilitator/Mentor will ask mentee(s) the question if anyone knows the difference between a career and a job?

Mentor will mention 10 occupations and ask the participants whether they think it's a career or a job. (During your prep time create a list of 10 occupations that the mentee(s) may know)

Mentor will share their first job and how they ended up in their current role.

2. Lead Guided and Independent Practice **(25 min)**

Conduct a group or mentor/mentee discussion using some or all the following language as a guide:
- How important is it to have a plan for your life?
- Is it important to just earn a paycheck?
- Does education alone help people move up in their careers?
- Why do you think some people stay at their places of employment for 20 years?

3. Close the Lesson and Assess Mastery **(15 min)**

Think of it this way: If life were a video game, a job would be just one level. Having a career means that you are committed to playing the game to get better over time and advance to higher levels.

The real difference between a job and a career is your attitude:

- People who want a career are always thinking about their long-term goals. They are thinking about what they can do now to make those goals happen in the future.
- Beginning job seekers often must work hard for little money. It might take a few years to earn bigger paychecks and have more interesting job duties, but these lower-level jobs can lead to great opportunities.

LOGISTICS: What materials, resources, and technology will I need to prepare and engage?

Computer
Microsoft Teams
Pencil and Paper

Pillar: Learning

WEEK 18

LESSON CYCLE:

1. Engage and Connect (10 min)

Watch this video on the difference between a career and a job

https://www.youtube.com/watch?v=_O7rSBH0mIk

2. Lead Guided and Independent Practice (25 min)

Facilitator defines Attitude: a set of emotions, beliefs, and behaviors toward a particular object, person, thing, or event.

Facilitator/Mentor will initiate a conversation with mentees about the importance of having a positive attitude in life. It is a strong predictor of improved performance. Especially when it comes to their future goals and plans. Mentor will comprise 6 situations where attitude can either help or hurt an employee in the future. For example: *"Get into a loud and very public disagreement with a co-worker or community worker"* or *"supervisor asks you to complete a task that you believe is beneath your position with the company; you explain that their request is beneath your position with the company and tells them to ask your subordinate."*

Participants will role play the two scenarios as described and the facilitator/mentor will provide alternate employee/community worker's attitudes and responses. Facilitator instructs participants to role play with the changes. After the role plays the facilitator instructs the participants to write down what they learned from each scenario where the employee/community worker has a bad attitude and when they have a good attitude. Ask them to share in their writings which they most connect with or use what they learned to improve their attitude and attain their professional and personal goals.

3. Close the Lesson and Assess Mastery (15 min)

Facilitator/Mentor will provoke critical thinking by asking the mentees what is one thing they learned that is motivating them to improve their attitude and/or attain their professional and personal goals.

LOGISTICS: What materials, resources, and technology will I need to prepare and engage?

Computer/Projector
Paper
Pencil/Pen

LESSON VOCABULARY WORDS

INSTRUCTIONS: Review vocabulary words listed below with the participants to ensure they have a good understanding of each before starting any of the activities.

1. **Career**: One or more jobs in the same area of interest.
2. **Job**: Work that one does for pay.
3. **Salary**: A fixed amount of pay for a certain period.
4. **Wages**: A fixed amount of money paid for each hour worked.
5. **Communication:** the imparting or exchanging of information or news.
6. **Guidance:** the act or process of guiding; advice on vocational or educational goals.

Discussion Questions:

1. Have you ever considered how Important is it to have a plan for your life?
   _____
   _____
   _____

2. Do you believe education alone helps people move up in their careers?
   _____
   _____
   _____

List of Careers and Jobs

Dentist	Cashier
Registered Nurse	Cook
Pharmacist	Automotive Technician
Information Security Analyst	Bartender
Software Developer	Office Assistant
Lawyer	Janitor
Physician	Assembly Line Technician
Veterinarian	Mailroom Clerk
Anesthesiologists	Front Desk Attendant
Occupational Therapist	Receptionist

Pillar: Learning

LESSON TITLE:

Social Media and Digital Responsibility

LEVEL: Youth

WEEKS 19-20

PACING: 55 minutes

OBJECTIVE(S): What will Participants know, understand, and be able to do?

Participants will be able to understand how to use social media and the importance of protecting themselves and others with what they post.

KEY VOCABULARY: What key terms will my Participants need to understand?

Social Media: Websites and applications that enable users to create and share content or to participate in social networking.

Social networking: The use of dedicated websites and applications to interact with other users, or to find people with similar interests to oneself.

Viral: An image or video that becomes popular through a viral process of internet sharing.

Cyber Bullying: A form of bullying or harassment using electronic means. Also known as online bullying.

Digital footprint: A trail of data you create while using the internet. It includes sites you visit, what you share, where you share, and links you click.

WEEK 19

LESSON CYCLE:

1. Engage and Connect (10 min)

Facilitator/Mentor will introduce the topic of the day "Social media and digital responsibility" and present the following video: https://www.youtube.com/watch?v=SgNIIUD_oQg

Discussion: *He will also ask the following questions*

1. *Who has a social media account or page?*
2. *What do you use your social media for?*
3. *What is a slam book/cyberbullying and how is it used on social media?*

Definition: *Slam book:* a sort of scrapbook of notes kids would write and pass around to denigrate other Participants or teachers. The entire purpose was to ridicule people.

Definition: *Cyberbullying:* the use of electronic communication to bully a person, typically by sending messages in an intimidating or threatening nature or posting inappropriate or personal information about a person online.

2. Lead Guided and Independent Practice (25 min)

Facilitator/Mentor will contribute the conversation on "Cyberbullying" and present the following video: https://youtu.be/4NXXJBMvJtc

Facilitate a discussion on the Cyberbullying and the impacts it has on the bully's and their victim's lives.

Discussion Topic 1: Ask participants if they've ever witnessed someone being bullied online. How did they feel? What was the outcome of the online bullying?

Discussion Topic 2: Ask participants to give examples of the types of Cyberbullying they have seen, experienced, etc. Ask *"what impact has it had on their life?"*

3. Close the Lesson and Assess Mastery (10 min)

Facilitator/Mentor will reiterate that cyberbullying can ruin lives, create scenario where it impacts another person's mental and emotional health and could lead to suicidal thoughts and/or suicide. In some cases, the person who is the bully is charged with a crime and becomes a felon. Encourage participants to post positive memes, pics, and quotes on their page and let them know you will be following up next week.

LOGISTICS: What materials, resources, and technology will I need to prepare and engage?

Computer
Microsoft Teams
Pencil and Paper

Pillar: Learning

WEEK 20

LESSON CYCLE:

1. Engage and Connect (10 min)

Review the vocabulary from last week, continue the conversation on Cyberbullying, and ask the participants if they witnessed any acts of Cyberbullying since last week's discussion? Did the conversation last week make them more aware of the issue and what to look for?

Follow up and see what the response on them was only posting positive pics, memes, videos, etc.

2. Lead Guided and Independent Practice (25 min)

Facilitator/Mentor will present the following video and get participant's feedback on the tips covered in the video. https://www.youtube.com/watch?v=X9Htg8V3eik, and information covered in https://www.youtube.com/watch?v=ottnH427Fr8

The following are the tips covered in the video they watched:

1. Don't give out personal information online (i.e. home address, school name, phone number, etc.)
2. Never send picture of you or your family to strangers.
3. Keep your passwords private except from parents.
4. Don't download anything without parental/guardian's permission.
5. Tell an adult if you receive a mean or strange message.
6. The dangers of oversharing online.

Ask participants if they've ever seen someone post something that wasn't nice on social media.

Share with participants that whatever they post online is in cyberspace forever, so post responsibly. Give examples of people that have lost jobs, and college scholarships due to what they posted on social media.

3. Close the Lesson and Assess Mastery (10 min)

Close out the lesson with final remarks and suggestions for social media and digital responsibility.

LOGISTICS: What materials, resources, and technology will I need to prepare and engage?

Computer
Microsoft Teams
Pencil and Paper

LESSON VOCABULARY WORDS

INSTRUCTIONS: Review vocabulary words listed below with the participants to ensure they have a good understanding of each before starting any of the activities.

1. **Social Media:** Websites and applications that enable users to create and share content or to participate in social networking.

2. **Social networking:** The use of dedicated websites and applications to interact with other users, or to find people with similar interests to oneself.

3. **Viral:** An image or video that becomes popular through a viral process of internet sharing.

4. **Cyber Bullying:** A form of bullying or harassment using electronic means. Also known as online bullying.

5. **Digital footprint:** A trail of data you create while using the internet. It includes sites you visit, what you share, where you share, and links you click.

Online Safety Tips

1. Don't give out personal information online (i.e. home address, school name, phone number, etc.)
2. Never send pictures of you or your family to strangers.
3. Keep your passwords private except from parents.
4. Don't download anything without your parent/guardian's permission.
5. Tell an adult if you receive a mean, vulgar and/or strange message.
6. Don't live your life online by oversharing.

Discussion Questions: Answer the following questions in preparation of the group discussion.

1. Do you have a social media account or page? Yes or No. (Circle your answer.)
2. What do you use your social media for?

_____
_____
_____

Pillar: Learning

3. What is Cyberbullying?
   _____
   _____
   _____

4. Can I be refused entrance into a university or college because of my online activities?
   _____
   _____
   _____

5. Have you ever seen someone post something that wasn't nice on social media?
   _____
   _____
   _____

Intentional Mentoring Mentor's Guide

LESSON TITLE:

Social Media and Digital Responsibility

LEVEL: Employee or Community Citizen

WEEKS 19-20

PACING: 55 minutes

OBJECTIVE(S): What will Participants know, understand, and be able to do?

Participants will be able to understand how to use social media and the importance of protecting themselves and others with what they post.

KEY VOCABULARY: What key terms will my Participants need to understand?

Social Media: Websites and applications that enable users to create and share content or to participate in social networking.

Social networking: The use of dedicated websites and applications to interact with other users, or to find people with similar interests to oneself.

Viral: An image or video that becomes popular through a viral process of internet sharing.

Cyber Bullying: A form of bullying or harassment using electronic means. Also known as online bullying.

Digital footprint: A trail of data you create while using the internet. It includes sites you visit, what you share, where you share, and links you click.

WEEK 19

LESSON CYCLE:

1. Engage and Connect (15 min)

Facilitator/Mentor will introduce the topic of the day "Managing Your Digital Footprint" and present the following video: https://www.youtube.com/watch?v=SgNIIUD_oQg *and managing your digital footprint video:* https://www.youtube.com/watch?v=OBg2YYV3Bts

Discussion: He will also ask the following questions

1. Who has a social media account or page?
2. What do you use your social media for?
3. What is a slam book/cyberbullying and how is it used on social media?

Definition: *Slam book:* a sort of scrapbook of notes kids would write and pass around to denigrate other Participants or teachers. The entire purpose was to ridicule people.

Definition: *Cyberbullying:* the use of electronic communication to bully a person, typically by sending messages in an intimidating or threatening nature or posting inappropriate or personal information about a person online.

Pillar: Learning

2. Lead Guided and Independent Practice **(20 min)**

Facilitator/Mentor defines the power of influence: *to have an effect on something; power to sway (Encarta Dictionary); "the act or power of producing an effect without apparent exertion of force or direct exercise of command; the power or capacity of causing an effect in indirect or intangible ways.* Provoke participants to think about the power of influence. Mention these names and ask the mentees what they think of their social media presence.

1) Travis Scott	2) Donald Trump
3) Kylie Jenner	4) Will Smith
5) Lebron James	6) Lil Baby
7) Cristiano Ronaldo	8) Megan thee Stallion
9) Nipsey Hussle	10) Beyoncé

3. Close the Lesson and Assess Mastery **(20 min)**

Questions to Ponder:
- Facilitator/Mentor will ask participants to reflect on the times when they have seen a fighting video, some unkind tweets, a personal and private image, or video online.
- How can we remain respectful and responsible online?
- How would they feel if someone posted something about you online that was not true?
- How would you feel if a mistake/poor decision you made became the trending story on social media?
- How can a bad online reputation impact your everyday life and/or career?

LOGISTICS: What materials, resources, and technology will I need to prepare and engage?
Computer
Microsoft Teams
Pencil and Paper

WEEK 20

LESSON CYCLE:

1. Engage and Connect (10 min)

Facilitator/Mentor will introduce the topic of the day "Managing Your Digital Footprint" and present the following video: https://www.youtube.com/watch?v=OBg2YYV3Bts *and being careful not to overshare in this video:* https://www.youtube.com/watch?v=ottnH427Fr8

Ask them to share their thoughts on this video.

2. Lead Guided and Independent Practice (35 min)

DISCUSSION: It's important to think about what you want your reputation to be online, and it's best to start now. This is where you can use technology to your advantage. In its most basic form, it's an online version of your résumé, but it can be much more than that. As schools and employers turn to the internet to find out more about potential candidates, it's clear that what we post online can have a real impact on our lives offline.

Recruiters often use networking and social media sites to find talent, with many indicating that they hired a candidate that they found via social media. Many employers have reported hiring a candidate for the good things they found about them online.

LEARNING OBJECTIVES:

- How digital footprints are formed
- How to be aware of and manage your digital footprint
- Ways to make it work to your advantage
- Discuss the ways in which one's online reputation might be under threat and how to defend it.

Activity 1: Have participants create a poster or pamphlet that provides information for others on how to protect their online reputation by coming up with strategies on how best to defend a person's online reputation against attacks.

Activity 2: Answer the questions.

1. What percentage of employers will use search engines to research people before offering them a position with their company? (Answer: 48%)
2. What is at risk when a negative light or posts are found about you online? (Answer: your online reputation)
3. Should you not be concerned about what you post? Yes or No

ONLINE SAFETY TIPS

1. Have security settings are set to a standard you are happy with to ensure only people you want to see your business gets access to it.
2. Delete any posts that you have put up in the past that do not represent who you are. It will make it difficult to find the post in the future.
3. If someone posts a piece of content that you are not happy with and tagged you in the post, untag yourself from the post and/or report it.
4. Delete or deactivate any unwanted or unused accounts.

Pillar: Learning

5. Regularly log out of all your online profiles. Including your social media accounts.
6. Use your preferred search engine and search for yourself. See what comes up and determine if any of the information is inappropriate or unwanted and go about removing it.

3. Close the Lesson and Assess Mastery **(5 min)**

REITERATE TO PARTICIPANTS: Your digital footprint yields information about you; your online reputation is how that information is interpreted by others to form an opinion of you as a person. Why Does It Matter? Your online reputation can affect relationships and potential jobs, and you may not even be aware that it's happening.

LOGISTICS: What materials, resources, and technology will I need to prepare and engage?

Computer
Microsoft Teams
Pen and Paper (optional)

LESSON VOCABULARY WORDS

INSTRUCTIONS: Review vocabulary words listed below with the participants to ensure they have a good understanding of each before starting any of the activities.

1. **Social Media:** Websites and applications that enable users to create and share content or to participate in social networking.

2. **Social networking:** The use of dedicated websites and applications to interact with other users, or to find people with similar interests to oneself.

3. **Viral:** An image or video that becomes popular through a viral process of internet sharing.

4. **Cyber Bullying:** A form of bullying or harassment using electronic means. Also known as online bullying.

5. **Digital footprint:** A trail of data you create while using the internet. It includes sites you visit, what you share, where you share, and links you click.

ONLINE SAFETY TIPS

1. Have security settings are set to a standard you are happy with to ensure only people you want to see your business gets access to it.

2. Delete any posts that you have put up in the past that do not represent who you are. It will make it difficult to find the post in the future.

3. If someone posts a piece of content that you are not happy with and tagged you in the post, untag yourself from the post and/or report it.

4. Delete or deactivate any unwanted or unused accounts.

5. Regularly log out of all your online profiles. Including your social media accounts.

6. Use your preferred search engine and search for yourself. See what comes up and determine if any of the information is inappropriate or unwanted and go about removing it.

Discussion Questions:

1. How are digital footprints are formed?

_____
_____
_____
_____

Pillar: Learning

2. How should you be aware of and manage your digital footprint?

3. How can your online reputation be threatened and how should you defend it?

4. Have you seen a fighting video, some unkind tweets, a personal and private image, or video online? What happened?

5. How can we remain respectful and responsible online?

6. How would they feel if someone posted something about you online that was not true?

7. How would you feel if a mistake/poor decision you made became the trending story on social media?

   _____
   _____
   _____
   _____

8. How can a bad online reputation impact your everyday life and/or career?

   _____
   _____
   _____
   _____

Activity 1: Poster/Pamphlet Activity:

Create a poster or pamphlet that provides information on how someone can protect their online reputation. Come up with strategies on how best to defend an online reputation against attacks.

Activity 2: Answer the questions.

1. What percentage of employers will use search engines to research people before offering them a position with their company? _____

2. What is at risk when a negative light or posts are found about you online? _____

3. Should you NOT be concerned about what you post? Yes or No (Circle your answer.)

Key Point: Digital footprints yield information about you. Your online reputation is how that information is interpreted by others to form an opinion of you as a person. Your online reputation can impact and affect relationships and potential jobs, and you may not even be aware of what is happening.

Pillar: Learning

LESSON TITLE:

Organization is Key

LEVEL: Youth

WEEKS 21-22

PACING: 55 minutes

OBJECTIVE(S): What will Participants know, understand, and be able to do?

Participants will understand the importance of being organized.

KEY VOCABULARY: What key terms will my Participants need to understand?

Organized: Arranged systematically, especially on a large scale.

Productivity: The effectiveness of productive effort; the state or quality of producing something.

Tasks: A piece of work to be done or undertaken.

Goals: The object of a person's ambition or effort; an aim or desired result.

Decluttering: Remove unnecessary items from an untidy or overcrowded place.

WEEK 21

LESSON CYCLE:

1. Engage and Connect (20 min)

Mentor will introduce the topic of the day as "**Organization is Key.**"

Take a Poll: Ask participants would they consider themselves to be organized? Why or why not?

Discussion: Ask participants about their understanding of what clutter is, and if they believe that it affects their learning environment at School and/or home. Ask Participants to reflect on the importance of being organized.

2. Lead Guided and Independent Practice (25 min)

Activity: Participants are to rate each concept from 1-5 (1 being not important 5 being very important) to determine how important being organized is in the situation.

1) Having friends over for the weekend
2) Cannot find your favorite toy or something you were looking for
3) Getting in trouble with your parents
4) You have chores to do at home
5) Your siblings following you around and telling everything that you do
6) Getting put in detention at school
7) Keeping a secret that needs to be told

3. Close the Lesson and Assess Mastery **(10 min)**

The facilitator will ask participants to think about one time in their lives when being unorganized caused them to miss out on something they really wanted to do? (i.e.: Could not find football cleats for the championship game, your parent asked you for something and you couldn't remember where you put it.)

LOGISTICS: What materials, resources, and technology will I need to prepare and engage?

Computer
Microsoft Teams
Pencil/Pen
Paper/Notebook

Pillar: Learning

WEEK 22

LESSON CYCLE:

1. Engage and Connect (10 min)

Recap the thoughts and themes expressed from last week about being organized. Facilitator/Mentor will play a video on the importance of being organized: https://www.youtube.com/watch?v=3Pi8ab-mkAo

2. Lead Guided and Independent Practice (20 min)

Being organized has many benefits that people underestimate. Facilitator/Mentor will lead a discussion on the importance of being organized including:

1) Being organized Reduces Stress
2) Getting organized boosts your self-confidence
3) Getting organized makes you more productive
4) Being organized enhances creativity
5) Getting organized enables you to adapt and become flexible
6) Being organized helps you to be a good role model
7) Getting organized improves our relationships

Facilitator/Mentor will cover the tips to be more organized:

1. **Break tasks into chunks.** Complete 20-minute tasks to become more organized or to complete household chores.
2. **Make a checklist and to-do lists to remain focused and on the task.** There's a sense of accomplishments when you can mark items off your list.
3. **Learn time-management skills.** It will help complete tasks and/or homework assignments on time.
4. **Establish daily routines.** Create a regular schedule so everyone knows what to expect and when tasks are to be completed.
5. **Help youth to think ahead.** Before bed have youth review the plans for the next day. It makes it easier to handle unexpected changes.

3. Close the Lesson and Assess Mastery (15 min)

The facilitator/mentor will ask the participants to reflect on the following question and write their thoughts on a separate sheet of paper.

Writing Prompt Topic: How can I practice being more organized in my daily life?

LOGISTICS: What materials, resources, and technology will I need to prepare and engage?

Computer
Microsoft Teams
Pencil
Paper/Notebook

LESSON VOCABULARY WORDS

INSTRUCTIONS: Review vocabulary words listed below with the participants to ensure they have a good understanding of each before starting any of the activities.

1. **Organized:** Arranged systematically, especially on a large scale.
2. **Productivity:** The effectiveness of productive effort; the state or quality of producing something.
3. **Tasks:** A piece of work to be done or undertaken.
4. **Goals:** The object of a person's ambition or effort; an aim or desired result.
5. **Decluttering:** Remove unnecessary items from an untidy or overcrowded place.

TIPS TO BE MORE ORGANIZED:

1. **Break tasks into chunks.** Complete 20-minute tasks to become more organized or to complete household chores.
2. **Make a checklist and to-do lists to remain focused and on the task.** There's a sense of accomplishments when you can mark items off your list.
3. **Learn time-management skills.** It will help complete tasks and/or homework assignments on time.
4. **Establish daily routines.** Create a regular schedule so everyone knows what to expect and when tasks are to be completed.
5. **Help youth to think ahead.** Before bed have youth review the plans for the next day. It makes it easier to handle unexpected changes.

Discussion Question:

1. Do you consider yourself organized? Why or why not?

   _____
   _____

2. What is clutter?

   _____
   _____

3. Does clutter affect your work environment at school and/or home?

   _____
   _____

Pillar: Learning

HOW IMPORTANT IS BEING ORGANIZED WORKSHEET

Rate each concept from 1-5 (1 being least important 5 being most important) to determine how important being organized is in the situation.

1) Having company over for the weekend _____

2) Having a stressful moment and cannot find anything you need _____

3) Writing things down as they come to your mind _____

4) You have chores to do at home _____

5) You have little kids looking up to you and following everything you do _____

6) Running late for a meeting _____

7) Donating some items to charity or a homeless shelter _____

Writing Prompt Topic: How can I practice being more organized in my daily life?

Pillar: Learning

LESSON TITLE:

Organization is Key

LEVEL: Employee or Community Citizen

WEEKS 21-22

PACING: 55 minutes

OBJECTIVE(S): What will Participants know, understand, and be able to do?

Participants will understand the importance of being organized.

KEY VOCABULARY: What key terms will my Participants need to understand?

Organized: Arranged systematically, especially on a large scale.

Productivity: The effectiveness of productive effort; the state or quality of producing something.

Tasks: A piece of work to be done or undertaken.

Goals: The object of a person's ambition or effort; an aim or desired result.

Decluttering: Remove unnecessary items from an untidy or overcrowded place.

WEEK 21

LESSON CYCLE:

1. Engage and Connect   **(20 min)**

Facilitator/Mentor will introduce the topic of the day as "*Organization is Key*."

Organizational skills include practices like time management, scheduling, prioritizing through to-do and to-don't list, project management skills, consistent communication, multi-tasking, and flexibility as well as adaptability. If you're disorganized, these skills will change your life!

Activity: Take a Poll: Ask participants do they believe they are organized? Why or why not?

Discussion: Ask participants about their understanding of what clutter is, and if they believe that it affects their work environment at work or home). Ask Participants to reflect again on the importance of being organized.

2. Lead Guided and Independent Practice   **(25 min)**

Facilitator/Mentor will facilitate an activity where participants rate each concept from 1-5 (1 being not important 5 being very important) to determine how important being organized is in the situation.

1) Having co-workers over for a dinner party, watch the Super Bowl or to hang out.
2) Having a stressful moment and cannot find anything you need.
3) Writing things down as they come to your mind.

4) You are supervising other employees and you assign their daily duties.
5) Running late for a meeting and don't have a good reason why.
6) Donating some items to charity or a homeless shelter.

3. *Close the Lesson and Assess Mastery* **(10 min)**

The facilitator will ask participants to think about the one time in their lives when being unorganized caused them to miss out on something important? (i.e., you forgot an important appointment, you missed an important call because you misplaced your phone, etc.)

LOGISTICS: What materials, resources, and technology will I need to prepare and engage?

Computer/Microsoft Teams
Pencil/
Paper/Notebook

Pillar: Learning

WEEK 22

LESSON CYCLE:

1. Engage and Connect (20 min)

Recap the thoughts and themes expressed from last week about being organized.

Facilitator/Mentor will share that organizational skills that are the practices and techniques someone uses to increase efficiency and productivity in their daily tasks. You might have heard the phrase, *"Discipline creates freedom,"* and that's exactly what organizational skills promote. By staying organized at work and home, you're better able to manage your schedule. As a result, this offers more time for rest, play, and doing the things you truly want to do.

2. Lead Guided and Independent Practice (25 min)

Facilitator/Mentor will play a video on the importance of being organized:
https://www.youtube.com/watch?v=88MjoZalHpM

Being organized has many benefits that people underestimate. Facilitator/Mentor will lead a discussion on the importance of being organized including:

1. Being organized Reduces Stress
2. Getting organized boosts your self-confidence
3. Getting organized makes you more productive
4. Being organized enhances creativity
5. Getting organized enables you to adapt and become flexible
6. Being organized helps you to be a good role model
7. Getting organized improves our relationships

FACILITATOR/MENTOR WILL COVER THE TIPS TO BE MORE ORGANIZED:

1. **Keep it simple.** Use the least number of steps as possible to complete your task. Choose a system that is easy to use.
2. **Make a checklist and/or to-do lists to remain focused and on the task.** There's a sense of accomplishments when you can mark items off your list. It takes planning to be organized.
3. **Don't be a perfectionist.** You don't have to be perfect to be organized. Prioritize tasks and determine where you can take shortcuts. Break your tasks down into small tasks. Complete 20-minute tasks to become more organized.
4. **Develop routines.** Create set routines about when and how you do them. It allows you to manage your time more effectively and reduces stress.
5. **Keep everything in its right place.** Assign the items you regularly use to a designated/dedicated storage space. **Moto:** Everything has a place, everything in its place.

6. **Toss Things Daily and Purge Routinely.** Take a few minutes to clean a previously used desk, delete old files on your computer, upload your picture to your cloud and erase them from your phone, delete old emails from your inbox, clean out your refrigerator (throw out expired food), etc.

3. *Close the Lesson and Assess Mastery* **(10 min)**

The facilitator will ask Participants to reflect on the following question and write their thoughts on a separate sheet of paper. How can I practice being more organized in my daily life?

LOGISTICS: What materials, resources, and technology will I need to prepare and engage?

Computer
Microsoft Teams
Pencil/Paper/Notebook

Pillar: Learning

LESSON VOCABULARY WORDS

INSTRUCTIONS: Review vocabulary words listed below with the participants to ensure they have a good understanding of each before starting any of the activities.

1. **Organized:** Arranged systematically, especially on a large scale.
2. **Productivity:** The effectiveness of productive effort; the state or quality of producing something.
3. **Tasks:** A piece of work to be done or undertaken.
4. **Goals:** The object of a person's ambition or effort; an aim or desired result.
5. **Decluttering:** Remove unnecessary items from an untidy or overcrowded place.

REASONS FOR BEING ORGANIZED:

1. Being organized Reduces Stress.
2. Getting organized boosts your self-confidence.
3. Getting organized makes you more productive.
4. Being organized enhances creativity.
5. Getting organized enables you to adapt and become flexible.
6. Being organized helps you to be a good role model.
7. Getting organized improves our relationships.

TIPS TO BE MORE ORGANIZED:

1. **Break tasks into chunks.** Complete 20-minute tasks to become more organized or to complete household chores.
2. **Make a checklist and to-do lists to remain focused and on the task.** There's a sense of accomplishments when you can mark items off your list.
3. **Learn time-management skills.** It will help complete tasks and/or homework assignments on time.
4. **Establish daily routines.** Create a regular schedule so everyone knows what to expect and when tasks are to be completed.
5. **Help youth to think ahead.** Before bed have youth review the plans for the next day. It makes it easier to handle unexpected changes.

Discussion Question:

1. Do you consider yourself organized? Why or why not?

   _____
   _____
   _____

2. What is clutter?

   _____
   _____
   _____

3. Does clutter negatively impact your work environment at school, work and/or home?

   _____
   _____
   _____

HOW IMPORTANT IS BEING ORGANIZED WORKSHEET

Rate each concept from 1-5 (1 being least important 5 being most important) to determine how important being organized is in the situation.

1) Having co-workers over for a dinner party, watch the Super Bowl or to hang out. _____

2) Having a stressful moment and cannot find anything you need. _____

3) Writing things down as they come to your mind. _____

4) You are supervising other employees and you assign their daily duties. _____

5) Running late for a meeting and don't have a good reason why. _____

6) Donating some items to charity or a homeless shelter. _____

Pillar: Learning

TO DO CHECKLIST

TO DO LIST

S M T W T F S

DATES: _____

TODAY'S GOALS

REMINDER & NOTES

Intentional Mentoring Mentor's Guide

LESSON TITLE:

Health and Well-being

LEVEL: Youth

WEEKS 23-24

PACING: 55 minutes

OBJECTIVE(S): What will Participants know, understand, and be able to do?

Participants will understand why health and well-being are essential to everyone, and ways they can implement daily.

KEY VOCABULARY: What key terms will my Participants need to understand?

Health: The general condition of the body and mind.

Healthy: Free from infirmity or disease.

Lifestyle: A manner of living that reflects one's values and attitudes.

Well-being: The state of being comfortable, healthy, or happy.

Physical Activity: Any bodily movement that uses energy.

Exercise: Planned, structured, and purposeful physical activity.

WEEK 23

LESSON CYCLE:

1. Engage and Connect **(10 min)**

a. Facilitator/Mentor will introduce the lesson by asking participants would they consider themselves to be healthy. (Yes or No)
   1. Ask participants to define well-being in their own words (Optional: Facilitator/Mentor writes down the answers).
   2. Mentor will show a brief video on why health is so important. https://www.youtube.com/watch?v=21s8-SMOSTY

2. Lead Guided and Independent Practice **(30 min)**

Facilitator/Mentor will share that health and well-being is the achievement and maintenance of physical fitness and mental stability. It is a combination of physical, social, intellectual, and emotional factors.

Activity: Participants will provide examples of individuals whose health and well-being play a huge role in how successful they are. For example: Simone Biles, James Harden, Stephen Curry, and JJ Wyatt (mention if they don't exercise, eat right and/or get adequate rest, they wouldn't be able to perform at such a high level).

Discussion: Common excuses why people say they cannot prioritize their physical health, mental health, etc.

3. Close the Lesson and Assess Mastery **(15 min)**

Have the mentees reflect and write out their answer on how they plan to implement health and well-being in their daily lives. Allow them to share what they wrote. This is a voluntary activity.

LOGISTICS: What materials, resources, and technology will I need to prepare and engage?

Computer
Microsoft Teams
Pencil/Paper/Notebook

WEEK 24

1. Engage and Connect   **(15 min)**

Recap from last week, ask participants what they remember about the discussions/lessons on health and wellness. Ask how many participants participated in the challenge.

Discussion Question: What would they do or eat if they did not have to worry about their health?

2. Lead Guided and Independent Practice   **(25 min)**

Mention to the participants the concept of getting healthy and staying healthy. Share with them the concept of quick fixes and not being sustainable for our lives. Have participants write down healthy habits they have on a sheet of paper, and not so healthy habits they have.

3. Close the Lesson and Assess Mastery   **(15 min)**

Question: "What steps can you take to make sure you are taking ownership of your health and not letting anyone disrupt your daily well-being?"

LOGISTICS: What materials, resources, and technology will I need to prepare and engage?

Computer
Microsoft Teams
Pen/pencil
Paper

Pillar: Learning

LESSON VOCABULARY WORDS

INSTRUCTIONS: Review vocabulary words listed below with the participants to ensure they have a good understanding of each before starting any of the activities.

1. **Health:** The general condition of the body and mind.//
2. **Healthy:** Free from infirmity or disease.
3. **Lifestyle:** A manner of living that reflects one's values and attitudes.
4. **Well-being:** The state of being comfortable, healthy, or happy.
5. **Physical Activity:** Any bodily movement that uses energy.
6. **Exercise**: Planned, structured, and purposeful physical activity.

WELLNESS WORKSHEET

1. Do you consider yourself to be healthy? Yes or No (Circle your answer.)

2. Define the Wellbeing in your own words.

   _____
   _____
   _____
   _____
   _____

3. Provide examples of individuals whose health and well-being play a huge role in how successful they are. (i.e., Simone Biles, James Harden, Stephen Curry, and JJ Wyatt).

   _____
   _____
   _____
   _____
   _____

4. "What steps can you take to make sure you are taking ownership of your health and not letting anyone disrupt your daily well-being?"

   _____
   _____
   _____
   _____

Pillar: Learning

LESSON TITLE:

Health and Well-Being

LEVEL: Employee or Community Citizen

WEEKS 23-24

PACING: 55 minutes

OBJECTIVE(S): What will Participants know, understand, and be able to do?

Participants will understand why health and well-being are essential to everyone, and ways they can implement them on a daily basis.

KEY VOCABULARY: What key terms will my Participants need to understand?

Health: The general condition of the body and mind.

Healthy: Free from infirmity or disease.

Lifestyle: A manner of living that reflects one's values and attitudes.

Well-being: The state of being comfortable, healthy, or happy.

Physical Activity: Any bodily movement that uses energy.

Exercise: Planned, structured, and purposeful physical activity.

WEEK 23

LESSON CYCLE:

1. Engage and Connect   (10 min)

When talking about achieving health and wellness, it is often only referred to becoming physically healthy by getting more exercise and eating healthier. But physical wellness is only one dimension of being a healthy person. To be truly healthy, consider all the other elements of health and wellness. Having a healthy, satisfying life happens when all of these elements interact seamlessly. (https://wellness411center.com/)

Discussion Questions:
1) Do you consider yourself to be healthy?
2) Define well-being in your own words (Optional: Mentor writes down answers).

Facilitator/Mentor will show a brief video on why health is important. https://www.youtube.com/watch?v=GGxPL37j234

2. Lead Guided and Independent Practice   (25 min)

Discussion: After seeing the video have an open discussion:
1) Various types of health (for example: mental health, emotional health, spiritual health, physical health, etc.).

2) Health within your family (Mentors can share personal stories, for example, an aunt that struggles with weight from lack of exercise or an uncle that has heart disease, cancer, diabetes, etc.).

Activity: Create a plan of action to implement health and well-being in their daily lives.

(https://www.healthierwork.act.gov.au/wp-content/uploads/2015/01/HW_Action_Plan_template.pdf)

3. Close the Lesson and Assess Mastery   **(10 min)**

- Ask the mentees share their plan of action for one aspect of their health and wellbeing.
- Challenge participants to add more fruit, veggies, adequate sleep, and less screen time to their day.

LOGISTICS: What materials, resources, and technology will I need to prepare and engage?

Computer
Pencil/Paper/Notebook

Pillar: Learning

WEEK 24

LESSON CYCLE:

1. Engage and Connect   **(10 min)**

Recap from last week, ask participants what they remember about the discussions/lessons on health and wellness. Ask how many participants participated in the challenge.

Discussion Question: What would they do or eat if they did not have to worry about their health?

2. Lead Guided and Independent Practice   **(25 min)**

Mention to the participants the concept of getting healthy and staying healthy?
   a. Share with them the concept of quick fixes and not being sustainable for our lives.
   b. Have Participants write down healthy habits they have on a sheet of paper, and not-so-healthy habits they have.
   c. Facilitator/Mentor to go over the steps/ways to improve their health/wellness.

10 SIMPLE WAYS TO IMPROVE YOUR HEALTH:

1.	Enjoy de-stressing	Experts recommend regular exercise, meditation and breathing techniques to reduce stress.
2.	Get to bed earlier.	Set a regular sleep and wake schedule and stick to it — even on days off. Going to bed even 15 minutes earlier every night could help.
3.	Check your posture and ergonomics.	Take a moment to think about your posture. Then straighten up your back, tuck in your stomach and put your feet flat on the floor with your legs uncrossed. You'll feel more relaxed right away.
4.	Make a few dietary substitutions.	Munch on a carrot instead of a cookie. They're rich in fiber and contain lots of water, so they'll leave you full and satisfied without a lot of calories and fat.
5.	Exercise regularly.	The next time you're going to a higher floor, bypass the elevator and climb the stairs instead. Take a few minutes to stretch out before and after you exercise.

3. Close the Lesson and Assess Mastery   **(10 min)**

Pose the question: *"How can you incorporate the previously discussed steps to ensure you take ownership of your health?"*

LOGISTICS: What materials, resources, and technology will I need to prepare and engage?

Computer
Microsoft Teams
Pencil or pen/Paper or notebook

Pillar: Learning

LESSON VOCABULARY WORDS

INSTRUCTIONS: Review vocabulary words listed below with the participants to ensure they have a good understanding of each before starting any of the activities.

1. **Health:** The general condition of the body and mind.
2. **Healthy:** Free from infirmity or disease.
3. **Lifestyle:** A manner of living that reflects one's values and attitudes.
4. **Well-being:** The state of being comfortable, healthy, or happy.
5. **Physical Activity:** Any bodily movement that uses energy.
6. **Exercise**: Planned, structured, and purposeful physical activity.

HEALTH & WELLNESS: When talking about achieving health and wellness, it is often only referred to becoming physically healthy by getting more exercise and eating healthier. But physical wellness is only one dimension of being a healthy person. To be truly healthy, consider all the other elements of health and wellness. Having a healthy, satisfying life happens when all the elements interact seamlessly. (https://wellness411center.com/)

Activity: After watching the video clip, create a plan of action to implement health and well-being in your daily life.
(https://www.healthierwork.act.gov.au/wp-content/uploads/2015/01/HW_Action_Plan_template.pdf)

10 SIMPLE WAYS TO IMPROVE YOUR HEALTH:

1. Enjoy de-stressing	Experts recommend regular exercise, meditation and breathing techniques to reduce stress.
2. Get to bed earlier.	Set a regular sleep and wake schedule and stick to it — even on days off. Going to bed even 15 minutes earlier every night could help.
3. Check your posture and ergonomics.	Take a moment to think about your posture. Then straighten up your back, tuck in your stomach and put your feet flat on the floor with your legs uncrossed. You'll feel more relaxed right away.
4. Make a few dietary substitutions.	Munch on a carrot instead of a cookie. They're rich in fiber and contain lots of water, so they'll leave you full and satisfied without a lot of calories and fat.
5. Exercise regularly.	The next time you're going to a higher floor, bypass the elevator and climb the stairs instead. Take a few minutes to stretch out before and after you exercise.

TO DO CHECKLIST

TO DO LIST

S M T W T F S

DATES: _____

TODAY'S GOALS

REMINDER & NOTES

PILLAR: LAUGHING

PILLAR: LAUGHING

Throughout life, many have been told not to take themselves too seriously. To enjoy life and to laugh more. In the previous chapters, the mentee has learned invaluable lessons, grown into who they are meant to be in this season of their life, learned the importance of giving themselves the gift of love and how to share it with others, and they have learned that their future is bright with opportunities and possibilities. All of which is necessary! Now it is time to learn how to LAUGH! Ella Wheeler Wilcox wrote, "*Laugh, and the world laughs with you; weep, and you weep alone.*" In her musings, it became clear she implied that cheerful people draw cheerful people to them. She encourages people to keep their sense of humor! In this chapter, the mentee will build upon what they have learned and LAUGH!

THE IMPORTANCE OF LAUGHTER/LAUGHING

Wow, considering how to present this chapter on laughter, I came across the following "*laughter is the language of the soul,*" - Pablo Neruda. It sets the tone and direction I will use to describe the different uses for laughter and its healing properties. All of which speak to its necessity in our lives. Robert Provine says, "*…laughter is specifically a social structure, something that connects humans with one another in a profound way.*" In his study, he found people are 30% more likely to laugh in a social setting that warrants it than when alone with humor dash inducing media. Which supports his previous statement that humans are more likely to laugh with friends than when experiencing some comedic event alone.

There are many ways in which people resort to laughter: contagious laughter, nervous laughter, and canned laughter. If you think about it, 90% of our laughter has nothing to do with responding to the joke someone told, but for various other reasons. The following are three different types of laughter and the reasons why we may use them.

CONTAGIOUS LAUGHTER: Think about the last time you were with friends or at a family gathering and someone tells a joke. A joke that isn't funny at all, but the person telling the joke laughs to the point of tears. Their laughter causes others to laugh and then you find yourself laughing. Laughing more because everyone else is laughing and not because the joke was funny. Which supports the belief that humans have laughed detectors. His belief was based on providing an explanation to why people automatically respond to laughter with laughter.

NERVOUS LAUGHTER: Nervous laughter is used to protect a person's dignity and/or to maintain control of a situation. However, a small giggle or laugh can easily turn into uncontrollable laughter without warning. Nervous laughter is usually a person's subconscious attempt to reduce stress in an attempt to calm down, but in most cases, it does the complete opposite. It usually heightens the uncomfortableness of the situation.

CANNED LAUGHTER: Canned laughter is genuine laughter that is taken completely out of context and place. Canned laughter is usually used to influence or cause an audience to find humor in the comedic material being shared or in response to it. This type of laughter is designed with contagious laughter in mind and was introduced in television in the 1950s.

CRUEL LAUGHTER: Cruel laughter is laughter that is used at another person's expense. It is considered as being cruel and insensitive. Most people who participate in cruel laughter did not initially set out to do so. Someone falls and hurts himself/herself, and an onlooker laughs. Other witnesses look at him/her, thinking their laughter is inappropriate. The person laughing realizes its inappropriateness and tries to stop laughing, and sometimes they are successful but not always. However, at other times, they force themselves to leave because they cannot stop laughing. Their laughter isn't because they aren't concerned with the other individual's wellbeing, it is because something in the action of falling caused them to laugh.

Pillar: Laughing

LAUGHTER'S HEALING CAPABILITIES

Nothing releases endorphins from your brain, reduces the level of stress in your body, and strengthens the immune system than laughing. It is proven that laughter therapy, also known as humor therapy, can reduce negativity, emotional stress, and physical discomfort.

1. **Laughter is a natural painkiller**: Laughing produces hormones (happy brain chemicals) that act as a natural painkiller (soothing stress, reducing anxiety, easing chronic pain, and makes a person feel happy).
2. **Strengthens your heart.** Laughing is a cardio activity for the heart because it speeds up a person's heart rate.
3. **Wards off disease**: Laughing is a form of protection for your body. The more you laugh and approach life positively, the fewer chronic diseases you will develop.
4. **Tones your abs**: The action of laughing causes the muscles in your abdomen to contract (or flex) and relax (like when doing Ab crunches).
5. **Boosts immunity**: Laughing activates your body's T-cells (are immune system cells) to help ward off germs and illness.
6. **Decreases blood pressure**: Laughter decreases and maintains healthy blood pressure levels and lowers the risk of a heart attack and stroke.
7. **Banishes stress**: A few moments of laughter will reduce the level of stress hormones (i.e., cortisol) coursing around your abdomen area.
8. **Helps those suffering from depression**: Laughing can improve one's overall outlook on life; and eases emotional and physical discomfort and pain significantly.

COMBAT STRESS

1. **Stimulates many organs:** Laughing enhances your intake of oxygen rich air, stimulates your heart, lungs and muscles, and increases the endorphins released by your brain.
2. **Activate your stress response**: Laughing cools down your stress release and increases your heart rate and decreases your blood pressure, leaving you feeling peaceful and relaxed.
3. **Soothes tension:** Laughing stimulates circulation and aids in muscle relaxation to release some of the physical symptoms of stress.

In every instance where there's laughter, it begins with a SMILE! Smiling activates tiny molecules in your brain that fends off stress and releases dopamine, endorphins and serotonin that lowers your anxiety while increasing feelings of happiness.

Pillar: Laughing

LESSON TITLE:

Laugh Therapy

LEVEL: Youth

WEEKS 25-26

PACING: 55 minutes

OBJECTIVE(S): What will Participants know, understand, and be able to do?

Understanding how laughter is connected to your health, be able to seek out more opportunities for humor and laughter.

KEY VOCABULARY: What key terms will my Participants need to understand?

Shared laughter: Signals that you see the world the same way as others, boost the sense of connection.

Simulated laughter: Laughing without experiencing a funny event.

WEEK 25

LESSON CYCLE:

1. Engage and Connect **(10 min)**

Share these health benefits of laughter- boosts the immune system, lowers stress, decreases pain, relaxes muscles, and prevents heart disease. Get the Participant's thoughts on the health benefits. Are you surprised?

2. Lead Guided and Independent Practice **(25 min)**

If you had to create a list of 3 of the funniest movies or TV shows you ever saw to save the world health complications, what would you choose?

- 1...
- 2...
- 3...

Discuss the choices and see who has the funniest list of all time.

3. Close the Lesson and Assess Mastery **(10 min)**

Promote health through laughter by encouraging the Participants to watch a movie/show that was shared over the weekend.

LOGISTICS: What materials, resources, and technology will I need to prepare and engage?

Computer
Pencil, pen, Paper or notebook
Wellness Worksheet
T-Chart

WEEK 26

LESSON CYCLE:

1. Engage and Connect   **(10 min)**

Start off with this quote and get everyone's thoughts. "*Laughter can transport you to a relaxed, positive, and joyful destination. Laughter helps with releasing anger and forgiving sooner.*"

True or False? Why?

2. Lead Guided and Independent Practice   **(25 min)**

Allow for the Participants to make a T-chart with "The past week I laughed at…" on the left, and "I can laugh tomorrow by" on the right.

EX:

The past week I laughed at…	I can laugh tomorrow by…
My puppy did a flip	Watching something funny on YouTube
My friend told me a joke	Reading something funny online
I saw a funny movie	Doing something silly

Give the Participants time to complete the chart and share a few stories.

3. Close the Lesson and Assess Mastery   **(10 min)**

Close the lesson with these tips:

- Count your blessings- considering the positive in your life will distance you from the negative.
- Smile- smiling is the beginning of laughter.
- Spend time with fun people- we tend to laugh more when we are with others vs alone.
- Do not take yourself too seriously- it's ok to laugh at yourself sometimes.

LOGISTICS: What materials, resources, and technology will I need to prepare and engage?

Computer
Pencil, pen
Paper or notebook
Wellness Worksheet
T-Chart

Pillar: Laughing

LESSON VOCABULARY WORDS

INSTRUCTIONS: Review vocabulary words listed below with the participants to ensure they have a good understanding of each before starting any of the activities.

1. **Shared laughter:** Signals that you see the world the same way as others, boost the sense of connection.
2. **Simulated laughter:** Laughing without experiencing a funny event.

WELLNESS WORKSHEET

1. Make a list of 3 of the funniest movies or TV shows you ever saw to save the world health complications. What would you choose?

   _____
   _____
   _____

2. "Laughter can transport you to a relaxed, positive, and joyful destination. Laughter helps with releasing anger and forgiving sooner." True or False? Why? (Circle your answer.)

   _____
   _____
   _____
   _____
   _____

3. Provide examples of individuals whose health and well-being play a huge role in how successful they are. (i.e., Simone Biles, James Harden, Stephen Curry, and JJ Wyatt).

   _____
   _____
   _____
   _____
   _____
   _____
   _____
   _____
   _____

Pillar: Laughing

T-Chart

The past week I laughed at...	I can laugh tomorrow by...

Intentional Mentoring Mentor's Guide

LESSON TITLE:

Laugh Therapy

LEVEL: Employee or Community Citizen

WEEKS 25-26

PACING: 45 minutes

OBJECTIVE(S): What will Participants know, understand, and be able to do?

Understanding how laughter is connected to your health, be able to seek out more opportunities for humor and laughter.

KEY VOCABULARY: What key terms will my Participants need to understand?

CONTAGIOUS LAUGHTER: a person's laughter causes others to laugh and then you find yourself laughing.

NERVOUS LAUGHTER: nervous laughter is used to protect a person's dignity and slash or to maintain control of a situation.

CANNED LAUGHTER: real laughter that is taken completely out of context and place to influence or cause an audience to find humor.

CRUEL LAUGHTER: is inappropriate, cruel, and insensitive laughter used at another person's expense because something in the action caused them to laugh.

WEEK 25

LESSON CYCLE:

1. Engage and Connect   **(15 min)**

Discuss the health benefits of laughter – boosts immune system, lowers stress, decreases pain, relaxes muscles, and prevents heart disease.

Get the Participant's thoughts on the health benefits and ask them if they know anyone that battles with any of these conditions. How does it feel knowing that something as simple as laughing can help heal?

2. Lead Guided and Independent Practice   **(30 min)**

Complete the fill in the blank exercise where the participant determines which scenario goes with the scenario.

Activity 1: From the definitions provided above, select the correct type of laughter from those listed in the vocabulary for the example:

(1 Linda is going up the steps and trips. As she is falling, she attempts to brace her fall but breaks her finger. Samantha sees Linda fall and laughs hysterically. Even after hearing she broke her finger, Samantha cannot stop laughing. (Cruel Laughter)

Pillar: Laughing

(2 Tonya walks into the room and everyone stops talking. She walks up to Al and asks what he is eating. Al responds a chicken sandwich and chips and asks Tonya where she is coming from. Tonya laughs before saying she had a meeting wither supervisor. (Nervous Laughter)

(3 While watching the Kings of Comedy, Marcia begins laughing at Steve Harvey's jokes. Her friend, Tammy, overhears her and begins laughing. Not because she heard the joke but because Marcia was laughing so hard. (Contagious Laughter)

(4 At the beginning of the Laugh Out Loud Comedy Show, local comedians entertained the audience to get them prepared for the headliners. The audience begin laughing and after a while the whole room was laughing hysterically. (Canned Laughter)

(5 _____ can reduce negativity, emotional stress, and physical discomfort. (Laughter Therapy)

Activity 2: Fill in the blank with the correct answers from the lesson on the pillar, Learning.

(1 Where there is laughter, it begins with a _____. (smile)

(2 _____ is released in the brain when someone laughs. (Serotonin)

(3 Pablo Neruda said "laughter is the language of the _____. (soul)

(4 Laughing is a _____ activity for the heart because it strengthens the hurt. (cardio)

(5 _____ and the world _____ with you; _____ and you _____ alone. (laugh/weep)

3. Close the Lesson and Assess Mastery **(10 min)**

Promote health through laughter by encouraging the Participants to watch a movie/show that were mentioned over the weekend.

LOGISTICS: What materials, resources, and technology will I need to prepare and engage?

Computer
Microsoft Teams
Pencil, pen
Paper or notebook

WEEK 26

LESSON CYCLE:

1. Engage and Connect **(15 min)**

Laughter decreases stress hormones and increases immune cells and infection-fighting antibodies, thus improving your resistance to disease. Laughter triggers the release of endorphins, the body's natural feel-good chemicals. Endorphins promote an overall sense of well-being and can even temporarily relieve pain.

Have each participant to smile a real smile. If they are struggling, ask them to think of a moment in time when they were genuinely happy. Have them envision it and smile while thinking about it. After about 2 minutes, ask: compared to when you came into the room/building to now; how are you feeling.

2. Lead Guided and Independent Practice **(30 min)**

Allow for the participants to make a T-chart with "The past week I laughed at…" on the left, and "I can laugh tomorrow by" on the right.

EX:

The past week I laughed at…	I can laugh tomorrow by…
My puppy did a flip	Watching something funny on YouTube
My friend told me a joke	Reading something funny online
I saw a funny movie	Doing something silly

Give the Participants time to complete the chart and share a few stories.

3. Close the Lesson and Assess Mastery **(10 min)**

Close the lesson with these tips:

- Count your blessings- considering the positive in your life will distance you from the negative.
- Smile- smiling is the beginning of laughter.
- Spend time with fun people- we tend to laugh more when we are with others vs alone.
- Do not take yourself too seriously- it's ok to laugh at yourself sometimes.

LOGISTICS: What materials, resources, and technology will I need to prepare and engage?

Computer
Microsoft Teams
Pencil, pen
Paper or notebook

Pillar: Laughing

LESSON VOCABULARY WORDS

INSTRUCTIONS: Study the vocabulary words listed below for a good understanding of each one.

1. **CONTAGIOUS LAUGHTER:** a person's laughter causes others to laugh and then you find yourself laughing.

2. **NERVOUS LAUGHTER:** nervous laughter is used to protect a person's dignity and slash or to maintain control of a situation.

3. **CANNED LAUGHTER:** real laughter that is taken completely out of context and place to influence or cause an audience to find humor.

4. **CRUEL LAUGHTER:** is inappropriate, cruel, and insensitive laughter used at another person's expense because something in the action caused them to laugh.

LAUGHING WORKSHEET

Complete the fill in the blank exercise where the participant determines which scenario goes with the scenario.

Activity 1: From the definitions provided above, select the correct type of laughter for the example:

(1 Linda is going up the steps and trips. As she is falling, she attempts to brace her fall but breaks her finger. Samantha sees Linda fall and laughs hysterically. Even after hearing she broke her finger, Samantha cannot stop laughing. _____

(2 Tonya walks into the room and everyone stops talking. She walks up to Al and asks what he is eating. Al responds a chicken sandwich and chips and asks Tonya where she is coming from. Tonya laughs before saying she had a meeting wither supervisor. _____

(3 While watching the Kings of Comedy, Marcia begins laughing at Steve Harvey's jokes. Her friend, Tammy, overhears her and begins laughing. Not because she heard the joke but because Marcia was laughing so hard. _____

(4 At the beginning of the Laugh Out Loud Comedy Show, local comedians entertained the audience to get them prepared for the headliners. The audience begin laughing and after a while the whole room was laughing hysterically. _____

(5 _____ can reduce negativity, emotional stress, and physical discomfort.

Activity 2: Fill in the blank with the correct answers from the lesson on the pillar, Learning.

(1 Where there is laughter, it begins with a _____.

(2 _____ is released in the brain when someone laughs.

(3 Pablo Neruda said "laughter is the language of the _____.

(4 Laughing is a _____ activity for the heart because it strengthens the hurt.

(5 _____ and the world _____ with you; _____ and you _____ alone.

Pillar: Laughing

T-Chart

| The past week I laughed at... | I can laugh tomorrow by... |

LESSON TITLE:

Anger Management

LEVEL: Youth   **WEEKS 27-28**

PACING: 55 minutes

OBJECTIVE(S): What will Participants know, understand, and be able to do?

Normalize anger and discuss techniques to manage anger while reflecting on past experiences.

KEY VOCABULARY: What key terms will my Participants need to understand?

Healthy anger: Demands reflection and requires that time is taken to exert the effort to empower the rational mind to override the emotional mind.

Anger explosions: Sudden episodes of impulsive and aggressive behavior.

Emotional triggers: Statement that may cause you to feel many emotions.

Consequence: A result or effect of an action or condition.

WEEK 27

LESSON CYCLE:

1. Engage and Connect   **(10 min)**

Lead with this quote: *"Anger is a normal and healthy emotion- the difference is how we choose to express it."*

Discussion: Agree or disagree? Why?

2. Lead Guided and Independent Practice   **(30 min)**

While anger is a normal and can even be a healthy and productive, anger that is expressed in a destructive or dangerous manner is dysfunctional. If a person expresses anger in the form of yelling, violence, threats, bullying or breaking the law, it can destroy their school life experience, academics, career, and relationships. Many youths have a hard time controlling anger because their brains are still developing (and won't fully develop until their early to mid-20s). Areas of the brain that control impulse control and planning are some of the last to develop. Therefore, many teens find anger management quite difficult. Despite this difficulty, there are many activities and exercises that can be beneficial for teens in helping them control their anger.

Instruct the participants to write about 2 experiences that made them angry this week or month, and how you responded to them. Allow a select number of participants to share 1 experience each.

Discuss: Alternatives to negatively expressing anger:

- Deep Breathing
- Exercise

- Learning to Express Feelings
- Talking to a Friend
- Journaling

(https://study.com/academy/lesson/anger-management-activities-exercises-for-teens)

3. *Close the Lesson and Assess Mastery* **(15 min)**

Close the lesson by giving your take on how it is imperative that everyone controls their anger and practices positive anger management activities.

LOGISTICS: What materials, resources, and technology will I need to prepare and engage?

Computer
Microsoft Teams
Pencil, pen
Paper or notebook

WEEK 28

LESSON CYCLE:

1. Engage and Connect   **(10 min)**

Anger is a complicated emotion, and the more youth can understand how it operates the better they'll be at getting ahead of it. Anger often serves as a protector or mask for other deep vulnerable emotions. It's easier to feel angry than ashamed, embarrassed, or hurt. Our subconscious wants to protect us, so it sends in its defense team. The anger iceberg metaphor is a fantastic visual that depicts this for youth and builds self-awareness. Any given day they have events, emotions, and stressors that lie under the surface of can be seen.

2. Lead Guided and Independent Practice   **(35 min)**

Activity 1: Teach participants how to use an Anger Iceberg. Explain that conflicts happen, and when they do, it's important for all parties to have a basic understanding that anger may not be the primary emotion at play. Understanding that anger is often protecting you from the deeper, more vulnerable emotions involved in loss which are more challenging to express can help respond instead of reacting when angered. The iceberg makes you aware that you need to look further into why you are feeling angry and what other emotions have led to the anger you are currently experiencing. And just as important as understanding your own anger is understanding anger that's directed toward you from another. When we recognize another's anger as something deeper, like pain or shame, we can approach conflict more compassionately, without reacting negatively/defensively.

1. **Understand what triggered you.** Ask yourself, where this emotion coming from? (Pay attention to the things, thoughts, feelings and/or experiences that let to your anger.)

2. **Identify what's going on underneath the tip of the iceberg.** Now you can get to the root of the deeper emotion and prioritize that over your anger. You may have to look at past experiences or limiting beliefs you have about yourself. It helps you unpack your anger to understand yourself with more clarity.

3. **Help yourself feel calmer.** Resolve the need to self-soothe and emotionally regulate. Take a walk, focus on some deep breaths, journal, do something physical and/or relax the tension you are experiencing in your body.

4. **Channel your energy.** When our emotions are overwhelming (and confusing) us, it can be difficult to focus on anything else. Understanding them will help you channel that energy into things you'd rather focus on, volunteer at a charity/charitable organization, go running/jogging, workout, ride a bike, etc.

Activity 2: Provide each participant with a notebook with a white cardboard cover. While you are reviewing this lesson, have them design the cover of their journal (supply a separate journal or notebook with white cardboard cover). Encourage them to use it to write about their anger-inspired experiences.

Activity 3: Yoga and Anger Management. There are many healthy ways to deal with anger, and one of the most effective ways to release anger is yoga. In fact, according to a study published in the publication, Frontiers Practicing Yoga, can help control anger and improve the impulses that surround anger. Regular yoga practice can train your brain to stop and calm itself, which can help you manage your anger. While yoga is not a solution for all of life's problems, including anger issues; it may be able to provide some relief from the impulses that surround anger management issues. (*If possible, invite a yoga instructor to come in and teach the five yoga poses that releases anger. If you do not have access to a yoga instructor show pictures of each pose.*)

5 YOGA POSES TO RELEASE ANGER:

1. **Easy Seated Pose (Sukhasana) With Breath of Fire.** Sukhasana, easy pose, is a simple cross-legged sitting asana in hatha yoga, sometimes used for meditation. For a full 60 seconds, commit to releasing any built-up anger that you have been suppressing while in this pose. Allow the anger to rise to the surface and as you exhale, let it go. When you're done, open your palms and stretch your arms overhead. This provides a direct channel to release your anger.

2. **Camel Pose (Ustrasana).** Begin in a kneeling position with your hips stacked over your knees. Place your palms against your low back, bringing your elbows in toward the center of your back. Begin to gently press your hips forward as you lift from the chest and send your gaze towards the ceiling. stay there for five deep breaths. When you're ready, come out of Camel Pose slowly and rest your seat to your heels. Bring your hands into your lap and sit quietly with your eyes open (so you don't get dizzy) breathing deeply for another 5-10 breaths, noticing how you feel both emotionally and physically.

3. **Revolved Crescent Lunge (Parivrtta Anjaneyasana).** Start in Low Crescent Lunge Pose with your right foot forward. Bring your hands to heart center and keeping your spine lengthened, hinge your torso forward slightly as you hook your left elbow to the outside of your right knee. Slowly straighten into your back leg (you can keep a micro bend in your back knee) and press down through your back left heel. As you twist, pull in your lower abdomen, and lift your torso away from your thigh. Stay in this pose for 30-60 seconds (or longer if it's part of your practice), and then repeat on the other side.

4. **Goddess Pose (Utkata Konasana) with Ganesha Mudra.** Mudras, which translates to "seal" in Sanskrit, are symbolic gestures of the hands to support the flow of energy within the body. Different parts of the hands are linked to different areas in the body and brain. By placing our hands in mudras, we stimulate specific areas, which can alter our state of mind. Bring your left hand in front of your sternum, palm facing outward with your thumb pointing down. Bring your right hand in front of the left, palm facing toward you, with your thumb pointing up. Bend your fingers and hook the right fingers with the left fingers, your elbows pointing outward. Inhale deeply and as you exhale, pull your elbows away from one another, keeping your fingers interlocked. Take five deep breaths here.

5. **Corpse Pose (Savasana).** As a pose of total relaxation and deep restoration, Savasana is a great way to complete your yoga to release anger practice. To begin, lie on your back with your legs extended long and arms by your sides with your palms facing up. Keep your eyes closed, breathe naturally, and allow your body to sink into the mat – from the tips of your toes all the way up to your eyebrows and forehead, fully relax and soften. Starting from the soles of your feet and moving to the top of your head, release any lingering tension. Invite peace and calm into your mind, body, and spirit. Stay in this position for five minutes.

(https://www.yogiapproved.com/yoga-poses-to-release-anger-2/)

3. Close the Lesson and Assess Mastery **(10 min)**

Ask participants what they learned and how it can help them control their anger in the future. Share there are other healthy activities they can use to reduce their anger: deep breathing, meditation, exercising, team sports, yoga, and laughter.

LOGISTICS: What materials, resources, and technology will I need to prepare and engage?

Computer
Microsoft Teams
Pencil, pen
Paper or notebook

LESSON VOCABULARY WORDS

INSTRUCTIONS: Review vocabulary words listed below with the participants to ensure they have a good understanding of each before starting any of the activities.

1. **Healthy anger:** Demands reflection and requires that time is taken to exert the effort to empower the rational mind to override the emotional mind.

2. **Anger explosions:** Sudden episodes of impulsive and aggressive behavior.

3. **Emotional triggers:** Statement that may cause you to feel many emotions.

4. **Consequence:** A result or effect of an action or condition.

Writing Prompt Topic: Write about 2 experiences that made you angry this week or month, and how you responded to them.

Pillar: Laughing

ANGER ICEBERG

Introduction: conflicts happen, and when they do, it's important for all parties to have a basic understanding that anger may not be the primary emotion at play. Understanding that anger is often protecting you from the deeper, more vulnerable emotions involved in loss which are more challenging to express can help respond instead of reacting when angered. The iceberg makes you aware that you need to look further into why you are feeling angry and what other emotions have led to the anger you are currently experiencing. And just as important as understanding your own anger is understanding anger that's directed toward you from another. When we recognize another's anger as something deeper, like pain or shame, we can approach conflict more compassionately, without reacting negatively/defensively.

Instructions: Using steps 1 and 2, complete the Anger Iceberg on the next page.

1. **Understand what triggered you.** Ask yourself, where this emotion coming from? (Pay attention to the things, thoughts, feelings and/or experiences that let to your anger.)

2. **Identify what's going on underneath the tip of the iceberg.** Now you can get to the root of the deeper emotion and prioritize that over your anger. You may have to look at past experiences or limiting beliefs you have about yourself. It helps you unpack your anger to understand yourself with more clarity.

3. **Help yourself feel calmer.** Resolve the need to self-soothe and emotionally regulate. Take a walk, focus on some deep breaths, journal, do something physical and/or relax the tension you are experiencing in your body.

4. **Channel your energy.** When our emotions are overwhelming (and confusing) us, it can be difficult to focus on anything else. Understanding them will help you channel that energy into things you'd rather focus on, volunteer at a charity/charitable organization, go running/jogging, workout, ride a bike, etc.

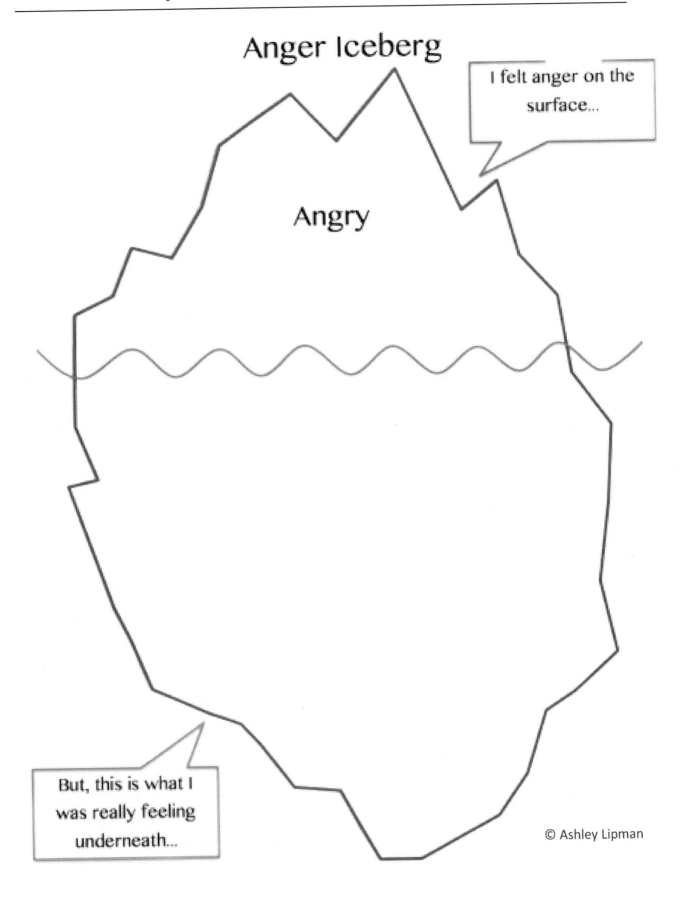

Pillar: Laughing

5 Yoga Poses to Release Anger:

1. **Easy Seated Pose (Sukhasana) With Breath of Fire**

    Find Sukhasana, or Easy Seated Pose, and take a moment to feel grounded and connected to the earth here. This simple step of mindfulness will help center you and start pulling you from the grips of anger.

    Now you're ready to practice **Breath of Fire Pranayama** for a full 60 seconds. Commit to releasing any built-up anger that you have been suppressing. Allow that anger to rise to the surface and as you exhale, let it go. *Not Sure How to Practice? Here's a Breath of Fire Pranayama Tutorial.* When you're done, open your palms and stretch your arms overhead. This provides a direct channel to release your anger. If you feel like you have any lingering emotions, scream for a few seconds to let it go.

    Screaming therapy, also known as **primal therapy**, is scientifically proven to be good for your health. So go ahead and let it all out! You'll feel better after you do. Then, let your arms fall down by your sides and sit in silence for a few minutes. Notice how you feel. Is there a shift in your emotional state? Do you feel like a weight has been lifted?

    How it helps release anger: Sukhasana helps you get grounded, which is the first step in releasing negative emotions. Breath of Fire deeply focuses the mind, detoxifies the body, and shifts the energy so you can let. it. go.

2. **Camel Pose (Ustrasana)**

    Begin in a kneeling position with your hips stacked over your knees. Place your palms against your low back, bringing your elbows in toward the center of your back. Begin to gently press your hips forward as you lift from the chest and send your gaze towards the ceiling.

    You can stay here. If Camel Pose is part of your practice and you'd like to take the final expression, slowly reach down, and grab your heels with each hand.

    Not Sure How to Practice? Here's How to Access Camel Pose Safely

    Wherever you are, stay there for five deep breaths. When you're ready, come out of Camel Pose slowly and rest your seat to your heels. Bring your hands into your lap and sit quietly with your eyes open (so you don't get dizzy) breathing deeply for another 5-10 breaths, noticing how you feel both emotionally and physically.

How it helps release anger:

Camel Pose is a big heart opener. Heart openers activate the Heart Chakra, inviting in and sending out love, helping to melt away the anger.

3. **Revolved Crescent Lunge (Parivrtta Anjaneyasana)**

Start in Low Crescent Lunge Pose with your right foot forward. Bring your hands to heart center and keeping your spine lengthened, hinge your torso forward slightly as you hook your left elbow to the outside of your right knee.

Option to push your elbow against the outside of your leg for a deeper twist. Make sure your shoulders are relaxed away from your ears. Slowly straighten into your back leg (you can keep a micro bend in your back knee) and press down through your back left heel. As you twist, pull in your lower abdomen, and lift your torso away from your thigh. Stay in this pose for 30-60 seconds (or longer if it's part of your practice), and then repeat on the other side.

How it helps release anger:

Twists nourish and massage the spinal column. When we're angry, we physically become closed off, rounding the spine and creating tension in the body. This twist helps release tension so you can then release your anger.

4. **Goddess Pose (Utkata Konasana) with Ganesha Mudra**

Mudras, which translates to "seal" in Sanskrit, are symbolic gestures of the hands to support the flow of energy within the body. Different parts of the hands are linked to different areas in the body and brain.

Common Mudras, Their Meaning, and How to Practice Them

By placing our hands in mudras, we stimulate specific areas, which can alter our state of mind. The Ganesha Mudra, named after the Hindu elephant deity who removes obstacles, is believed to help alleviate anger. Start in Goddess Pose with your heels in, toes out, and knees gently pressing outward. Bring your left hand in front of your sternum, palm facing outward with your thumb pointing down. Bring your right hand in front of the left, palm facing toward you, with your thumb pointing up. Bend your fingers and hook the right fingers with the left fingers, your elbows pointing outward. Inhale deeply and as you exhale, pull your elbows away from one another, keeping your fingers interlocked. Take five deep breaths here.

How it helps release anger:

The Ganesha Mudra combined with Goddess Pose promotes better blood circulation and releases tension in the shoulders and chest, helping to open up the Heart Chakra.

Goddess Pose also opens the hips and cultivates confidence and strength so you can release your anger and move on.

5. **Corpse Pose (Savasana)**

As a pose of total relaxation and deep restoration, Savasana is a great way to complete your yoga to release anger practice.

To begin, lie on your back with your legs extended long and arms by your sides with your palms facing up. Keep your eyes closed, breathe naturally and allow your body to sink into the mat – from the tips of your toes all the way up to your eyebrows and forehead, fully relax and soften. Starting from the soles of your feet and moving to the top of your head, release any lingering tension. Invite peace and calm into your mind, body and spirit. Stay in this position for five minutes.

How it helps release anger:

Practicing Savasana helps you rejuvenate and recharge by activating the parasympathetic nervous system, also known as the "rest and digest" reaction in the body. This pose lowers blood pressure and heart rate, which is particularly beneficial when it comes to releasing anger.

Intentional Mentoring Mentor's Guide

LESSON TITLE:

Anger Management

LEVEL: Employee or Community Citizen

WEEKS 27-28

PACING: 55 minutes

OBJECTIVE(S): What will Participants know, understand, and be able to do?

Normalize anger and discuss techniques to manage anger while reflecting on past experiences.

KEY VOCABULARY: What key terms will my Participants need to understand?

Healthy anger: Demands reflection and requires that time is taken to exert the effort to empower the rational mind to override the emotional mind.

Anger explosions: Sudden episodes of impulsive and aggressive behavior.

Emotional triggers: Statement that may cause you to feel many emotions.

Consequence: A result or effect of an action or condition.

WEEK 27

LESSON CYCLE:

1. Engage and Connect **(10 min)**

Lead with this quote: *"Anger is a normal and healthy emotion- the difference is how we choose to express it."*

Discussion: Agree or disagree? Why?

2. Lead Guided and Independent Practice **(25 min)**

While anger is a normal and can even be healthy and productive, anger that is expressed in a destructive or dangerous manner is dysfunctional. If a person expresses anger in the form of yelling, violence, threats, bullying or breaking the law, it can destroy their work life experience, academics, career, and relationships. Many adults have a hard time controlling anger because of the hurt, pain, and trauma they have experienced in their past. Which makes anger management somewhat difficult. Despite this difficulty, there are many activities and exercises that can be beneficial for traumatized adults in helping them control their anger.

Instruct the participants to write about 2 experiences that made them angry this week or month, and how they responded to them. Allow a select number of participants to share 1 experience each.

Discuss: Alternatives to negatively expressing anger:

- Deep Breathing
- Exercise

Pillar: Laughing

- Learning to Express Feelings
- Talking to a Friend
- Journaling

(https://study.com/academy/lesson/anger-management-activities-exercises-for-teens)

3. Close the Lesson and Assess Mastery **(10 min)**

Close the lesson by giving your take on how it is imperative that everyone controls their anger and practices positive anger management activities.

LOGISTICS: What materials, resources, and technology will I need to prepare and engage?

Computer
Microsoft Teams
Pencil, pen
Paper or notebook

WEEK 28

LESSON CYCLE:

1. Engage and Connect **(10 min)**

When it's all over, who loses when we make anger driven decisions? Explain your answer.

Discussion: Was it worth it?

2. Lead Guided and Independent Practice **(25 min)**

Activity 1: Start a discussion around the health facts below:

Long and short-term health problems linked to unmanaged anger: Headaches, digestion problems, insomnia, increased anxiety, depression, high blood pressure, heart attack, skin problems and stroke. Then, collectively create a list of ways you can control your anger.

Anger Management tools for the workplace or at an event:

1. **Stop and listen**. When you're in an angry argument, you might find yourself jumping to conclusions and saying things that are unkind. Try to stop and listen to the other person in the conversation before reacting can help your anger drop and allow you to better respond and resolve the situation. Think carefully before replying. Tell them you need to take a step away if you feel you need to cool down before you continue the conversation.

2. **Know your body**. When you get angry, your body tends to get very excited. Your heart rate, blood pressure, breathing speed, and body temperature may increase. Your body also releases certain stress hormones that put your body on high alert. Pay attention to your body when you're angry. Learn your body's anger warning signs. Next time you feel these warnings, you can step away from the situation or try a relaxation technique.

3. **Visualize yourself calm**. Imagining a relaxing place may help you reduce your anger. Sit in a quiet, comfortable space from your memory and close your eyes for a few moments. Let your imagination flow. For a quick way to manage anger, go for a brisk walk, bike ride, run. Or do some other form of physical activity when you feel anger growing.

4. **Learn to breathe**. When you're angry, you might notice your breathing gets quicker and shallower. One easy way to calm your body and reduce your anger is to slow and deepen your breathing. Try breathing slowly into your nose and out your mouth. Breathe deeply from your belly rather than your chest. Repeat breaths as necessary.

5. **Progressive muscle relaxation**. Muscle tension is another sign of stress in the body that you may feel when you're angry. To help calm down, you may want to try a progressive muscle relaxation technique. This involves slowly tensing and then relaxing each muscle group in the body, one at a time. Consider starting at the top of your head and move your way to your toes, or vice versa.

(https://www.healthline.com/health/anger-management-exercises#seeking-help)

Pillar: Laughing

Activity 2: Yoga and Anger Management. There are many healthy ways to deal with anger, and one of the most effective ways to release anger is yoga. In fact, according to a study published in Frontiers Practicing yoga can help control anger and improve the impulses that surround anger. Regular yoga practice can train your brain to stop and calm itself, which can help you manage your anger. While yoga is not a solution for all of life's problems, including anger issues; it may be able to provide some relief from the impulses that surround anger management issues. (*If possible, invite a yoga instructor to come in and teach the five yoga poses that releases anger. If you do not have access to a yoga instructor show pictures of each pose.*)

5 Yoga Poses to Release Anger:

1) **Easy Seated Pose (Sukhasana) With Breath of Fire.** Sukhasana, easy pose, is a simple cross-legged sitting asana in hatha yoga, sometimes used for meditation. For a full 60 seconds, commit to releasing any built-up anger that you have been suppressing while in this pose. Allow the anger to rise to the surface and as you exhale, let it go. When you're done, open your palms and stretch your arms overhead. This provides a direct channel to release your anger.

2) **Camel Pose (Ustrasana).** Begin in a kneeling position with your hips stacked over your knees. Place your palms against your low back, bringing your elbows in toward the center of your back. Begin to gently press your hips forward as you lift from the chest and send your gaze towards the ceiling. stay there for five deep breaths. When you're ready, come out of Camel Pose slowly and rest your seat to your heels. Bring your hands into your lap and sit quietly with your eyes open (so you don't get dizzy) breathing deeply for another 5-10 breaths, noticing how you feel both emotionally and physically.

3) **Revolved Crescent Lunge (Parivrtta Anjaneyasana)**. Start in Low Crescent Lunge Pose with your right foot forward. Bring your hands to heart center and keeping your spine lengthened, hinge your torso forward slightly as you hook your left elbow to the outside of your right knee. Slowly straighten into your back leg (you can keep a micro bend in your back knee) and press down through your back left heel. As you twist, pull in your lower abdomen, and lift your torso away from your thigh. Stay in this pose for 30-60 seconds (or longer if it's part of your practice), and then repeat on the other side.

4) **Goddess Pose (Utkata Konasana) with Ganesha Mudra.** Mudras, which translates to "seal" in Sanskrit, are symbolic gestures of the hands to support the flow of energy within the body. Different parts of the hands are linked to different areas in the body and brain. By placing our hands in mudras, we stimulate specific areas, which can alter our state of mind. Bring your left hand in front of your sternum, palm facing outward with your thumb pointing down. Bring your right hand in front of the left, palm facing toward you, with your thumb pointing up. Bend your fingers and hook the right fingers with the left fingers, your elbows pointing outward. Inhale deeply and as you exhale, pull your elbows away from one another, keeping your fingers interlocked. Take five deep breaths here.

5) **Corpse Pose (Savasana).** As a pose of total relaxation and deep restoration, Savasana is a great way to complete your yoga to release anger practice. To begin, lie on your back with your legs extended long and arms by your sides with your palms facing up. Keep your eyes closed, breathe naturally, and allow your body to sink into the mat – from the tips of your toes all the way up to your eyebrows and forehead, fully relax and soften. Starting from the soles of your feet and

moving to the top of your head, release any lingering tension. Invite peace and calm into your mind, body, and spirit. Stay in this position for five minutes.

(https://www.yogiapproved.com/yoga-poses-to-release-anger-2/)

3. Close the Lesson and Assess Mastery **(10 min)**

Learning to healthfully manage your anger is a process that happens more quickly for some than for others. If you feel that your anger gets overwhelming or if it's causing you to hurt yourself or those around you, it's time to get expert help. Reiterate the importance of getting professional help when the tips and tools you have tried no longer or do not work for you.

LOGISTICS: What materials, resources, and technology will I need to prepare and engage?

    Computer
    Microsoft Teams
    Pencil, pen
    Paper or notebook

LESSON VOCABULARY WORDS

INSTRUCTIONS: Review vocabulary words listed below with the participants to ensure they have a good understanding of each before starting any of the activities.

1. **Healthy anger:** Demands reflection and requires that time is taken to exert the effort to empower the rational mind to override the emotional mind.

2. **Anger explosions:** Sudden episodes of impulsive and aggressive behavior.

3. **Emotional triggers:** Statement that may cause you to feel many emotions.

4. **Consequence:** A result or effect of an action or condition.

Writing Prompt Topic: Write about 2 experiences that made you angry this week or month, and how you responded to them.

ANGER ICEBERG

Introduction: Conflicts happen, and when they do, it's important for all parties to have a basic understanding that anger may not be the primary emotion at play. Understanding that anger is often protecting you from the deeper, more vulnerable emotions involved in loss which are more challenging to express can help respond instead of reacting when angered. The iceberg makes you aware that you need to look further into why you are feeling angry and what other emotions have led to the anger you are currently experiencing. And just as important as understanding your own anger is understanding anger that's directed toward you from another. When we recognize another's anger as something deeper, like pain or shame, we can approach conflict more compassionately, without reacting negatively/defensively.

Instructions: Using steps 1 and 2, complete the Anger Iceberg on the next page.

1. **Understand what triggered you.** Ask yourself, where this emotion coming from? (Pay attention to the things, thoughts, feelings and/or experiences that let to your anger.)
2. **Identify what's going on underneath the tip of the iceberg.** Now you can get to the root of the deeper emotion and prioritize that over your anger. You may have to look at past experiences or limiting beliefs you have about yourself. It helps you unpack your anger to understand yourself with more clarity.
3. **Help yourself feel calmer.** Resolve the need to self-soothe and emotionally regulate. Take a walk, focus on some deep breaths, journal, do something physical and/or relax the tension you are experiencing in your body.
4. **Channel your energy.** When our emotions are overwhelming (and confusing) us, it can be difficult to focus on anything else. Understanding them will help you channel that energy into things you'd rather focus on, volunteer at a charity/charitable organization, go running/jogging, workout, ride a bike, etc.

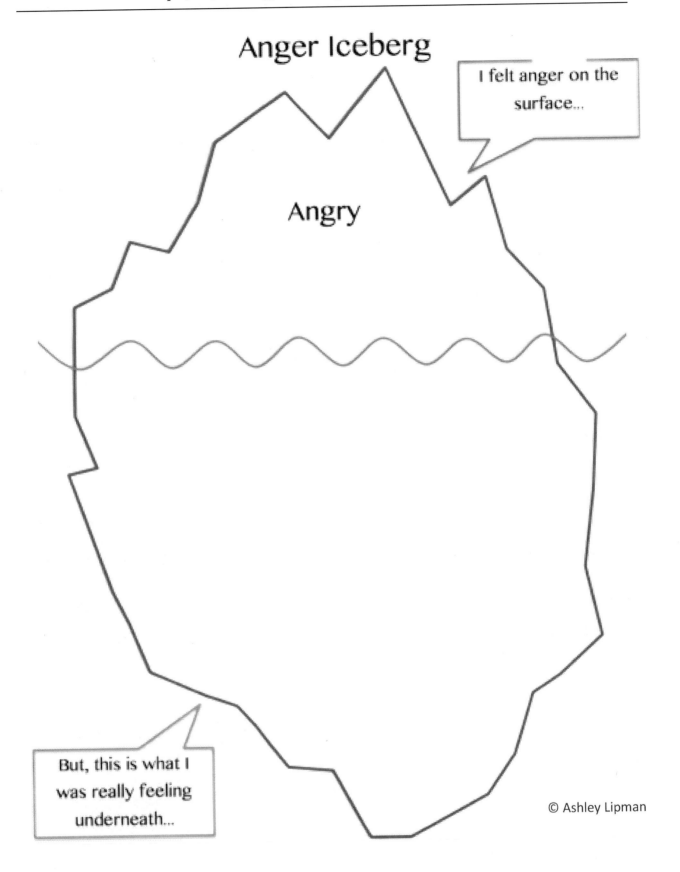

Pillar: Laughing

LESSON TITLE:

Overcoming Stress and Anxiety

LEVEL: Youth

WEEKS 29-30

PACING: 55 minutes

OBJECTIVE(S): What will Participants know, understand, and be able to do?

- Normalize stress and anxiety
- Learn ways to treat stress and anxiety
- Discover how struggling with your identity can trigger stress and anxiety in school
- List out specifics as it relates to how you view yourself and how others view you
- Have the desire to live your truth

KEY VOCABULARY: What key terms will my Participants need to understand?

Stress: A state of mental or emotional strain or tension resulting from adverse or very demanding circumstances.

Anxiety: A feeling of worry, nervousness, or unease, typically about an imminent event or something with an uncertain outcome.

False front: Putting forth a vision of yourself to someone that is anything other than the pure, undistorted truth.

WEEK 29

LESSON CYCLE:

1. Engage and Connect (10 min)

A false front is putting forth a vision of yourself to someone that is not the truth. Basically, being someone that you are not. This act causes a lot of stress and anxiety on Participants. Share this with the youth and ask who can name famous people that pretend to be someone they are not and what celebrated profession accepts this as normal.

2. Lead Guided and Independent Practice (35 min)

When it comes to our identity, we often stress over these 3 questions:

- What do other people think of me?
- What do I know of me?
- Who am I working to become?

Have the Participants create and complete the chart below with 3 examples each. Allow them to share a few.

Ex:

What do other people think of me?	What do I know of me?	Who am I working to become?
I get in trouble a lot	Misunderstood	Honor roll Participant
Hates school	Smart	1st in my family to graduate college
Not focused	Battle with ADD	A millionaire
Class clown	Introvert	Perfect attendance

(10 min)

3. Close the Lesson and Assess Mastery

Encourage the Participants that at the end of the day, it is better to just be yourself. Spend the rest of the time allowing the Participants to further describe the person they are working towards becoming.

LOGISTICS: What materials, resources, and technology will I need to prepare and engage?
Computer
Microsoft Teams
Pencil, pen
Paper or notebook

Pillar: Laughing

WEEK 30

LESSON CYCLE:

1. Engage and Connect (10 min)

Have the Participant answer these True or False questions: (All False)

_____ Only adults get stressed and deal with anxiety.

_____ Stress and anxiety are the same.

_____ Stress and anxiety aren't real.

2. Lead Guided and Independent Practice (25 min)

It is important to let the participants know that stress and anxiety are normal, and everyone deals with it. No matter how much money you have, your age or if you are male or female, everyone deals with it. Share the "How We Cope with Anxiety/Stress": https://www.youtube.com/watch?v=o18I23HCQtE or https://www.youtube.com/watch?v=sBH4HnuNTTY

As them to develop a list of ways to combat stress and anxiety. Share your list after participants have completed the exercise. Below are a few examples:

Ways to manage stress:

- Take a time-out
- Eat well-balanced meals
- Get enough sleep
- Exercise daily
- Take deep breaths

Ways to manage anxiety:

- Count to 10 slowly
- Accept that you cannot control everything
- Welcome humor, laugh, smile
- Learn what triggers your anxiety
- Talk to someone

3. Close the Lesson and Assess Mastery (10 min)

Type of the list and be sure to share it with the Participants. Encourage them to share with family members at home.

LOGISTICS: What materials, resources, and technology will I need to prepare and engage?

Computer
Microsoft Teams
Pencil, pen
Paper or notebook

Pillar: Laughing

LESSON VOCABULARY WORDS

INSTRUCTIONS: Review vocabulary words listed below with the participants to ensure they have a good understanding of each before starting any of the activities.

1. **Stress:** A state of mental or emotional strain or tension resulting from adverse or very demanding circumstances.

2. **Anxiety:** A feeling of worry, nervousness, or unease, typically about an imminent event or something with an uncertain outcome.

3. **False front:** Putting forth a vision of yourself to someone that is anything other than the pure, undistorted truth.

WHAT DO OTHERS THINK OF ME VS WHAT I KNOW ABOUT ME CHART

Activity 1: Complete the chart below using the 3 examples provided:

b. When I get in trouble at home or school.
c. When I stay out past my curfew or the time, I was told to be home by.
d. When I am disrespectful and will not listen.

Activity 2: Answer the following by responding true or false to each statement:

1. _____ Only adults get stressed and deal with anxiety.

2. _____ Stress and anxiety are the same.

3. _____ Stress and anxiety aren't real.

What do other people think of me?	What do I know of me?	Who am I working to become?

Pillar: Laughing

LESSON TITLE:

Overcoming Stress and Anxiety

LEVEL: Employee or Community Citizen

WEEKS 29-30

PACING: 55 minutes

OBJECTIVE(S): What will Participants know, understand, and be able to do?

- Normalize stress and anxiety
- Learn ways to treat stress and anxiety
- Discover how struggling with your identity can trigger stress and anxiety in school
- List out specifics as it relates to how you view yourself and how others view you
- Have the desire to live your truth

KEY VOCABULARY: What key terms will my Participants need to understand?

Stress: A state of mental or emotional strain or tension resulting from adverse or very demanding circumstances.

Anxiety: A feeling of worry, nervousness, or unease, typically about an imminent event or something with an uncertain outcome.

False front: Putting forth a vision of yourself to someone that is anything other than the pure, undistorted truth.

WEEK 29

LESSON CYCLE:

1. Engage and Connect **(10 min)**

A false front is putting forth a vision of yourself to someone that is anything other than the pure, undistorted truth. It is difficult to form meaningful relationships with someone if you are putting on a false front. It is difficult for people to know where you are emotionally and mentally when you are asked "*how are you doing?*" and you respond "*fine.*"

According to psychologists, the worst answer you can give when asked 'how are you doing' is 'I'm fine.' This is because it makes you look dishonest and can give your colleagues and friends a bad impression. You may think you are breezily replying to the question in a nonchalant way but, it's much more loaded than you think.

4 Better Ways to Respond to "How Are You?"

1. **My day has been great so far.** [Give a reason why]. When you're genuinely enthusiastic, it's truly difficult for others to resist your good mood. And note that your reason doesn't have to be incredibly impressive. You might say, "Thanks for asking! I'm having a great day."
2. **I'll be honest—I've had better days. Hopefully, tomorrow will be better!** Unless you're speaking to a total stranger, don't be afraid to be honest. Having a terrible day is hard enough – trying to cover it up can be even worse. Oftentimes, being a little vulnerable with people strengthens the relationship (and you never know when they'll say, "Ugh, me too! What's going

on with the universe today?!?") As long as you end on a slightly optimistic note—like, "tomorrow will be better"—sharing the less-good times is definitely kosher.

3. **Good, thank you. I'm just** [appreciating/looking forward to]... This response lets you acknowledge something you're happy about. The other person will appreciate your cheery response. Even better, it gives them something to ask you about.
4. **Hmmm...productive. Thanks for asking**! How are you? Sometimes, you're running around like crazy trying to get everything done. That probably means you're stressed—so you might not feel like saying you feel great. This response also gives the other person a chance to ask, "What have you been doing?" Discussing your current projects with your coworkers or friends is a great way to learn more about each other's work lives and even get suggestions or ideas.

(https://www.sigconsult.com/blog/2019/02/4-better-ways-to-respond-to-how-are-you-than-im-good?source=google.com)

2. Lead Guided and Independent Practice **(25 min)**

It's important to maintain your physical and mental wellbeing, especially at work. Anxiety and stress may seem minor, but all can lead to serious risks and accidents, as well as influence your physical and emotional health.

What is workplace anxiety?

Workplace anxiety is a learned response to stress and can be triggered from a range of factors. These symptoms are specifically related to the work environment. However, workplace anxiety may develop as either phobias or even hypochondrial anxieties regarding working conditions, interacting with colleagues and superiors, and fears of inadequacy or judgement. (https://www.airswift.com/about/safety/stress-and-anxiety-at-work)

What causes workplace anxiety? The main culprits of work-related anxiety:

- Deadlines
- Interpersonal relationships/Workplace Bullying
- Staff management
- Arisen issues/problems

While some workplace stress is normal, excessive stress can interfere with productivity and impact physical and emotional health. Your ability to deal with it can mean the difference between success or failure. You can't control everything in your work environment, but that doesn't mean you are powerless--even when you are stuck in a difficult situation. Finding ways to manage workplace stress isn't about making huge changes or rethinking career ambitions, but rather about focusing on the one thing that's always within your control: **you**.

Activity 1: Discussion: Instruct participants to share how they initially answered when asked "How are you doing?" Now that they have gone through the lesson, ask them how they would answer the question "How are you doing? Next, have them make a list of ways they can combat workplace anxiety/stress.

Pillar: Laughing

Activity 2: Fun, Stress-Relieving Activities. Have each participant commit to, plan out and complete one of the activities listed below and report back the next week about their experience.

1. **Take a group cooking class.** Learn a new skill while having fun with strangers who you do not have a relationship with. Use your five senses to reach a state of relaxation and peace.
2. **Try your hand at art.** Use chalk to draw a scene on your driveway with your child(ren) or alone, pick up a paintbrush and learn the different ways to paint, or color in a coloring book. There are coloring books specifically for adults with gorgeous nature scenes.
3. **Complete a puzzle.** Get a huge puzzle (we're talking 1,000 pieces) spread it out on the table or floor and have at it. Along with feelings of accomplishment, puzzles can spark feelings of nostalgia.
4. **Start or work in a Garden.** Spending time in the fresh air helps your body make melatonin, promoting a good night's sleep. (And restful sleep is key for lowering stress.) Planting flowers, herbs or plants and watching them grow is also satisfying to see your hard work flourish. If you live in an apartment building, get some pots, and get growing indoors, because merely playing in the dirt can promote feelings of happiness.
5. **Watch a movie.** Sometimes focusing on something else for a while allows you the time to get away and come back clear minded seeing what you could not see before. Watching a movie takes the spotlight off you and allows you to concentrate on something outside of yourself.

3. Close the Lesson and Assess Mastery   **(10 min)**

Ask each participant to think of a time they were fully engaged in an activity and lost track of time. They forgot about everything around them. Explain that they are singularly focused. Once someone becomes immersed in an activity that tests their skills (but isn't overwhelming) their attention is completely devoted to that one fun activity. Sometimes in these situations an individual is awarded with a sense of accomplishment from doing something they truly enjoy.

LOGISTICS: What materials, resources, and technology will I need to prepare and engage?

Computer
Microsoft Teams
Pencil, pen, Paper, or notebook

WEEK 30

LESSON CYCLE:

1. Engage and Connect (10 min)

Continue the discussion on workplace stress/anxiety. Ask participants which activity they completed and to share their experience.

2. Lead Guided and Independent Practice (25 min)

Introduce the term: PTSD: Post-traumatic stress disorder. PTSD is a disorder that develops in some people who have experienced a shocking, scary, or dangerous event. It is natural to feel afraid during and after a traumatic situation. Fear triggers many split-second changes in the body to help defend against danger or to avoid it.

Post-traumatic stress disorder symptoms may start within one month of a traumatic event, but sometimes symptoms may not appear until years after the event. These symptoms cause significant problems in social or work situations and in relationships. They can also interfere with your ability to go about your normal daily tasks. PTSD symptoms are generally grouped into four types: intrusive memories, avoidance, negative changes in thinking and mood, and changes in physical and emotional reactions. Symptoms can vary over time or vary from person to person.

CAUSES:

You can develop post-traumatic stress disorder when you go through, see, or learn about an event involving actual or threatened death, serious injury or sexual violation. Doctors aren't sure why some people get PTSD. As with most mental health problems, PTSD is probably caused by a complex mix of:

- Stressful experiences, including the amount and severity of trauma you've gone through in your life
- Inherited mental health risks, such as a family history of anxiety and depression
- Inherited features of your personality — often called your temperament
- The way your brain regulates the chemicals and hormones your body releases in response to stress

Discussion: Talk about PTSD and how it not only impacts the lives of veterans but everyday human beings. Ask participants to share what they have learned and how it has impacted their life.

3. Close the Lesson and Assess Mastery (10 min)

Many people have PTSD-like symptoms at first, such as being unable to stop thinking about what's happened. Fear, anxiety, anger, depression, guilt — all are common reactions to trauma. However, many people exposed to trauma do not develop long-term post-traumatic stress disorder. Getting timely help and support may prevent normal stress reactions from getting worse and developing into PTSD. This may mean turning to family and friends who will listen and offer comfort. It may mean seeking out a mental health professional for a brief course of therapy. Some people may also find it helpful to turn to their faith community. Support from others also may help prevent you from turning to unhealthy coping methods, such as misuse of alcohol or drugs.

LOGISTICS: What materials, resources, and technology will I need to prepare and engage?

Computer
Microsoft Teams
Pencil, pen, Paper or notebook

LESSON VOCABULARY WORDS

INSTRUCTIONS: Review vocabulary words listed below with the participants to ensure they have a good understanding of each before starting any of the activities.

1. **Stress:** A state of mental or emotional strain or tension resulting from adverse or very demanding circumstances.

2. **Anxiety:** A feeling of worry, nervousness, or unease, typically about an imminent event or something with an uncertain outcome.

3. **False front:** Putting forth a vision of yourself to someone that is anything other than the pure, undistorted truth.

OVERCOMING STRESS AND ANXIETY

4 Better Ways to Respond to "How Are You?"

1. **My day has been great so far.** [Give a reason why]. When you're genuinely enthusiastic, it's truly difficult for others to resist your good mood. And note that your reason doesn't have to be incredibly impressive. You might say, "Thanks for asking! I'm having a great day."

2. **I'll be honest—I've had better days. Hopefully, tomorrow will be better!** Unless you're speaking to a total stranger, don't be afraid to be honest. Having a terrible day is hard enough—trying to cover it up can be even worse. Oftentimes, being a little vulnerable with people strengthens the relationship (and you never know when they'll say, "Ugh, me too! What's going on with the universe today?!?") As long as you end on a slightly optimistic note—like, "tomorrow will be better"—sharing the less-good times is definitely kosher.

3. **Good, thank you. I'm just** [appreciating/looking forward to]… This response lets you acknowledge something you're happy about. The other person will appreciate your cheery response. Even better, it gives them something to ask you about.

4. **Hmmm…productive. Thanks for asking**! How are you? Sometimes, you're running around like crazy trying to get everything done. That probably means you're stressed—so you might not feel like saying you feel great. This response also gives the other person a chance to ask, "What have you been doing?" Discussing your current projects with your coworkers or friends is a great way to learn more about each other's work lives and even get suggestions or ideas.

(https://www.sigconsult.com/blog/2019/02/4-better-ways-to-respond-to-how-are-you-than-im-good?source=google.com)

Activity 1: What is workplace anxiety?

(1 What causes workplace anxiety? (Select the best answer.)
    a. Deadlines
    b. Interpersonal relationships/Workplace Bullying
    c. Staff management

Pillar: Laughing

    d. Arisen issues/problems
    e. No being able to take a smoke break
    f. All of the above.
    g. None of the above.

(2) _____ can interfere with productivity and impact physical and emotional health.

(3) What/Who is the one thing that's always within your control?

_____

_____

_____

Activity 2: Make a list of ways you can combat workplace anxiety/stress.

Pillar: Laughing

PTSD: TOP 5 SIGNS OF PTSD YOU NEED TO KNOW

Posted on 03/05/18 01:36:pm

According to the National Center for PTSD, posttraumatic stress disorder, about 8 million Americans have PTSD during any given year. While the signs of PTSD in women don't differ greatly from signs of PTSD in men, women are more likely to develop PTSD, with a lifetime incidence of 1 in 10. For men, it's 1 in 25. Yet an even higher number of Americans experience and show signs of trauma each year. So when does suffering a traumatic event lead to suffering from PTSD?

"PTSD is a mental health diagnosis characterized by five events or symptoms," says Dr. Chad Wetterneck, PhD, clinical supervisor for Rogers Behavioral Health.

Here, Dr. Wetterneck walks us through each sign of PTSD:

1. **A life-threatening event.** This includes a perceived-to-be life threatening event. Whether or not it actually is, it's really about the perception of the person who experienced or witnessed the event that it could happen to them again.

2. **Internal reminders of a traumatic event.** These signs of trauma typically present as nightmares or flashbacks. It's important to realize that these are not simply memories. They are unwanted, intrusive episodes in which a person feels as though they are in the life-threatening situation again – like they're watching a movie or seeing it unfold in front of them. It feels very real to them.

3. **Avoidance of external reminders.** Those with PTSD often do whatever they can to not think about their traumatic event, to suppress the feelings associated with it. They might avoid alleys if they were assaulted in one, or they might refuse to drive if they were in a car accident.

4. **Altered anxiety state.** PTSD can leave people feeling on edge and looking out for danger (hypervigilance). Really, what it boils down to is that people feel more anxious. Their startle response is exaggerated. They're jumpy or looking over their shoulder more often. It's a physical sign of PTSD and reaction to the body's increased anxiety and the need to be aware of possible threats.

5. **Changes in mood or thinking.** People with PTSD can see the world as a very dangerous place. And because they focus on protecting themselves from it, it's often difficult for them to go out in public. The isolation can lead to depression, or sometimes a person may act in an opposite way when they see no future. In that case, they may take more risks or engage in risky behaviors.

"While we are continuing to learn more about it's complicated symptoms and diagnosis, there is no 'cure' for PTSD— we cannot fully remove a traumatic memory from the brain," says Dr. Wetterneck.

"However, there are proven treatments that greatly reduce the symptoms and help people move forward with healthy lives."

Concerned you or a loved one may be suffering from the signs of trauma or PTSD? You can take a short, confidential quiz to check your symptoms. If you believe you or a loved one needs help, please request a free screening online or give us a call at 800-767-4411.

(https://rogersbh.org/about-us/newsroom/blog/ptsd-5-signs-you-need-know)

Pillar: Laughing

Mindfulness Time!

Issue Number 1

NAME: _____

TODAY'S JOKE: Wear a watch and you'll always know what time it is. Wear two watches and you'll never be sure.

Grade the joke above: A+ or D- ?

Thought for Today

Whether one has natural talent or not, any learning period requires the willingness to suffer uncertainty and embarrassment.
Gail Sheehy

My rating for this quote = ____ /10

List your top 3 goals for today in the space below.

1.

2.

3.

Draw a picture of a face that is representative of how you are feeling today.

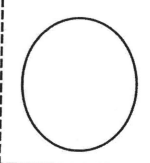

The Big Question!
Have you travelled to any different countries? Which ones?

Make a sentence where each word begins with these letters in order:

O_____ K_____ T_____ R_____ F_____

List 5 positive attributes or personal characteristics that you have.

1.

2.

3.

4.

5.

Draw a picture that combines these two words: Shrek and Acceptance.

LESSON TITLE:

Express Yourself

LEVEL: Youth

WEEKS 31-32

PACING: 55 minutes

OBJECTIVE(S): What will Participants know, understand, and be able to do?

Participants will be able to make connections with their own feelings and when expressing them.

KEY VOCABULARY: What key terms will my Participants need to understand?

Self-Awareness: Conscious knowledge of one's own character, feelings, motives, and desires.

Self-Expression: The expression of one's feelings, thoughts, or ideas, especially in writing, art, music, or dance.

Self-Representation: The way we represent ourselves to others within a particular culture.

WEEK 31

LESSON CYCLE:

1. Engage and Connect **(15 min)**

The facilitator/mentor will lead by asking what are ways an individual can express themselves? Allow participants an opportunity to share. (ex. what we say, clothing choices, through art, body language).

The facilitator will define self-expression: "Self-expression is an individual's expression of their thoughts and feelings. These expressions can be accomplished through words, choices, or actions." (Kim & Ko, 2007). Provide examples of how an individual can express themselves through their words, choices, and actions.

2. Lead Guided and Independent Practice **(25 min)**

Activity 1: Make your own flag. (Facilitator/Mentor will provide the construction paper, crayons, markers, etc.) Facilitator/Mentor: "There are many different flags that stand for many different things. Flags use symbols, colors, and words that represent an important part of a country, state, culture, family, or movement." Participants will have a chance to create their own flag that is an expression of them. (https://digitalsynopsis.com/design/flag-stories-colors-symbols-data-infographics/)

The facilitator/mentor will lead a discussion with the participants as they describe their flags at the close of the lesson segment.

Pillar: Laughing

Sample guiding questions:
1. What symbols did you use? Why?
2. Why did you choose those colors?
3. What does your flag represent overall?

Activity 2: Discussion: Ask participants to share how people on social media and well-known stars express themselves.

3. Close the Lesson and Assess Mastery　　　　　　　　　　　　　　　　**(15 min)**

Youth express themselves through art, words, clothing, choices, actions, etc. This includes their feelings and thoughts of their world. It is the hope that through understanding the participant's perspective using their own voice that we are be able to understand how to support and respond to people's needs and understand implications felt today and that of future generations.

BE BOLD, BE FEARLESS…EXPRESS YOURSELF

LOGISTICS: What materials, resources, and technology will I need to prepare and engage?
Computer
Pencil, Pen, Paper, or Notebook
Construction paper, crayons, markers, etc.

WEEK 32

LESSON CYCLE:

1. Engage and Connect   **(10 min)**

The facilitator will kick off the lesson by playing a snippet of the song *"Express Yourself."* https://www.youtube.com/watch?v=jW4VZ6J0fNQ

- Remind Participants about the importance of self-expression. Examples:
    - Builds self-confidence
    - Enhance relationships with yourself and others
    - Boost creativity
    - Conquer your fear and soothe your anxiety

2. Lead Guided and Independent Practice   **(30 min)**

Activity #1: Participants will make decisions based on the TV show *"What Would You Do?"* This activity provides participants an opportunity to discuss ways that positively assert themselves in a variety of situations with a goal to *"do the right thing"* in situations that call for them to make quick decisions. Play the following video: https://www.youtube.com/watch?v=fi0Jacu70dI (Play a snippet and not the whole video.)

Have participants to answer the following questions in their workbook (provide them with ample time to answer the questions before beginning the discussion):

1. What is the video about?
2. Why is there an issue? And what is the issue?
3. How is the topic impacting the characters' lives?
4. What does each participant have to say about the subject of the video?

Activity 2: Have participants discuss ways that positively assert themselves in the following situations with a goal to *"do the right thing"*:

a. You are at a school party with kids from your school. When you get there, some of the other kids start teasing your friend, but they do not know your friends with him. What do you do?
b. You oversee the care of your neighbor's dog while they are out of town. You are told to feed him and play with him but not let other people in the gate or take the dog out. Two very good friends come by and ask you to take the dog out and go to the park. You know nothing bad could possibly happen. What do you do?
c. You are eating dinner at a friend's house, and his mother serves you this horrible-looking, smelly stuff everyone is sitting around the table enjoying it. What do you do?
d. You are taking a test and you notice that a classmate, who is a popular kid around the school, is sitting next to you. You notice that they are copying your test answers and that the teacher is walking up and down the aisle. What do you do?

Pillar: Laughing

3. Close the Lesson and Assess Mastery **(15 min)**

Close the lesson with a quote by Oprah Winfrey, *"Don't get confused with what people say you are, boldly and intentionally be who you know you are."* Be authentically and unapologetically **YOU**!

LOGISTICS: What materials, resources, and technology will I need to prepare and engage?

Computer/Projector
Paper
Pencil/Markers

LESSON VOCABULARY WORDS

INSTRUCTIONS: Review vocabulary words listed below with the participants to ensure they have a good understanding of each before starting any of the activities.

1. **Self-Awareness:** Conscious knowledge of one's own character, feelings, motives, and desires.

2. **Self-Expression:** The expression of one's feelings, thoughts, or ideas, especially in writing, art, music, or dance.

3. **Self-Representation:** The way we represent ourselves to others within a particular culture.

Pillar: Laughing

"WHAT WOULD YOU DO?" ACTIVITY

INSTRUCTIONS: After watching the video clip, answer the following questions:

1. What is the video about?

2. Why is there an issue? And what is the issue?

3. How is the topic impacting the characters' lives?

4. What does each participant have to say about the subject of the video?

Intentional Mentoring Mentor's Guide

LESSON TITLE:

Express Yourself

LEVEL: Employee o Community Citizen

WEEKS 31-32

PACING: 55 minutes

OBJECTIVE(S): What will Participants know, understand, and be able to do?

Participants will be able to make connections with their own feelings and expressing them.

KEY VOCABULARY: What key terms will my Participants need to understand?

Self-Awareness: Conscious knowledge of one's own character, feelings, motives, and desires.

Self-Expression: The expression of one's feelings, thoughts, or ideas, especially in writing, art, music, or dance.

Self-Representation: The way we represent ourselves to others within a particular culture.

WEEK 31

LESSON CYCLE:

1. Engage and Connect (15 min)

The facilitator/mentor will introduce this week's topic: **Workplace Bullying** and share the definition with the participants. Workplace bullying can be defined as the repeated less favorable treatment of a person by another or others in the workplace, which may be considered unreasonable and inappropriate workplace practice. It includes behavior that intimidates, offends, degrades, isolates, or humiliates a worker, possibly in front of co-workers, clients, or customers.

- Bullies can be supervisors, subordinates, co-workers, and colleagues
- Bullies often operate within the established rules and policies of their organization
- While actions are not necessarily illegal and may not even be against the policies, the damage that such actions cause–both to the targeted employee and to workplace morale is significant.

2. Lead Guided and Independent Practice (30 min)

The facilitator/mentor will play the "Impact of bullying in the workplace" video: https://www.youtube.com/watch?v=mx3bwmm3CbU

Activity 1: Discuss: ***What impact does bullying in the workplace have on its victims?*** (Answer: It can increase the risk for negative physical health effects and lead to decreased mental wellbeing for both the victims of bullying and their co-workers.)

1. **Isolation and exclusion.** Is there a member of staff who always sits on their own and is never involved in the office chit-chat? Someone who is never invited to social events or other group

Pillar: Laughing

activities, and conversations stop when they approach or walk into the room, are they being excluded intentionally?

2. **Lateness and absenteeism.** If someone's attendance and timekeeping is usually impeccable, but they've started to regularly phone in sick or arrive late to work, they might be avoiding someone in the office who's giving them a hard time or making them feel uncomfortable

3. **Criticism and credit-taking.** Constructive criticism is perfectly valid and acceptable. It helps people to do their job to the best of their abilities, but if the criticism is unwarranted and undermines or humiliates an individual, then this is bullying. Another form of bullying to look out for is one team member constantly taking the praise and credit for the work of another without giving them due acknowledgment.

Activity 2: Write a letter to your 12-year-old self and include what advise you would give to him/her, share important lessons you have learned, how to navigate their teenage and early adult years (if applicable), and how to take care of him/herself.

3. *Close the Lesson and Assess Mastery* **(10 min)**

Share with the participants: *"Bullying is tricky to define. It definitely is not a one-off event, or it would be harassment. Bullying on the other hand is deliberately intended to dominate, cause distress and fear in the intended victim. Bullying often happens in private settings and by a person in authority and difficult to find material evidence for. Bullying doesn't happen "by accident", it is a deliberate action, and even though perpetrators might say they "meant no harm" when reprimanded, bullying often involves a planned campaign by the bully with the likelihood of negative intent. It can be difficult to understand what is happening. It creates self-doubt in the individual or victim."*

(https://www.forbes.com/sites/pragyaagarwaleurope/2018/07/29/workplace-bullying-here-is-why-we-need-to-talk-about-bullying-in-the-work-place/?sh=25bac1a63259)

"BE BOLD, BE FEARLESS…EXPRESS YOURSELF

LOGISTICS: What materials, resources, and technology will I need to prepare and engage?

Computer/Projector
Paper
Pencil

WEEK 32

LESSON CYCLE:

1. Engage and Connect (10 min)

The facilitator will kick off the lesson by playing a snippet of the song "Express Yourself."
https://www.youtube.com/watch?v=jW4VZ6J0fNQ

Article 19 of the Universal Declaration of Human Rights, adopted in 1948, states that: Everyone has the right to freedom of expression. This right shall include freedom to hold opinions and receive and impart information and ideas without interference by public authority and regardless of frontiers. It also underpins most other rights and allows them to flourish. The right to speak your mind freely on important issues in society, access information and hold the powers that be to account, plays a vital role in the healthy development process of any society.

2. Lead Guided and Independent Practice (35 min)

The facilitator/mentor will play the song "Enough."
https://www.youtube.com/watch?v=jWnQcOK7588

Lead a discussion with: When it comes to your self-worth, only one opinion truly matters — ***your own***. Healthy self-esteem is a realistic, appreciative opinion of oneself. And even that one should be carefully evaluated; we tend to be our own harshest and worst critic. Examples:

a. **Be mindful.** We can't change something if we don't recognize that there is something to change. By simply becoming aware of our negative self-talk, we begin to distance ourselves from the feelings it brings up.
b. **Change the story.** We all have a narrative or a story we've created about ourselves that shapes our self-perceptions, upon which our core self-image is based. If we want to change that story, we have to understand where it came from and where we received the messages, we tell ourselves.
c. **Avoid falling into the compare-and-despair rabbit hole.** In all of this there are two key things: to practice acceptance and stop comparing yourself to others.
d. **Forgive.** Forgiving self and others has been found to improve self-esteem and connects us with our innately loving nature and promotes an acceptance of people, despite their flaws. Forgiveness can be practiced at any time.
e. **Remember that you are not your circumstances.** Learning to differentiate between your circumstances and who you are is key to self-worth. You are not your last poor choice or bad act is one of the hardest things to accept "*Recognizing inner worth, and loving one's imperfect self, provide the secure foundation for growth,*" says Schiraldi. "*With that security, one is free to grow with enjoyment, not fear of failure — because failure doesn't change core worth.*"

3. Close the Lesson and Assess Mastery (5 min)

The facilitator/mentor will share: "*We are all born with infinite potential and equal worth as human beings. That we are anything less is a false belief that we have **learned** over time. Therefore, with hard work and self-*

compassion, self-destructive thoughts and beliefs can be unlearned. Taking the steps outlined above is a start in the effort to increase self-worth, or as Schiraldi says, to "recognize self-worth. It already exists in each person."

(https://www.psychologytoday.com/us/blog/nurturing-self-compassion/201703/8-steps-improving-your-self-esteem)

LOGISTICS: What materials, resources, and technology will I need to prepare and engage?

Computer/Projector
Paper
Pencil

LESSON VOCABULARY WORDS

INSTRUCTIONS: Review vocabulary words listed below with the participants to ensure they have a good understanding of each before starting any of the activities.

1. **Self-Awareness:** Conscious knowledge of one's own character, feelings, motives, and desires.

2. **Self-Expression:** The expression of one's feelings, thoughts, or ideas, especially in writing, art, music, or dance.

3. **Self-Representation:** The way we represent ourselves to others within a particular culture.

WHAT IS WORKPLACE BULLYING?

Workplace bullying is harmful, targeted behavior that happens at work. It might be spiteful, offensive, mocking, or intimidating. It forms a pattern, and it tends to be directed at one person or a few people.

A few examples of bullying include:

- targeted practical jokes
- being purposely misled about work duties, like incorrect deadlines or unclear directions
- continued denial of requests for time off without an appropriate or valid reason
- threats, humiliation, and other verbal abuse
- excessive performance monitoring
- overly harsh or unjust criticism

Criticism or monitoring isn't always bullying. For example, objective and constructive criticism and disciplinary action directly related to workplace behavior or job performance aren't considered bullying.

But criticism meant to intimidate, humiliate, or single someone out without reason would be considered bullying. According to the Workplace Bullying Institute, more than 60 million working people in the United States are affected by bullying. Existing federal and state laws only protect workers against bullying when it involves physical harm or when the target belongs to a protected group, such as people living with disabilities or people of color. Since bullying is often verbal or psychological in nature, it may not always be visible to others. Read on to learn more about ways to identify workplace bullies, how workplace bullying can affect you, and safe actions you can take against bullying. Identifying workplace bullying

Bullying can be subtle. One helpful way to identify bullying is to consider how others might view what's happening. This can depend, at least partially, on the circumstances. But if most people would see a specific behavior as unreasonable, it's generally bullying.

TYPES OF BULLYING

Bullying behaviors might be:

- **Verbal.** This could include mockery, humiliation, jokes, gossip, or other spoken abuse.
- **Intimidating.** This might include threats, social exclusion in the workplace, spying, or other invasions of privacy.
- **Related to work performance.** Examples include wrongful blame, work sabotage or interference, or stealing or taking credit for ideas.
- **Retaliatory.** In some cases, talking about the bullying can lead to accusations of lying, further exclusion, refused promotions, or other retaliation.
- **Institutional.** Institutional bullying happens when a workplace accepts, allows, and even encourages bullying to take place. This bullying might include unrealistic production goals, forced overtime, or singling out those who can't keep up.

Bullying behavior is repeated over time. This sets it apart from harassment, which is often limited to a single instance. Persistent harassment can become bullying, but since harassment refers to actions toward a protected group of people, it's illegal, unlike bullying.

Early warning signs of bullying can vary:

- Co-workers might become quiet or leave the room when you walk in, or they might simply ignore you.
- You might be left out of office culture, such as chitchat, parties, or team lunches.
- Your supervisor or manager might check on you often or ask you to meet multiple times a week without a clear reason.
- You may be asked to do new tasks or tasks outside your typical duties without training or help, even when you request it.
- It may seem like your work is frequently monitored, to the point where you begin to doubt yourself and have difficulty with your regular tasks.
- You might be asked to do difficult or seemingly pointless tasks and be ridiculed or criticized when you can't get them done.
- You may notice a pattern of your documents, files, other work-related items, or personal belongings going missing.

These incidents may seem random at first. If they continue, you may worry something you did caused them and fear you'll be fired or demoted. Thinking about work, even on your time off, may cause anxiety and dread.

(https://www.healthline.com/health/workplace-bullying#What-is-workplace-bullying?)

WRITE A LETTER TO YOUR 12-YEAR-OLD SELF

Instructions: Make a list of 4-5 things you would like to say to your 12-year-old self and create a letter that will help build his/her self-esteem, self-image, and overall concept of self. Knowing what you know now, what would you say to him/her?

Pillar: Laughing

PILLAR: LEADING

Before anyone can become a leader of many, they must first become a leader of one: SELF. The core values the mentee has learned while on this journey are invaluable and transferable. However, to become an effective leader, the mentee must develop or enhance their leadership skills. Leadership is about serving others and isn't self-serving. As we step into these lessons on LEADERSHIP, I challenge you not to lose sight of the self-work you have already done. That work should begin revealing the mentee's life plan and the journey he/she is to take. Some people are natural born leaders while others are taught to be leaders. Regardless which category the mentee falls into, to be an effective leader he/she must be concerned with people and their ability to learn the core values, systems, and processes that are the nuts and bolts of the company or organization in which they work. The expectations, skills and tools needed to secure a successful education; and their personal values, insight, and willingness to serve others are all the framework of an effective leader.

This pillar on leading begins first with the mentor before the mentee enters the picture. The mentor MUST understand that to be an effective leader, he/she must serve. John Maxwell shares his leadership philosophy as *"One life influencing another. This is the heart of leadership. One person casting vision. One person forging legacy, so that their influence incites the same passion in those they seek to lead. Afterall, people are our most valuable asset. [Affording] …you the power to impact those lives, to motivate teams, to transform organizations… We believe leadership is a process marked by constant growth."* (*John Maxwell on Leadership*, https://www.td.org/magazines/td-magazine/john-maxwell-on-leadership, by ATD Staff, February 8, 2013). Mentoring is the truest form of leadership any person can participate in. Leadership, in a nutshell, takes everything covered in the previous pillars and brings it into perspective for the mentor to understand their role in the mentor-mentee relationship. In the article, *Develop Leadership Skills with a Mentor*, (https://www.togetherplatform.com/blog/mentoring-develop-leadership-skills-with-a-mentor, by Matthew Reeves, August 1, 2021) the author says, *"Mentorship. Leaders learn through direct experience and the advice of others… mentors provide role models and guidance that future leaders can aspire to be like. Mentorship, in short, builds leadership skills."* The mentor's ability to see past their hopes, dreams, and desires to serve as a life or career guide to another person identifies within themselves their leadership qualities. The same qualities that will be modeled in front of the mentee as they learn how to navigate their journey called life. Tony Dungy shared in the *4 Essential Traits of a Mentor Leader*, (https://www.allprodad.com/4-essential-traits-of-a-mentor-leader/) *"In my life and career, I have seen all kinds of leaders. The ones who have had the greatest positive impact on my life are the select few who have been not only leaders, but also mentors. Here are four essential traits of a mentor leader to keep in mind:*

1. *Becoming a mentor leader is not rocket science. Leadership comprises of principles and skills that are accessible to anyone and everyone. They aren't necessarily intuitive, but they aren't terribly difficult, either.*
2. *Mentor leadership can be taught and learned; but in order to be absorbed, it must be practiced. The best way to evaluate leadership philosophies and find your own style is by testing them in action.*
3. *Mentor leadership focuses on developing the strengths of individuals. It might be in a narrowing way, such as building a specific skill, or more broadly focused, such as teaching employees to be proactive about meeting others' needs so they can better support the organization. Successful mentor leaders make the people they lead better players, workers, students, or family members and, ultimately, better people.*
4. *Mentor leadership works best when the ones being mentored are aware that the mentor leader has a genuine concern for their development and success. Those we lead will be more receptive if they believe we genuinely want them to succeed."*

As I was reading through Tony's essential mentor leadership traits, I thought about the many mentors I have had throughout my life and career, and how each of them instilled something in me I still use today. The same journey I took to get to where I am today, is the same journey mentors will take mentees to help them maximize the mentoring experience and take the skills they've gained, lessons they have learned and the experience that have totally changed their lives to become the best version of themselves possible. As Tony said, "*…this isn't rocket science…*," it is an opportunity to give back and to impart knowledge into another person who helps them see beyond their limitations into the expansive world which is theirs to experience however they deem necessary.

ROLE MODELING

The article, *Positive role models and mentors have an important role to play in promoting pro-environmental behaviors*, (https://research.childrenandnature.org/research/positive-role-models-and-mentors-have-an-important-role-to-play-in-promoting-pro-environmental-behaviors/, Prince, H.E., (2017). Outdoor experiences and sustainability. Journal of Adventure Education and Outdoor Learning, 17(2), 161-171.) says, "*Social learning theory includes the idea that people learn behaviors by observing others. This theory supports the utilization of role models and mentors in educational programs designed to influence the behaviors of children and youth.*" The article goes on to say, "*Through role modeling, mentoring, and coaching, educators can also promote students' sense of empowerment and commitment to sustainability. Effective mentorship provides benefits for both the mentor and mentee. The mentee gains increased confidence and skill, while the mentor experiences renewed enthusiasm.*"

To better understand the role of the mentor and an important aspect of their mentor-mentee relationship, let's inspect what a role model is. According to *Role Model vs. Mentor: Compare & Contrast*, https://study.com/academy/lesson/role-model-vs-mentor-compare-contrast.html, by Artem Cheprasov) *"A role model is an individual whose example, such as their behaviors or successes, are looked up to and imitated by others... Mentors are like personal role models. More formally, we can state that mentors are trusted individuals with more experience and wisdom than another person who helps guide that person with respect to a particular concern or desire. There is a personal, two-way relationship here. Mentors want to see you succeed, while role models may not even know who you are!* As I was reading this article, it became apparent that a mentor MUST choose to be a role-model and model the behavior, attributes and/or abilities of a leader in front of their mentee for them to observe it, internalize it and model it in their daily life. In the chapter on LEARNING, *I shared, "LEARNING only happens where we see the value in acquiring or obtaining the information for internal or external use. Sometimes the information is only valuable to you because of your own personal values and the accomplishments you desire for your life.* [It provides] *the freedom to make a decision that changed their perspective regarding the situation and make the decision that was the right one for them in that moment."* Think about that for a moment! In the same way that a mentee determines which information offered by the mentor is valuable, the mentor must determine what information to share that will be of value to the mentee. That alone can change the mentee's perspective, behaviors and/or attitude toward life, school, their community, and the world. That's the power of mentors being a role model and leading their mentees by example. They take the best they have to offer and that is relevant in that moment. The mentor has the potential of impacting their mentee's life in a way that empowers and enables them to activate and model what they have observed and learned.

LEADERSHIP SKILLS/QUALITIES

Now that we have spoken to the mentor, let's talk about the information that will help the mentor equip and empower the mentee to step into the role of a leader as a result of participating in an effective and successful mentoring program. As we discuss leadership qualities, the mentor is to impart to the mentee keep in mind that "...*mentoring is a process for the informal transmission of knowledge, social capital and the psychosocial support perceived by the recipient as relevant to work, career or professional development; mentoring entails informal communication, usually face-to-face and during a sustained period of time, between a person who is perceived to have greater relevant knowledge, wisdom or experience (the mentor) and a person who is perceived to have less (the protégé or mentee).*" (*Develop Leadership Skills by Mentoring*, https://www.reliableplant.com/Read/29332/mentoring-develops-leadership, by Debbie Zmorenski, from excerpt by Bozeman, Feeney, 2007,)

1. **COMMUNICATION.** Having excellent communication skills is an essential leadership competency. The best leaders are skilled communicators who can communicate in a variety of ways, from transmitting information to inspire others to coaching direct reports. And you must be able to listen to, and communicate with, a wide range of people across roles, geographies, social identities, and more.

2. **TIME-MANAGEMENT.** Time has a monetary value today. Time-management requires a person to organize and prioritize tasks to be more effective with consideration to any competing priorities.

3. **CRITICAL THINKING.** Critical thinking is one of the topmost important skills required of successful leaders. Critical thinkers are intelligent decision makers, highly analytical and always rational. A leader must be able to stand firm on his/her decisions. Because he/she is a critical thinker, it should be safe to assume that every decision he/she makes is well researched, objectively scrutinized and that all potential outcomes were assessed, and therefore, their eventual choice is the best course of action.

4. **RESPECT.** In today's society, there seems to be a misnomer that states ***to get respect, you must give respect***. Although that may be the way of the world. It is not the sign of a good leader. A good leader gives respect understanding that by doing so, he/she is teaching others how to respect and treat them. Respect is inherent (*existing in something as a permanent, essential*). It is not about the absence of disrespect, but about how a leader can INFLUENCE (*authentically and transparently being able to convince people through logical, emotional, or cooperative appeals*) others while building and sustaining mutually beneficial relationships that are built on a foundation of RESPECT.)

5. **LEARNING AGILITY.** A leader who has learned the importance of being a life learner is one who learns from their mistakes and those of others, seek opportunities to grow while asking insightful and informative questions, and are open to hear other's opinions and feedback on relevant topics. This leader realizes that there are truly no failures in life, only opportunities to learn how to do something more efficiently and/or differently. This includes recognizing when new behaviors, leadership skills, and/or attitudes are needed and seeking opportunities to develop them.

6. **CHANGE MANAGEMENT AND INNOVATION SKILLS.** Change happens whether or not you want it to and being able to manage change in both your life and in business is essential when leading yourself and people. Wikipedia defines change management as a *collective term for all approaches to prepare, support and help individuals, teams, and organizations in making organizational or structural change.*

Before change can occur, there must be some sign that change is needed. I think Oprah said it best, *"The greatest discovery of all time is that a person can change his future by merely changing his attitude."* Think about that for a moment. Change happens every second of every day, whether or not we acknowledge it. It singularly can usher an individual into the next season of life or be the reason they are left behind because they refuse to accept and do what is necessary to manifest it in their life. This is an aspect of being a life learner (Learning Agility) especially when a leader recognizes *"…when new behaviors, leadership skills, and/or attitudes are needed and [seeks] opportunities to develop them."* That's when genuine change happens!

7. **SERVICE-MINDED.** A servant leader feels responsible to help people learn and grow, feel purposeful, motivated, and energized, as he/she contributes to the betterment of the people and not merely selfish gain. He/She realizes this calling isn't about him/her but about the people! Simply put, servant leaders have the humility, insight, and courage to accept, acknowledge and understand that their greatest lessons have come from the people they interact with and/or surround themselves with. Leaders understand that as they accept their right to their views and/or opinions they must also do so with others simply because they are a member of humanity. A servant leader searches for opportunities to serve others with the understanding that before he/she can effectively serve anyone else, they MUST first be a servant to themselves. Malcolm X said, *"We can't teach what we don't know, and we can't LEAD where we can't [or won't] go."* The following are some significant attributes of a service-minded leader (*6 Reasons Why Servant Leadership is Best*, https://www.rootinc.com/why-servant-leadership-really-works/, by Jim Haudan, October 26, 2020):

   a. **Encourages others to think for themselves.** It is not that we don't know. Sometimes we must talk it out to hear the solution as we speak. Which builds character, and confidence in themselves and their abilities while helping them realize their place in the world.

   b. **Believe that all people are valuable and have something great to contribute.** He/She refuses to believe that anyone has the right or should throw people away as irrelevant. A service-minded leader builds trust with others from the care and genuine concern they show regularly. He/She believes in investing in people in the same way that others have invested in him/her.

   c. **Lives their life of service by asking one question: How may I help?** This question empowers people to step up and say what they need help with. It *"…highlights the best in others, which will create far better results than if the leader dictated directions from their removed perspective. Servant* *leaders believe this approach reveals the untapped creative and performance capabilities of* [all] *people…" (Servant Leader as Change Agents - A Lean Journey,* by Tim McMahon, April 11, 2022, http://www.aleanjourney.com/2022/04/servant-leader-as-change-agents.html) This is necessary, regardless if the mentee is a youth, frontline employee, and/or community worker.

Pillar: Legacy

LESSON TITLE:

Leading Social Change

LEVEL: Youth

WEEKS 33-34

PACING: 55 minutes

OBJECTIVE(S): What will Participants know, understand, and be able to do?

- Participants will be able to define a social movement.
- Participants will be able to explain different types of social movements.
- Participants will be able to explain the causes of social movements.
- Participants will be able to explain what makes social movements successful.

KEY VOCABULARY: What key terms will my Participants need to understand?

Social movement- an organized effort by a large number of people to bring about or impede social, political, economic, or cultural change. There are five types of social movements.

Reform movement- movement that seeks some sort of change to some aspect of a nation's political, economic, or social systems. The goal is to improve conditions within the nation's current regime, not overthrow.

Self-help movements- movement that involves people trying to improve aspects of their personal lives; examples of self-help groups include Alcoholics Anonymous and Weight Watchers.

Religious movements- a movement started to reinforce religious beliefs among their members and to convert other people to these beliefs.

Reactionary movement- a movement initiated to block social change or to reverse social changes that have already been achieved.

Revolutionary movement- a movement that want to replace already existing orders with a totally different structure

Key Points:

1) Social movements are started because people are dissatisfied with the way things are. There must be certain political, economic, or other problems to prompt people to want to start or join a social movement. People tend to start or join social movements because they are unhappy about something.

2) Example of problems could be lack of political freedom or discrimination based on gender, race or ethnicity, or sexual orientation.

WEEK 33

LESSON CYCLE:

1. Engage and Connect   (20 min)

Show participants this video about the civil rights movement
https://www.youtube.com/watch?v=tT3EIKmKpaQ

As participants watch the video, ask them to be attentive for the discussion afterwards. After watching the video, conduct a discussion with Participants revolving around the questions below. Ensure that participants can answer the questions using examples from the video they watched. Discussion questions:

a. What was the cause of the civil rights movement?
b. What were people dissatisfied with or unhappy with?
c. What were some ways that people-initiated change?
d. Has America changed since the civil rights movement? Yes or No? Why or Why not?

Introduce them to the term: "***social movements***." Write "*social movements*" on the board **with** the definition. Call on a Participant to read the definition. Ask if any participants have any questions about the definition.

Teach participants about the different types of social movements using the definitions. Stamp the **key point** of the lesson after participants read the definition. Ensure that participants understand that social movements arise because people are unhappy and/or dissatisfied with the status quo. That frustration regarding a political, social, or economic issue can bring about a social movement if enough people are frustrated.

2. Lead Guided and Independent Practice   (25 min)

Now that participants understand what social movements are, their causes, and the different types. They also have seen an example of one from the brain pop video of the civil rights movement.

Briefly talk to the Youth about the different movements below. Give them a sheet of paper and have the participants draw a picture that represents at least one of the movements. Older Youth can draw a picture and provide a description of the movement.

- Women's Movement
- Disability Rights Movement
- LGBT Movement
- Environmental Movement
- Labor Movement
- Reproductive Justice Movement
- Anti-War Movement

By the end, participants should have a paper where they have their chosen movement written down and a picture and/or description for it. Participants should be able to describe the movement using the picture that they drew.

3. Close the Lesson and Assess Mastery **(10 min)**

Review with the participants the purpose of social movements. Share one reason why you believe social movements are important. Have Participants share one thing they have learned from the lesson.

LOGISTICS: What materials, resources, and technology will I need to prepare and engage?

Computer/Projector
Index Cards/Post-it Notes/Paper/Writing Utensils
Anchor Chart paper
Index Cards/Post-it Notes

WEEK 34

LESSON CYCLE:

1. Engage and Connect (20 min)

Participants should quickly review the social movements from last class with their mentor/facilitator. Facilitator/Mentor will lead the discussion and review with participants the definition of social movements. They should reflect on the pictures that they drew (and the descriptions).

Participants should be prepared to do 2-minute presentations on their movement, summarizing the key points.

2. Lead Guided and Independent Practice (25 min)

While the facilitator/mentor is reviewing the different social movements and will go into more detail about each of the movements. Last session was more general and surface, but today, the facilitator/mentor will discuss each of the movements in depth, answering each of the questions below. Show the "Kids can change the world" video: https://www.youtube.com/watch?v=nBi0o9YVErU

  a. What is the video about?
  b. How did the movement start?
  c. What was the cause of the movement?
  d. Explain the importance of youth involvement within the movement.
      1. Were there any youth leaders in the movement?
      2. What role did they play?
      3. Any concrete examples?

Instruct participants to think about issues in their community they would like to address. Remind them that today's youth can change the world through the role they have played.

Discussion Question: What are some issues in your community that you would like to address, change and/or improve? How would you go about addressing those issues? How can you have a positive impact on your community? If participants cannot name issues that they would like to change in their community, name some for them and help the participants think through ways they can make a difference in their community.

3. Close the Lesson and Assess Mastery (10 min)

Share the closing quote with the Participants from Malcolm X, *"A man who stands for nothing will fall for anything."* Tell participants that the reason why the social justice lessons were taught was because participants need to know they have a voice and the ability to have a positive impact in their community and that there is a way to be an advocate for change in a respectful way.

LOGISTICS: What materials, resources, and technology will I need to prepare and engage?

Computer/Projector
Index Cards/Post-it Notes
Paper/Chart Paper
Writing Utensils

Pillar: Legacy

LESSON VOCABULARY WORDS

INSTRUCTIONS: Review vocabulary words listed below with the participants to ensure they have a good understanding of each before starting any of the activities.

1. **Social movement-** an organized effort by a large number of people to bring about or impede social, political, economic, or cultural change. There are five types of social movements.

2. **Reform movement-** movement that seeks some sort of change to some aspect of a nation's political, economic, or social systems. The goal is to improve conditions within the nation's current regime, not overthrow.

3. **Self-help movements-** movement that involves people trying to improve aspects of their personal lives; examples of self-help groups include Alcoholics Anonymous and Weight Watchers.

4. **Religious movements-** a movement started to reinforce religious beliefs among their members and to convert other people to these beliefs.

5. **Reactionary movement-** a movement initiated to block social change or to reverse social changes that have already been achieved.

6. **Revolutionary movement-** a movement that want to replace already existing orders with a totally different structure.

SOCIAL MOVEMENTS

1. **Women's Movement:** The feminist movement (also known as the women's movement, or feminism) refers to a series of social movements and Political campaigns for radical and liberal reforms on women's issues created by the inequality between men and women.

2. **Disability Rights Movement:** a global movement that advocates for and secures equal rights and opportunities for people who have disabilities. In the United States, and around the world, the movement has been successful in changing laws and social attitudes to make societies more inclusive.

3. **LGBT Movement:** Lesbian, gay, bisexual, and transgender (LGBT) movements are social movements that advocate for LGBT people in society. Some focus on equal rights, such as the ongoing movement for same-sex marriage, while others focus on liberation, as in the gay liberation movement of the 1960s and 1970s.

4. **Environmental Movement:** (sometimes referred to as the ecology movement) is a diverse philosophical, social, and political movement for addressing environmental issues.

5. **Labor Movement:** consists of two main wings: the trade union movement (British English) or labor union movement (American English) on the one hand, and the political labor movement on the other. Consists of the collective organization of working people developed to represent and campaign for better working conditions and treatment from their employers and, by the implementation of labor and employment laws, from their governments. The standard unit of organization is the trade union. A political party that represents the interests of employees.

6. **Reproductive Justice Movement:** is the human right to maintain personal bodily autonomy, have children, not have children, and parent the children we have in safe and sustainable communities. The reproductive justice framework encompasses a wide range of issues affecting the reproductive lives of marginalized women, including access to: contraception, comprehensive sex education, prevention and care for sexually transmitted infections, alternative birth options, adequate prenatal and pregnancy care, domestic violence assistance, adequate wages to support families, and safe homes.

7. **Anti-War Movement:** is a social movement, usually in opposition to a particular nation's decision to start or carry on an armed conflict, unconditional of a maybe-existing just cause. It is also the opposition to all use of military force during conflicts, or to anti-war books, paintings, and other works of art.

SOCIAL MOVEMENT QUESTIONS

1. What are some issues in your community that you would like to address, change and/or improve?

_____

_____

_____

Pillar: Legacy

2. How would you go about addressing those issues? How can you have a positive impact on your community?

   _____
   _____
   _____

Junior Scholastic
SKILLS SHEET   Name: Date:

Analyzing a Primary Source

Why We Can't Wait

KEY STANDARD: RH.6-8.1

Before he was assassinated on April 4, 1968, civil rights leader Martin Luther King Jr. was jailed dozens of times in his pursuit of racial equality in the United States.

One of those jailings occurred in April 1963 in Birmingham, Alabama. King described Birmingham in the 1960s as "the most thoroughly segregated city in the United States." Rather than integrate its public parks and playgrounds, the city closed them. And opponents of civil rights for African Americans bombed black homes and businesses.

In the spring of 1963, King and other civil rights leaders converged on Birmingham to organize demonstrations against the inequality and violence. King's actions landed him in Birmingham City Jail, where he wrote one of the most important documents of the civil rights movement. The 21-page, 7,000-word *Letter From Birmingham Jail* was written in response to a group of white religious leaders who asked African Americans to wait patiently for equal rights.

Read this excerpt from King's letter, then answer the questions.

Letter From Birmingham Jail, April 16, 1963

My Dear Fellow Clergymen:

While confined here in the Birmingham City Jail, I came across your recent statement calling my present activities "unwise and untimely." . . .

We know through painful experience that freedom is never voluntarily given by the oppressor; it must be demanded by the oppressed. . . . For years now I have heard the word "Wait!" It rings in the ear of every Negro* with piercing familiarity. This "Wait" has almost always meant "Never." We must come to see . . . that "justice too long delayed is justice denied."

We have waited for more than 340 years for our constitutional and God-given rights. The nations of Asia and Africa are moving with jetlike speed toward gaining political independence, but we still creep at horse-and-buggy pace toward gaining a cup of coffee at a lunch counter.

Perhaps it is easy for those who have never felt the stinging darts of segregation to say, "Wait." But when you have seen vicious mobs lynch your mothers and fathers at will and drown your sisters and brothers at whim; when you have seen hate-filled policemen curse, kick, and even kill your black brothers and sisters; when you see the vast majority of your 20 million Negro brothers smothering in an airtight cage of poverty . . . then you will understand why we find it difficult to wait.

There comes a time when the cup of endurance runs over, and men are no longer willing to be plunged into the abyss of despair. I hope, sirs, you can understand our legitimate and unavoidable impatience. . . .

Yours for the cause of Peace and Brotherhood,
Martin Luther King Jr.

*African American (Once a standard term, *Negro* is now considered dated and often offensive.)

Questions

1. What does Martin Luther King Jr. think *wait* means for African Americans? Cite evidence from the text.
2. What metaphors does King use to describe segregation and living in poverty?
3. Compare and contrast King's observations of progress in Asia and Africa with that in the United States. What comment is he making about the U.S.?
4. What examples of racial violence does King include in his letter?
5. What descriptive language does King use to show that African Americans were tired of waiting for racial equality?

https://junior.scholastic.com/pages/content-hubs/the-civil-rights-movement.html

Pillar: Legacy

SOCIAL MOVEMENTS WORKSHEET

Name _____ Date _____

Crossword Puzzle:
American Civil Rights Movement

Use the clues below to complete the crossword puzzle.

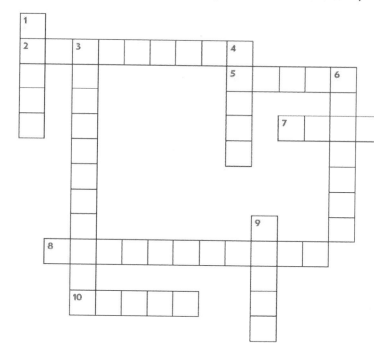

A civil rights march in 1965

Across

2 Woman known as the "mother of the civil rights movement" after refusing to give up her seat on a bus

5 A doctrine that supported racial segregation by saying "separate but _____"

7 A group of students known as the "Little Rock _____" who were the first Black students to enter Little Rock's desegregated Central High School

8 A set of laws in the South that enforced racial segregation

10 In 1964, Martin Luther King Jr. received the _____ Peace Prize for his leadership

Down

1 _____ v. Board of Education was a 1954 ruling that declared racial segregation in public schools unconstitutional

3 The practice or policy of keeping people of different races separate from each other

4 The _____ to Montgomery marches were a series of civil rights protest marches in 1965 to support voting rights

6 Dr. Martin Luther King Jr. gave his famous "I Have a Dream" speech at the _____ memorial in Washington, D.C.

9 Over 200,000 people participated in the _____ on Washington for Jobs and Freedom in 1963 to fight for civil and economic rights of Black Americans

Martin Luther King Jr. addressing crowds in Washington, D.C., 1963

Find worksheets, games, lessons & more at education.com/resources

© 2007 - 2022 Education.com

LESSON TITLE:

Leading Social Change

LEVEL: Employee or Community Citizen

WEEKS 33-34

PACING: 55 minutes

OBJECTIVE(S): What will Participants know, understand, and be able to do?

- Participants will be able to define a social movement.
- Participants will be able to explain different types of social movements.
- Participants will be able to explain the causes of social movements.
- Participants will be able to explain what makes social movements successful.

KEY VOCABULARY: What key terms will my Participants need to understand?

Social movement- an organized effort by a large number of people to bring about or impede social, political, economic, or cultural change. There are five types of social movements.

Reform movement- a movement that seeks some sort of change to some aspect of a nation's political, economic, or social systems. The goal is to improve conditions within the nation's current regime, not overthrow it.

Self-help movements- a movement that involves people trying to improve aspects of their personal lives; examples of self-help groups include Alcoholics Anonymous and Weight Watchers.

Religious movements- a movement started to reinforce religious beliefs among their members and to convert other people to these beliefs.

Reactionary movement- a movement initiated to block social change or to reverse social changes that have already been achieved.

Revolutionary movement- a movement that wants to replace already existing orders with a totally different structure

KEY POINTS:

1) Social movements are started because people are dissatisfied with the way things are. There must be certain political, economic, or other problems to prompt people to want to start or join a social movement. People tend to start or join social movements because they are unhappy about something.

2) Example of problems could be lack of political freedom or discrimination based on gender, race or ethnicity, or sexual orientation.

Pillar: Legacy

WEEK 33

LESSON CYCLE:

1. Engage and Connect   **(15 min)**

Show Participants the Civil Rights video: https://www.youtube.com/watch?v=9ppTiyxFSs0 and https://www.youtube.com/watch?v=QZE0a5-p9pg

As participants to answer the following questions:

- What was the cause of the civil rights movement?
- What were people dissatisfied with or unhappy with?
- What were some ways that people-initiated change?

After watching the videos, conduct a discussion with participants revolving around the questions posed above, and have participants answer the questions using evidence from the videos they watched.

Introduce them to the term: "social movements." Write "*social movements*" on the board **with** the definition. Call on a participant to read the definition. Ask the participants what the different types of social movements are using the definitions. Ensure that participants understand that social movements arise because people are unhappy and/or dissatisfied with the status quo and frustrated with the political, social, or economic issue that can bring about a social movement.

2. Lead Guided and Independent Practice   **(30 min)**

Now, Participants understand what social movements are, their causes, and the different types. Divide participants into small, even groups, if possible. Assign each of the groups to one of the following movements:

- The Glass Ceiling (The Glass Ceiling by Parity.org - YouTube)
- Voter's Suppression (Voter Suppression: It's the American Way - YouTube /Voter suppression - YouTube)
- LGBT Movement (Wanda Sykes Takes Us Through the History of LGBTQ+ — Now You Know - YouTube)
- Gender Pay Gap (How Iceland is Fighting the Gender Pay Gap - BBC Stories - YouTube)
- Racism in America (Oprah Winfrey: Racism over when we release fear - Bing video)

Participant groups will <u>begin</u> the process of researching their different social movements. When participants are researching, they should be able to answer the following questions:

1) When did the movement start?
2) What was the cause of the movement?
3) Explain the importance of the supporters' involvement within the movement.
      a) Were there any unexpected leaders in the movement?
      b) What role did they play?

c) Any concrete examples?

Provide participants with chart paper to respond to the questions and prepare for the next class.

3. *Close the Lesson and Assess Mastery* **(10 min)**

Review with the Participants the purpose of social movements. Share one reason you believe social movements are important. Have participants share one thing they have learned from the lesson.

LOGISTICS: What materials, resources, and technology will I need to prepare and engage?

Computer/Projector
Index Cards/Post-it Notes
Paper/Writing Utensils

Pillar: Legacy

WEEK 34

LESSON CYCLE:

1. Engage and Connect (15 min)

Participants will begin this session by completing the research on their assigned social movement and prepare for their presentation of their findings. Each participant group will answer the following questions based on their research:

a. When did the movement start?
b. What was the cause of the movement?
c. Explain the importance of the adults/supporters' involvement within the movement.
   1. Were there any youth leaders in the movement?
   2. What role did they play?
   3. Any concrete examples?

Participants should be prepared to do 2-minute presentations on their movement, summarizing the key points.

2. Lead Guided and Independent Practice (30 min)

Participants will conduct their 2-minute presentations. Facilitator/Mentor will use timers to hold participants to the assigned time.

After presentations on the social movements are complete, participants will consider issues in their community they would like to address. Participants should watch the "Stepping up: The Social Justice Activist" video: https://www.youtube.com/watch?v=FED6MenLsuA of a young activist as they think about issues they would like to address in their community or the world at large.

Discussion Question:

Facilitator/Mentor asks: Now that you have had a chance to learn about different social movements and you have researched social movements, and their causes. What are some issues in your community that you would like to address, change and/or improve? How would you go about addressing those issues? How can you have a positive impact on your community?

3. Close the Lesson and Assess Mastery (10 min)

Share the closing quote with the Participants from Malcolm X, *"A man who stands for nothing will fall for anything."* Tell participants the reason why social justice lessons were taught because each participant needs to know they do have a voice and the ability to have a positive impact in their community regardless of their age, race, gender, sexual orientation, etc.

LOGISTICS: What materials, resources, and technology will I need to prepare and engage?

Computer/Projector
Index Cards/Post-it Notes
Paper
Writing Utensils

Pillar: Legacy

LESSON VOCABULARY WORDS

Instructions: Review the different social movements listed below with the participants to ensure they have a good understanding of each before starting any of the activities.

1. **Social movement**- an organized effort by a large number of people to bring about or impede social, political, economic, or cultural change. There are five types of social movements.
2. **Reform movement**- a movement that seeks some sort of change to some aspect of a nation's political, economic, or social systems. The goal is to improve conditions within the nation's current regime, not overthrow it.
3. **Self-help movements**- a movement that involves people trying to improve aspects of their personal lives; examples of self-help groups include Alcoholics Anonymous and Weight Watchers.
4. **Religious movements**- a movement started to reinforce religious beliefs among their members and to convert other people to these beliefs.
5. **Reactionary movement**- a movement initiated to block social change or to reverse social changes that have already been achieved.
6. **Revolutionary movement**- a movement that wants to replace already existing orders with a totally different structure

Activity 1: Facilitator/Mentor will split the participants into group. Each group will be assigned a social movement from the list below.

1. The Glass Ceiling (The Glass Ceiling by Parity.org - YouTube)
2. Voter's Suppression (Voter Suppression: It's the American Way - YouTube/Voter suppression - YouTube)
3. LGBT Movement (Wanda Sykes Takes Us Through the History of LGBTQ+ — Now You Know - YouTube)
4. Gender Pay Gap (How Iceland is Fighting the Gender Pay Gap - BBC Stories - YouTube)
5. Racism in America (Oprah Winfrey: Racism over when we release fear - Bing video)

Each group will research their assigned social movement. On the chart paper provided, each group will answer the following questions:

1) When did the movement start?
2) What was the cause of the movement?
3) Explain the importance of youth involvement within the movement.
   a) Were there any youth leaders in the movement?
   b) What role did they play?
   c) Any concrete examples?

SOCIAL MOVEMENTS

1. **Women's Movement**: The feminist movement (also known as the women's movement, or feminism) refers to a series of social movements and Political campaigns for radical and liberal reforms on women's issues created by the inequality between men and women.

2. **Disability Rights Movement**: a global movement that advocates for and secures equal rights and opportunities for people who have disabilities. In the United States, and around the world, the movement has been successful in changing laws and social attitudes to make societies more inclusive.

3. **LGBT Movement**: Lesbian, gay, bisexual, and transgender (LGBT) movements are social movements that advocate for LGBT people in society. Some focus on equal rights, such as the ongoing movement for same-sex marriage, while others focus on liberation, as in the gay liberation movement of the 1960s and 1970s.

4. **Environmental Movement**: (sometimes referred to as the ecology movement) is a diverse philosophical, social, and political movement for addressing environmental issues.

5. **Labor Movement**: consists of two main wings: the trade union movement (British English) or labor union movement (American English) on the one hand, and the political labor movement on the other. Consists of the collective organization of working people developed to represent and campaign for better working conditions and treatment from their employers and, by the implementation of labor and employment laws, from their governments. The standard unit of organization is the trade union. A political party that represents the interests of employees.

6. **Reproductive Justice Movement**: is the human right to maintain personal bodily autonomy, have children, not have children, and parent the children we have in safe and sustainable communities. The reproductive justice framework encompasses a wide range of issues affecting the reproductive lives of marginalized women, including access to: contraception, comprehensive sex education, prevention and care for sexually transmitted infections, alternative birth options, adequate prenatal and pregnancy care, domestic violence assistance, adequate wages to support families, and safe homes.

7. **Anti-War Movement**: is a social movement, usually in opposition to a particular nation's decision to start or carry on an armed conflict, unconditional of a maybe-existing just cause. It is also the opposition to all use of military force during conflicts, or to anti-war books, paintings, and other works of art.

Social Movement Questions

1. What are some issues in your community that you would like to address, change and/or improve?

   _____
   _____
   _____

Pillar: Legacy

2. How would you go about addressing those issues? How can you have a positive impact on your community?

   _____
   _____
   _____

LESSON TITLE:

Financial Literacy

LEVEL: Youth

WEEKS 35-36

PACING: 55 minutes

OBJECTIVE(S): What will Participants know, understand, and be able to do?

Participants will understand the basics of financial literacy and responsible decision-making.

KEY VOCABULARY: What key terms will my Participants need to understand?

Wants: Things people like to have, but do not need.

Needs: Things that people must have to live.

Save: To keep your money to use later.

Volunteer: A person who works for no pay to help others.

Tax: A compulsory contribution to state revenue, levied by the government on workers' income and business profits, or added to the cost of some goods, services, and transactions.

Tip: A sum of money given to someone as a reward for their service.

Credit score: A number assigned to a person that indicates to lenders their capacity to repay a loan.

Living wage: A wage that is high enough to maintain a normal standard of living.

WEEK 35

LESSON CYCLE:

1. Engage and Connect (10 min)

Lead a discussion with the participants about the importance of money and the dangers that can come from mismanagement of money. Play the BrainPop Jr. Video on "Saving and Spending." https://www.youtube.com/watch?v=gNwOmJPq9X4. Pause the video accordingly to clarify any vocabulary or misunderstandings.

2. Lead Guided and Independent Practice (25 min)

Participants will participate in a *"Want vs. Need"* activity. Explain a "need" is something we must have to survive, like food, water, clothing, and shelter. Impress upon the participants, for us to be successful all our basic needs must be met. Explain that a "want" is something we can live without, even though we may have a strong desire for it. Participants can create their own needs vs wants t-chart. **Challenge question:** Will your needs and wants change during high school, college, a working adult, etc.? Give examples. Have participants fill out the "Needs vs Wants Chart.

Pillar: Legacy

3. Close the Lesson and Assess Mastery **(20 min)**

Tell the participants they have just won a prize for their project they submitted to Google. For their excellent work Google is going to give them some money. They can take one check for $60 now or get $10 each month for the next year (hint: if they get $10 a month, they will end up with $120 total but must wait monthly for a payment). Which payout of the money would you like to have? Does a person's situation change the decision, such as a person who must pay their light bill or buy food for their family? Close out the lesson by reminding Participants that our choices we make with money must go with responsible decision making.

LOGISTICS: What materials, resources, and technology will I need to prepare and engage?

Computer/Projector
Needs vs Wants Activity Sheet
Mr. Gruber Reading
Financial Literacy on Kahoot

WEEK 36

LESSON CYCLE:

1. Engage and Connect **(15 min)**

The facilitator will begin the lesson with the reading from Mr. Gruber on "Needs vs. Wants." Once the story is over, ask the participants if they agree or disagree with Mr. Gruber.

2. Lead Guided and Independent Practice **(30 min)**

The participants will have an opportunity to participate in a Financial Literacy Game on Kahoot. Participants will engage in the financial vocabulary connected to real-world scenarios.

3. Close the Lesson and Assess Mastery **(10 min)**

Close out the lesson by showing the "Happiness" video. At the end of the video remind Participants that money and having a lot of "stuff" does not make us happy. We must work hard to earn money and be responsible with our decisions on how we save, spend, and share it.

Video link: https://houstonpbs.pbslearningmedia.org/resource/lpsc10.sci.life.happy/happiness/

LOGISTICS: What materials, resources, and technology will I need to prepare and engage?

Computer/Projector
Needs vs Wants Activity Sheet
Mr. Gruber Reading (Needs and Wants)
Financial Literacy on Kahoot

Pillar: Legacy

LESSON VOCABULARY WORDS

INSTRUCTIONS: Review vocabulary words listed below with the participants to ensure they have a good understanding of each before starting any of the activities.

1. **Wants:** Things people like to have, but do not need.
2. **Needs:** Things that people must have to live.
3. **Save:** To keep your money to use later.
4. **Volunteer:** A person who works for no pay to help others.
5. **Tax:** A compulsory contribution to state revenue, levied by the government on workers' income and business profits, or added to the cost of some goods, services, and transactions.
6. **Tip:** A sum of money given to someone as a reward for their service.
7. **Credit score:** A number assigned to a person that indicates to lenders their capacity to repay a loan.
8. **Living wage:** A wage that is high enough to maintain a normal standard of living.

NEEDS AND WANTS
Story By: Andrew Frinkle

"*What is success?*" Mr. Gruber asked his 6th grade business class. It was his opening conversation for the first class of the semester. "*Success is rolling in a sweet car, watching an 80-inch TV, and living in a place with at least twelve rooms.*" One student answered, earning a chorus of laughter.

Mr. Gruber smiled but shook his head. "*Tom, that is excess. That is not success.*" "*How about being able to provide for your family?*" A blonde girl named Sandy in the front suggested as an answer. "*Now we're getting closer,*" Mr. Gruber smiled, "*but try thinking about it in terms of what you need and what you want.*" "*Getting everything you want.*" Tom shouted out an answer again, trying for more laughs. Mr. Gruber sighed. "*I believe we've already talked about excess versus success.*" "*Getting everything you need, but some of what you want?*" James, sitting in the back, wondered aloud.

"*Exactly!*" Mr. Gruber clapped. "*Success is getting everything you need and some of what you want. The more you get that you want, the more successful you are. You do reach a point where you are living in excess, though.*" "*What does this have to do with business?*" Tom demanded. It seemed if it wasn't funny, he wasn't happy.

"*Well, Tom, think of it this way: the point of business is to make a living to support your family. Once you have properly seen to their needs, you can then see to getting the extras that you want.*" "*What if I don't have a family?*" He continued to be difficult. "*Then you have to provide for yourself, a family of one.*" "*He has goldfish to think about!*" Peter, Tom's friend, shouted out. "*Then he needs to provide for a family of one with a fishbowl.*" Mr. Gruber corrected himself. Tom nodded, satisfied with that answer.

"*So, in the next nine weeks, we're going to study basic business situations, like having a checking account, balancing household budgets, and understanding credit cards.*" Tom rubbed his hands together excitedly. "*When do we get to start spending?*" "*You already are, Tom. You're spending time with us!*" Mr. Gruber laughed. "*Now, let's see what you guys know about credit cards…*"

Pillar: Legacy

INSTRUCTIONS: Use the information in the *"Needs vs Wants"* story to answer the questions below. (Circle the correct answer.)

1. What class does Mr. Gruber teach?
   a. history
   b. science
   c. math
   d. business
2. What is the main point of this discussion?
   a. Get what you want
   a. Wants vs. Needs
   b. Money
   c. How to play the stock market
3. Which student doesn't seem to be taking the class seriously?
   a. Tom
   b. James
   c. Peter
   d. Sandy
4. How does Mr. Gruber try to keep the students interested?
   a. He is showing a movie.
   b. He is giving a lecture where only he talks.
   c. He is involving the students in a discussion.
   d. He is reading from a textbook.
5. Based on the story, how could you NOT describe Mr. Gruber?
   a. patient
   b. humorous
   c. involved
   d. grumpy

© HaveFunTeaching.com

A need is something you have to have to live.

A want is something you would like to have, but can live without.

Needs

Wants

Directions: Place each picture in the correct group.

| ice cream | house | bike | toothpaste | pet |
| dinner | necklace | clothes | football | medicine |

LIVEWORKSHEETS

Pillar: Legacy

THE BIGGEST LOOSER
FINANCIAL LITERARY ACTIVITY

This is a financial literacy game to help the participants to understand the necessity of being financially responsible with their money.

Materials: Play Money (dollars of all denominations and coins)

Instructions: Facilitator/Mentor will give each participant $200 and instruct them they will have to apply for more money if they run out of money or borrow it from a friend or family member.

Read the following: Tonya and Brian are starting new jobs on Monday and they both need to prepare for their first day. Tonya needs a pair of work shoes, khaki pants and some socks or footies. Brian needs a tie, some khaki pants and a belt. (The girls will buy as if they are Tanya and the boys will buy as if they are Brian.) The following are the stores closest to them to purchase their items from: Goodwill, Target, Macy's, Shoe Carnival and/or Finish Line. The following is the price list for each store:

Goodwill Store:
1. Female Work Shoes..................$12.00
2. Male Work Shoes.....................$15.00
3. Khaki Pants – Female...............$10.00
4. Khaki Pants – Male..................$13.00
5. Belts..$5.00
6. Ties...$2.00
7. Polo Shirts – Female................$7.00
8. Polo Shirts – Male...................$9.00

Target:
1. Female Work Shoes..................$34.99
2. Male Work Shoes.....................$39.99
3. Khaki Pants – Female...............$15.99
4. Khaki Pants – Male..................$18.99
5. Belts..$12.99
6. Ties...$6.99
7. Polo Shirts – Female................$14.99
8. Polo Shirts – Male...................$15.99

Macy's (All popular name brand items):
1. Female Work Shoes..................$49.99
2. Male Work Shoes.....................$65.99
3. Khaki Pants – Female...............$24.99
4. Khaki Pants – Male..................$29.99
5. Belts..$15.99
6. Ties...$9.99
7. Polo Shirts – Female................$19.99
8. Polo Shirts – Male...................$21.99

Shoe Carnival:
1. Female Work Shoes (Timberlands)..............$59.99
2. Male Work Shoes (Timberlands).................$64.99
3. Belts..$14.99

Finish Line:
1. Female Work Shoes (Nike)........................$34.99
2. Male Work Shoes (Nike)...........................$54.99
3. Belts (Name Brand).................................$9.99
4. Polo Shirts – Female (Name Brand)...........$12.99
5. Polo Shirts – Male (Name Brand).............$16.99

Have each participant decide where they will shop and make their selections. They are to deduct the amount spent from their money on hand ($200). Once they have made their selections, give money to the Facilitator/Mentor, who will act as the bank (if actualy play money is used). Note: Banker refuse all loan requests as applicant hasn't been on their job long enough and there isn't a guarantee of repayment.

Instruct the participants they have added expenses that they will have to deduct from their money:
1. Two week bus pass..................................$25.00
2. Lunch for two weeks
   a. Purchasing lunch items from store: ..$25.00 (carrying lunch to work)
   b. Eating at the food court daily..........$50.00

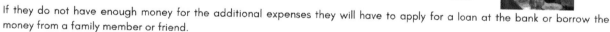

If they do not have enough money for the additional expenses they will have to apply for a loan at the bank or borrow the money from a family member or friend.

Have participants count how much money they have left over to put into their rainy day fund savings account.

Whoever has the most money left will have their money doubled to go shopping for more needed items or to save.

The next highest will receive an additional 75% of their remaining money to go shopping for more needed items or to save.

The third highest will receive an additional 50% of their remaining money to go shopping for more needed items or to save.

The fourth highest will receive an addition 25% of their remaining money to go shopping for more needed items or to save.

If there is anyone who had to borrow from the bank, friend or family member. They will not receive any additional funds and will be seen as the biggest loser.

LESSON TITLE:

Financial Literacy

LEVEL: Employee or Community Citizen

WEEKS 35-36

PACING: 55 minutes

OBJECTIVE(S): What will Participants know, understand, and be able to do?

Participants will understand the basics of financial literacy and responsible decision making.

KEY VOCABULARY: What key terms will my Participants need to understand?

Wants: Things people like to have, but do not need.

Needs: Things that people must have to live.

Save: To keep your money to use later.

Volunteer: A person who works for no pay to help others.

Tax: A compulsory contribution to state revenue, levied by the government on workers' income and business profits, or added to the cost of some goods, services, and transactions.

Tip: A sum of money given to someone as a reward for their service.

Credit score: A number assigned to a person that indicates to lenders their capacity to repay a loan.

Living wage: A wage that is high enough to maintain a normal standard of living.

WEEK 35

LESSON CYCLE:

1. Engage and Connect (15 min)

Lead a discussion with the participants about the importance of money and the dangers that can come from mismanagement of money. Allow the Mentee to explain any struggles and successes they have/had with money.

2. Lead Guided and Independent Practice (30 min)

Participants will participate in a *"Want vs. Need"* activity. Explain a "need" is something we must have to survive, like food, water, clothing, and shelter. Stress that to meet our needs; all we must have our basic needs met. Explain that a "want" is something we can live without, even though we may have a strong desire for it. Participants can create their own needs vs wants t-chart. ***Challenge question:*** Will your needs and wants change during high school, college, a working adult, etc.? Give examples. Have participants fill out the "Needs vs Wants Chart.

Pillar: Legacy

3. Close the Lesson and Assess Mastery **(10 min)**

Tell the participants they have just won the lottery. They must decide if they want the lump sum payout or the monthly payout. They can take lump sum payout for $6,875,000 now or get $3,000 each week for life (hint: if they get $3,000 a week, they will end up with $15,600,000 total if you live for 25 years, but they must wait for their weekly payment). Which payout of the money would you like to have? Does a person's situation change the decision, such as a person who must pay their light bill or buy food for their family? Challenge the participants to create a weekly/monthly budget. Participants can use the next week/month to track where they are earning, spending, and saving money. Close out the lesson by reminding participants that the choices we make with money must go with responsible decision making.

LOGISTICS: What materials, resources, and technology will I need to prepare and engage?

Computer/Projector
The Tonya Scenario
Financial Literacy on Kahoot

WEEK 36

LESSON CYCLE:

1. Engage and Connect   **(20 min)**

The facilitator will begin the lesson with the reading the "Needs vs. Wants" story. Tonya is a professional woman who works hard and has recently been promoted to her dream job making the salary she has always wanted. With the new job came a new commitment to save money, pay off some bills and purchase a new condo. Tonya sat down and created her monthly budget. She pulled out all her bills, other expenses, and her take home pay. She determined which bills/expenses would be paid when, how much she would keep and how much she would put in her savings. Tonya decided she would pay 10% in tithes, 10% in savings, 5% for everyday odds and ends and the remaining to pay her bills/expenses. While on social media, Tonya saw a pair of shoes she really wanted was on sale. And even though they were 80% off, they were p0riced outside of her budgeted amount. Tonya had been eyeing those shoes for a while, and felt she needed them because they matched an outfit she had previously purchased.

Discussion: Are the shoes a need or a want based upon the definitions previously provided? Should Tonya honor her commitment and tick to her budget or purchase the shoes? Yes or no? Why or why not? What would you do if you were in Tonya's shoes?

2. Lead Guided and Independent Practice   **(30 min)**

The participants will have an opportunity to engage in a Financial Literacy activity on Kahoot. Participants will engage in the financial literacy vocabulary connected to real-world scenarios.

3. Close the Lesson and Assess Mastery   **(5 min)**

Ask participants what terms/concepts they learned and how they can apply then to their life. Participants/Mentee can explain any struggles and successes they have/had with money.

LOGISTICS: What materials, resources, and technology will I need to prepare and engage?

Computer/Projector
The Tonya Scenario
Financial Literacy on Kahoot

Pillar: Legacy

LESSON VOCABULARY WORDS

INSTRUCTIONS: Review vocabulary words listed below with the participants to ensure they have a good understanding of each before starting any of the activities.

1. **Wants:** Things people like to have, but do not need.
2. **Needs:** Things that people must have to live.
3. **Save:** To keep your money to use later.
4. **Volunteer:** A person who works for no pay to help others.
5. **Tax:** A compulsory contribution to state revenue, levied by the government on workers' income and business profits, or added to the cost of some goods, services, and transactions.
6. **Tip:** A sum of money given to someone as a reward for their service.
7. **Credit score:** A number assigned to a person that indicates to lenders their capacity to repay a loan.
8. **Living wage:** A wage that is high enough to maintain a normal standard of living.

Name: _____

Needs and Wants

Directions: Categorize the list of words below into what a person **needs** to survive, and what a person **wants** to have in his or her life.

| food   bicycle   ice cream   air   television   water |
| shelter   cell phone   clothing   family   toys |
| games   bed   music   trees   electricity   shoes |

Directions: Discuss your choices with a partner. Are there any choices you made with which your partner disagrees? Explain your choices.

© www.HaveFunTeaching.com

Pillar: Legacy

HOW TO MAKE A BUDGET

Surprises are nice, but not when it comes to your money. If you're scrambling to pay the bills each month, you would probably benefit from having a budget. Below are three methods for helping you organize and manage your monthly expenses.

FIXED AND FLEX

The first budgeting technique involves grouping your expenses into two categories—"fixed," which are must-haves like food and utilities, and "flex," the nice-to-haves like a new watch or a day at the spa. Keeping these definitions in mind, follow the four-step process below:

- ☐ Gather 6 to 12 months of bank statements, receipts, and other financial records.
- ☐ Separate those expenses into "Fixed" and "Flex" columns.
- ☐ Add up your monthly "Fixed" expenses, then subtract the total from your monthly income.
- ☐ What's left over is your "Flex" spending money.

Although you're still dealing with the same amount of money, looking at your finances in a more organized way can help get your spending under control.

THE 50/30/20 RULE

Another budgeting technique is the 50/30/20 rule. It involves dividing your monthly income into three "buckets":

- ☐ 50% (or less) goes to necessities such as housing, student loans, and utilities. These are expenses you have to pay every month.
- ☐ 30% (or less) goes to nice-to-haves, such as entertainment, hobbies, and travel.
- ☐ 20% (or more, if possible) goes toward savings and paying down debt.

You can adjust the 50/30/20 rule based on your short- and long-term goals but be careful about confusing "nice-to-haves" for "necessities." Several dinners out each week and unlimited data plans may be nice to have, but they aren't essential.

TRACKING

Tracking takes the most time, but it provides the greatest insight into your spending habits.

- ☐ Use a spreadsheet, an online service or, if you prefer to go "low tech," a notebook and pen will work just fine.
- ☐ First, create columns for your spending categories (e.g., groceries, gas, utilities, medical, entertainment, and childcare). Add a "miscellaneous/unexpected" and a "savings" category, as well.
- ☐ Next, divide your monthly income among the categories and then pay your bills/save accordingly. It's important to list all items and subtract the amount you spend in each category, so you know where your money is going. Once a category is "out of money":
- ☐ Stop spending in that category, if possible, until you get your next paycheck
- ☐ Consider making trade-offs by moving money around from other categories

You stretch your money in many directions. Daily expenses, entertainment, life events, and long-term goals all compete for the same dollar. Budgeting can help ensure you're covering the necessary monthly expenses, saving for the future, and—maybe—have some extra cash to reward yourself for your good work. (https://www.tiaa.org/public/learn/personal-finance-101/how-to-make-a-budget)

Pillar: Legacy

EXPENSE TRACKER

DATE	DESCRIPTION	AMOUNT SPENT	CASH	CREDIT	NEED	WANT
			☐	☐	☐	☐
			☐	☐	☐	☐
			☐	☐	☐	☐
			☐	☐	☐	☐
			☐	☐	☐	☐
			☐	☐	☐	☐
			☐	☐	☐	☐
			☐	☐	☐	☐
			☐	☐	☐	☐
			☐	☐	☐	☐
			☐	☐	☐	☐
			☐	☐	☐	☐
			☐	☐	☐	☐
			☐	☐	☐	☐
			☐	☐	☐	☐
			☐	☐	☐	☐
			☐	☐	☐	☐
			☐	☐	☐	☐
			☐	☐	☐	☐
			☐	☐	☐	☐
			☐	☐	☐	☐
			☐	☐	☐	☐

www.ShiningMom.com

Name: _____

Needs and Wants

Directions: Categorize the list of words below into what a person **needs** to survive, and what a person **wants** to have in his or her life.

food   bicycle   ice cream   air   television   water
shelter   cell phone   clothing   family   toys
games   bed   music   trees   electricity   shoes

Directions: Discuss your choices with a partner. Are there any choices you made with which your partner disagrees? Explain your choices.

© www.HaveFunTeaching.com

Pillar: Legacy

THE BIGGEST LOOSER
FINANCIAL LITERARY ACTIVITY

This is a financial literacy game to help the participants to understand the necessity of being financially responsible with their money.

Materials: Play Money (dollars of all denominations and coins)

Instructions: Facilitator/Mentor will give each participant $200 and instruct them they will have to apply for more money if they run out of money or borrow it from a friend or family member.

Read the following: Tonya and Brian are starting new jobs on Monday and they both need to prepare for their first day. Tonya needs a pair of work shoes, khaki pants and some socks or footies. Brian needs a tie, some khaki pants and a belt. (The girls will buy as if they are Tanya and the boys will buy as if they are Brian.) The following are the stores closest to them to purchase their items from: Goodwill, Target, Macy's, Shoe Carnival and/or Finish Line. The following is the price list for each store:

Goodwill Store:
1. Female Work Shoes................$12.00
2. Male Work Shoes....................$15.00
3. Khaki Pants – Female..............$10.00
4. Khaki Pants – Male.................$13.00
5. Belts..$5.00
6. Ties..$2.00
7. Polo Shirts – Female...............$7.00
8. Polo Shirts – Male...................$9.00

Target:
1. Female Work Shoes................$34.99
2. Male Work Shoes...................$39.99
3. Khaki Pants – Female.............$15.99
4. Khaki Pants – Male.................$18.99
5. Belts......................................$12.99
6. Ties..$6.99
7. Polo Shirts – Female..............$14.99
8. Polo Shirts – Male..................$15.99

Macy's (All popular name brand items):
1. Female Work Shoes................$49.99
2. Male Work Shoes...................$65.99
3. Khaki Pants – Female.............$24.99
4. Khaki Pants – Male................$29.99
5. Belts......................................$15.99
6. Ties..$9.99
7. Polo Shirts – Female..............$19.99
8. Polo Shirts – Male..................$21.99

Shoe Carnival:
1. Female Work Shoes (Timberlands)..............$59.99
2. Male Work Shoes (Timberlands)................$64.99
3. Belts..$14.99

Finish Line:
1. Female Work Shoes (Nike)........................$34.99
2. Male Work Shoes (Nike)...........................$54.99
3. Belts (Name Brand)..................................$9.99
4. Polo Shirts – Female (Name Brand)............$12.99
5. Polo Shirts – Male (Name Brand)...............$16.99

Have each participant decide where they will shop and make their selections. They are to deduct the amount spent from their money on hand ($200). Once they have made their selections, give money to the Facilitator/Mentor, who will act as the bank (if actualy play money is used). Note: Banker refuse all loan requests as applicant hasn't been on their job long enough and there isn't a guarantee of repayment.

Instruct the participants they have added expenses that they will have to deduct from their money:
1. Two week bus pass................................$25.00
2. Lunch for two weeks
   a. Purchasing lunch items from store: ..$25.00 (carrying lunch to work)
   b. Eating at the food court daily..........$50.00

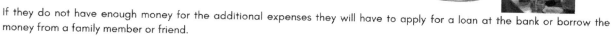

If they do not have enough money for the additional expenses they will have to apply for a loan at the bank or borrow the money from a family member or friend.

Have participants count how much money they have left over to put into their rainy day fund savings account.

Whoever has the most money left will have their money doubled to go shopping for more needed items or to save.
The next highest will receive an additional 75% of their remaining money to go shopping for more needed items or to save.
The third highest will receive an additional 50% of their remaining money to go shopping for more needed items or to save.
The fourth highest will receive an addition 25% of their remaining money to go shopping for more needed items or to save.
If there is anyone who had to borrow from the bank, friend or family member. They will not receive any additional funds and will be seen as the biggest loser.

LESSON TITLE:

Character Development

LEVEL: Youth

WEEKS 37-38

PACING: 55 minutes

OBJECTIVE(S): What will Participants know, understand, and be able to do?

Participants will learn that when it comes to character development, actions speak louder than words. Though you cannot control what others do, their everyday actions will teach them the importance of integrity.

KEY VOCABULARY: What key terms will my Participants need to understand?

Character Trait: a way to describe someone.

Character: how your habits, motives, thoughts, and so on relate to morality, particularly as it concerns integrity.

Values: the things that you believe are important in the way you live and work.

Mentor: An experienced and trusted advisor

Transformation: A thorough or dramatic change in form or appearance.

WEEK 37

LESSON CYCLE:

1. Engage and Connect (10 min)

Being the lesson by showing the "What is Character" video: https://www.youtube.com/watch?v=G1YeaOh4gHQ

2. Lead Guided and Independent Practice (30 min)

Facilitator/Mentor will review the definition for Character and share how to develop character.

How to Develop Character?

There are many things that engrave our character upon the clay of our lives and shape our character for better and for worse into a unique set of scratches and grooves. Our character begins to be shaped from the very time we are born and is influenced by where we grow up, how we are raised, the examples our parents provide, religious and academic education, and so on. Our character can be dramatically altered by a life-changing tragedy. One of the greatest influences on our character is those with whom we surround ourselves. As we can see, many factors, some beyond our control, play a role in molding our character. But the single greatest influence on our character is that which we have ultimate power over how we respond to circumstances.

CHARACTER TRAITS:

Generosity: seeing what others need and giving my resources to help them.

Adaptability: eagerly embracing a change in plans without complaint.

Pillar: Legacy

Cooperation: finding ways to understand others and work together to achieve a goal.
Courage: confidently doing what is right even if I feel afraid.
Creativity: approaching a need, task, or idea from a unique or new perspective.
Decisiveness: resolving a tough choice by evaluating what will achieve the greatest good.
Dependability: building trust with others by doing what I say I will do.
Diligence: pursuing a task until it is finished.
Endurance: using my inward strength to accomplish what is difficult even when I feel like giving up.
Forgiveness: clearing the record of someone who has wronged me and showing them love instead.
Truthfulness: speaking only what is honest and factual.
Self-Control: choosing to do what is right when I feel like doing wrong.

There are more identified character traits than what is listed. Feel free to check them out on your own and/or when completing the activity. (https://www.craftionary.net/character-trait-crafts-activities-kids/)

Activity 1: Storyboard – Instruct participants to create a comic strip about character. This activity will provide insight into what is character.

3. *Close the Lesson and Assess Mastery* **(10 min)**

The facilitator/mentor will share: "*Schools and community organizations seek to instill the values of integrity, respect, responsibility, fairness, honesty, caring, and citizenship in youth to strengthen the social fabric of the school and community. But building character for youth can't just happen in the classroom. The qualities of character develop through an interplay of family, school, and community influences and each individual youth's temperament, experiences, and choices. Parents have many opportunities and tools to build their children's character. Using them will give you the joy and satisfaction of seeing the youth grow into people of integrity and compassion.*" (https://www.verywellfamily.com/ways-to-build-character-in-children-620266)

LOGISTICS: What materials, resources, and technology will I need to prepare and engage?

Computer
Microsoft Teams
Pencil, pen
Paper or notebook
Comic Strip Template (Canva.com)

WEEK 38

LESSON CYCLE:

1. Engage and Connect **(15 min)**

Recap from what was discussed last week and have participants present their comic strip to the group.

2. Lead Guided and Independent Practice **(30 min)**

Start discussion around the three questions:
   a. What does it mean to have good character?
   b. Identify five people who you respect and admire? Share what you respect and admire about them.
   c. What could make you no longer respect and admire them? (Discuss the Will Smith incident.)

3. Close the Lesson and Assess Mastery **(10 min)**

Ask participants to reflect and share their thoughts on this question: "What type of individual would you like to be when you grow up?"

Computer
Microsoft Teams
Pencil, pen
Paper or notebook
Character Comic Strip

Pillar: Legacy

LESSON VOCABULARY WORDS

INSTRUCTIONS: Review vocabulary words listed below with the participants to ensure they have a good understanding of each before starting any of the activities.

1. **Character Trait:** a way to describe someone.

2. **Character:** how your habits, motives, thoughts, and so on relate to morality, particularly as it concerns integrity.

3. **Values:** the things that you believe are important in the way you live and work.

4. **Mentor:** An experienced and trusted advisor.

5. **Transformation:** A thorough or dramatic change in form or appearance.

Comic Strip

Pillar: Legacy

LESSON TITLE:

Character Development

LEVEL: Employee or Community Citizen

WEEKS 37-38

PACING: 55 minutes

OBJECTIVE(S): What will Participants know, understand, and be able to do?

Participants will learn that when it comes to character development, actions speak louder than words. Though you cannot control what others do, their everyday actions will teach them the importance of integrity.

KEY VOCABULARY: What key terms will my Participants need to understand?

Adolescence: The period following the onset of puberty during which a young person develops from a child into an adult.

Maturity: The state, fact, or period of being mature.

Transformation: A thorough or dramatic change in form or appearance.

WEEK 37

LESSON CYCLE:

1. Engage and Connect   **(10 min)**

Lead with this quote: *"Your thoughts become your words. Your words become your actions. Your actions become your habits. Your habits become your character, and your character determines your destiny."*

Assign groups of participants (no more than 3-4) to create a list of what they believe are professional and personal characteristics. After a set time, instruct the groups to stand and share their characteristics. As this is happening, the remaining groups are listening; if the standing group calls out a characteristic that is on the list of groups still sitting, they will scratch that characteristic off their list and not share it when it's their turn to present.

2. Lead Guided and Independent Practice   **(30 min)**

Character traits are individual parts of your personality and behavior that express who you are as a person. Your character traits are based on your personality, morals, ethics, and beliefs. Knowing your best character traits can help you develop them further and use them to your advantage.

While there are many character traits that can contribute to career success, here are some of the top characteristics that can help you advance in a community setting or the workplace:

a. **Ambitious.** A strong desire to achieve success by meeting their goals and applied hard work and dedication to overcome a challenge or exceed goals/objectives.
b. **Creative.** Uses their imagination to make or invent something and is applicable when solving a difficult problem, presenting information in a clear, interesting way or finding better ways to complete tasks.

c. **Compassionate.** Someone who can both feel and express sympathy for others.
d. **Conscientious.** Someone who is careful and takes purposeful action and concerned with doing what is right to fulfill a duty.
e. **Courageous.** Someone who is not deterred by challenges and difficulties, takes calculated risks, and takes on projects others fear may be too hard or require too much work.
f. **Flexible.** Can quickly adapt to changes in plans and is critical to succeeding in various roles.
g. **Honest.** Someone who is sincere, honest, and generally does not feel comfortable participating in deceptive practices.
h. **Humble.** Someone who exercises humility, are respectful, and displays leadership traits.
i. **Honorable** (Integrity). Someone who acts according to their principles and ethics.
j. **Loyal.** Someone who is supportive and trustworthy.
k. **Patient.** Someone who can tolerate setbacks, delays, or unexpected challenges without becoming anxious or angry.
l. **Persistent.** Someone who is relentless in the pursuit of goals and continues along their path despite any obstacles or difficulties they may face.
m. **Resilient.** Someone who can quickly recover from setbacks, stress, adverse situations, or unexpected changes.
n. **Disciplined.** Someone who can overcome temptations, procrastination, and self-doubt.
o. **Curious.** Someone with the drive to want to know or learn new skills, information, and abilities strategically and with motivation.

These positive character traits are examples of sought-after personality and behaviors. Understanding your best and most relevant character traits can also support setting and attaining goals.

Activity 1: Make a list of four to six character traits that you intend to live by; words you believe describe the man or woman you hope to become by the end of your life. Share your list of "***core values***" with the group and tell why you chose those words.

Activity 2: Promises, Promises Activity

Have the participants write out some promises you made to your younger self. Make a list of them and be sure and include some you failed to keep. Next, select one of those unkept promises (to yourself or to someone else), and determine to keep that promise for one whole week. Fix your eyes on it as an attainable goal. Write it down and think of steps you can take to keep the promise. Choose another participant as an accountability partner who will hold you accountable, encourage and inspire you to continue working to attain your goal. Next week, share the goal you selected and your progress in honoring it for a week. Share what it means to keep a promise? How did it positively affect your character? Did it strengthen your discipline? Remember that it is better that you don't make a promise, than to make one you don't intend to fulfill.

Activity 3: Current Events Activity

Have the participants watch the evening news on television. Look for the news stories about people who either exhibited strong character (integrity and ethics) or failed to do so. (Trust me—these reports will not be hard to find.) Write out a summary of what you think made them act the way they did. Include in your summary, what values had they determined to live by: self-centered; self-promoting and self-protecting or civic-minded, others-centered and/or self-sacrificing.

Pillar: Legacy

Activity 4: I had to See it to Believe it Activity

Have the participants observe their workplace. Look for men or women who either exhibit strong character (integrity and ethics) or failed to do so. (Be honest and integral in your interpretation of their character traits.) Write out a summary of what positive/negative character traits he/she exhibited and why you think they acted the way they did. Include in your summary, what values you believe they have determined to live by: self-centered; self-promoting and self-protecting or civic-minded, others-centered and/or self-sacrificing.

3. Close the Lesson and Assess Mastery **(15 min)**

Pose the Question: Explain how positive character traits are displayed in everyday life, the workplace, and the community. Allow participants to answer the question one-by-one.

LOGISTICS: What materials, resources, and technology will I need to prepare and engage?

Computer
Microsoft Teams
Pencil/Pen
Paper or Notebook

WEEK 38

LESSON CYCLE:

1. Engage and Connect (10 min)

Recap from what was discussed last week. From whichever activity was completed ask each participant what they learned from the activity and what they have applied to their daily lives.

Ask them who is a man or woman in their lives that they respect, trust and can confide in?

2. Lead Guided and Independent Practice (30 min)

Start discussion around the two questions:
   a. What does it mean to have good character?
   b. Identify five people who you respect and admire in your personal or professional life? Share what you respect and admire about them. Clearly identify the positive character traits you see in them.
   c. What could make you no longer respect and admire them? (Discuss the Jada/Will Smith incident (https://www.youtube.com/watch?v=myjEoDypUD8). Be sure to tell them to excuse the profanity in the video clip.)

3. Close the Lesson and Assess Mastery (15 min)

Ask Participants to reflect on the quote: *"Your reputation is what others think of you; your character is who you truly are. Reputations can be manipulated; character can only be developed and maintained."*

LOGISTICS: What materials, resources, and technology will I need to prepare and engage?

Computer
Pencil, pen
Paper

Pillar: Legacy

LESSON VOCABULARY WORDS

INSTRUCTIONS: Review vocabulary words listed below with the participants to ensure they have a good understanding of each before starting any of the activities.

1. **Adolescence:** The period following the onset of puberty during which a young person develops from a child into an adult.

2. **Maturity**: The state, fact, or period of being mature.

3. **Transformation**: A thorough or dramatic change in form or appearance.

LESSON TITLE:

Lead by Example

LEVEL: Youth

WEEKS 39-40

PACING: 55 minutes

OBJECTIVE(S): What will Participants know, understand, and be able to do?

Participants will be able to understand the importance of leading by example.

KEY VOCABULARY: What key terms will my Participants need to understand?

Leadership: The action of leading a group of people or an organization.

Example: A thing or characteristic of its kind or illustrating a general rule.

Impact: The effect or influence of one person, thing, or action, on another.

Guidance: Advice or information aimed at resolving a problem or difficulty, especially as given by someone in authority.

WEEK 39

LESSON CYCLE:

1. Engage and Connect (15 min)

Start by introducing the topic of *"Leading by Example"* to the participants.

- Ask if they would consider themselves a leader.
- What does it mean to be a leader?
- Ask them to name one leader in their family, and one leader at their school.

2. Lead Guided and Independent Practice (25 min)

Show participants this video clip and discuss afterwards. https://www.youtube.com/watch?v=ZnjJpa1LBOY

Ask participants how important is working with others and collaborating?

3. Close the Lesson and Assess Mastery (15 min)

Ask the participants if it is hard for them to admit their mistakes? Why or Why not?

Explain that as a leader, you are not going to be perfect and to build trust when working with others you must be responsible and admit when you've made a mistake. Being a leader does not make people superhuman.

Pillar: Legacy

LOGISTICS: What materials, resources, and technology will I need to prepare and engage?

Computer
Pencil/Pen
Paper

WEEK 40

LESSON CYCLE:

1. Engage and Connect   **(15 min)**

Recap the concept and theme of "*Leading by Example*" to your participants.

Ask them if they demonstrated any leadership qualities since the last time, we met.

Ask: "How can someone be a leader even at home, while a lot of Participants are learning virtually?

2. Lead Guided and Independent Practice   **(25 min)**

Ask participants to identify 3 leaders they admire who are celebrities? What character traits do they possess?

If they are having trouble coming up with names propose the names:

Common	Kobe Bryant
Stephen Curry	Kamala Harris
Oprah	Kim Kardashian
LL Cool J	Serena Williams
Joe Biden	Future

3. Close the Lesson and Assess Mastery   **(15 min)**

Ask the questions: Who Should not become a leader and lead people?

Can everyone become a leader?

LOGISTICS: What materials, resources, and technology will I need to prepare and engage?

Computer
Microsoft teams
Pen/Paper/Notebook
Leading by Example Activity
Journal Pages

Pillar: Legacy

LESSON VOCABULARY WORDS

INSTRUCTIONS: Review vocabulary words listed below with the participants to ensure they have a good understanding of each before starting any of the activities.

1. **Leadership**: The action of leading a group of people or an organization.
2. **Example:** A thing or characteristic of its kind or illustrating a general rule.
3. **Impact**: The effect or influence of one person, thing, or action, on another.
4. **Guidance:** Advice or information aimed at resolving a problem or difficulty, especially as given by someone in authority.

LEADING BY EXAMPLE

1. Do you consider yourself a leader?

   _____
   _____
   _____
   _____

2. What does it mean to be a leader?

   _____
   _____
   _____
   _____

3. Name one leader in your family, and one at your school.

   a. _____

   b. _____

4. Is it hard for you to admit to your mistakes? Why or why not?

   _____
   _____
   _____
   _____

5. Who should not become a leader and lead people? Can everyone become a leader?

   _____
   _____
   _____
   _____

Pillar: Legacy

6. Discussion questions: How can someone be a leader even at home, while a lot of participants are learning virtually?

   _____
   _____
   _____

7. Have you demonstrated any leadership qualities since the last meeting?

   _____
   _____
   _____

LESSON TITLE:

Lead by Example

LEVEL: Employee or Community Citizen

WEEKS 39-40

PACING: 55 minutes

OBJECTIVE(S): What will Participants know, understand, and be able to do?

Participants will be able to understand the importance of leading by example.

KEY VOCABULARY: What key terms will my Participants need to understand?

Leadership: The action of leading a group of people or an organization.

Example: A thing or characteristic of its kind or illustrating a general rule.

Impact: The effect or influence of one person, thing, or action, on another.

Guidance: Advice or information aimed at resolving a problem or difficulty, especially as given by someone in authority.

WEEK 39

LESSON CYCLE:

1. Engage and Connect (15 min)

Start by introducing the topic of "*Leading by Example*" to the participants.

- Ask them would they consider themselves to be a leader.
- What does it mean to be a leader?
- Ask them to name one leader in their family, and one leader in the community.

2. Lead Guided and Independent Practice (25 min)

Show participants this video clip and discuss afterwards. https://www.youtube.com/watch?v=VmQVNE-MbKI

Ask participants how important is working with others and collaborating?

3. Close the Lesson and Assess Mastery (15 min)

Ask the participants if it is hard for them to admit their mistakes? Why or Why not?

Explain that as a leader, you are not going to be perfect and to build trust when working with others you must be responsible and admit when you've made a mistake. Being a leader does not make people superhuman.

Pillar: Legacy

LOGISTICS: What materials, resources, and technology will I need to prepare and engage?

Computer, Microsoft Teams
Pencil, pen,
Paper or notebook

WEEK 40

LESSON CYCLE:

1. Engage and Connect **(10 min)**

Recap thoughts, and themes from last week about *Leading by Example* with your participants.

2. Lead Guided and Independent Practice **(30 min)**

Show participants this video clip and discuss afterwards. https://www.youtube.com/watch?v=VmQVNE-MbKI

Discussion: Review the 7 Keys to Creative Collaboration that was covered in the video and how it can be used in your life and in business. Here are the seven ideas:

1. **Ownership**: Members need to be empowered from the start.
2. **Dependability**: Creative collaboration requires members to hit their deadlines and develop creative endurance.
3. **Trust**: When members trust one another, they work interdependently and genuinely listen to one another and assume the best in each other. Over time, they become transparent and even vulnerable.
4. **Structure**: The structure should be loose and flexible. But you need to have structure in creative collaboration.
5. **A Shared Vision**: This isn't conducive to a vision statement. Its more like of a sense of direction. A shared desire, a goal you are aiming for, and picture of what you will produce.
6. **Fun**: The best collaborative groups are the ones where you want to be together, laugh and work towards a shared vision. It boosts both convergent thinking and divergent thinking.
7. **Candor**: It's the idea that groups need to be honest about what's working and failing. This honesty allows you to adjust and iterate and ultimately create something awesome.
    a. **Propose a scenario** What if you were working on a group project, and you were the only person that did any work, how would you respond? Allow your creativity to inspire you to come up with workable scenarios.

Activity: Play the "*What If*" game.

Propose a scenario (for example: what if you were working on a group project, and you were the only person that did any work, how would you respond? You should be able to come up with at least 5 scenarios.

Question: What makes creative collaboration work effectively?

3. Close the Lesson and Assess Mastery **(15 min)**

Discuss the Quote: "*Collaboration captures collective intelligence. Coming together is a beginning. Keeping together is progress. Working together is success.*"

Ask participants if they think it is important to NOT lead with a "*Do as I say, not as I do approach?*"

Pillar: Legacy

LOGISTICS: What materials, resources, and technology will I need to prepare and engage?

Computer
Microsoft teams
Leader in Me Self-Evaluation
Leading by Example Activity Worksheet
2 Activities that Showcase Different Leadership Styles Worksheet
Journal Pages

Intentional Mentoring Mentor's Guide

LESSON VOCABULARY WORDS

INSTRUCTIONS: Review vocabulary words listed below with the participants to ensure they have a good understanding of each before starting any of the activities.

1. **Leadership:** The action of leading a group of people or an organization.

2. **Example:** A thing or characteristic of its kind or illustrating a general rule.

3. **Impact:** The effect or influence of one person, thing, or action, on another.

4. **Guidance:** Advice or information aimed at resolving a problem or difficulty, especially as given by someone in authority.

_____
_____
_____
_____
_____
_____

Discuss the Quote: *"Collaboration captures collective intelligence. Coming together is a beginning. Keeping together is progress. Working together is success."*

Ask participants if they think it is important to NOT lead with a *"Do as I say, not as I do approach?"*

_____
_____
_____
_____
_____
_____
_____

Pillar: Legacy

LEADING BY EXAMPLE

1. Do you consider yourself a leader?

   _____
   _____
   _____
   _____

2. What does it mean to be a leader?

   _____
   _____
   _____
   _____
   _____

3. Name one leader in your family, and one at your community.

   a. _____

   b. _____

4. Is it hard for you to admit to your mistakes? Why or why not?

   _____
   _____
   _____
   _____

5. Who should not become a leader and lead people? Can everyone become a leader?

   _____
   _____
   _____
   _____
   _____

6. Discussion questions: How can someone be a leader even at home, while a lot of participants are learning virtually?

   _____
   _____
   _____

7. Have you demonstrated any leadership qualities since the last meeting?

   _____
   _____
   _____

Pillar: Legacy

THE LEADER IN ME SELF EVALUATION

Instructions: Circle the smiley face that closely represents the truthfulness of the statement.

Habit 1: Be Proactive

1. I am responsible	☹ 😐 🙂
2. I take initiative	☹ 😐 🙂
3. I have a good attitude most of the time	☹ 😐 🙂
4. I make good choices	☹ 😐 🙂
5. I do the right thing without being asked	☹ 😐 🙂

Habit 2: Begin with the End in Mind

1. I plan ahead	☹ 😐 🙂
2. I set goals	☹ 😐 🙂
3. I am a good citizen	☹ 😐 🙂
4. I contribute to my school's mission/vision	☹ 😐 🙂

Habit 3: Put First Things First

1. I set priorities	☹ 😐 🙂
2. I am organized	☹ 😐 🙂
3. I am disciplined	☹ 😐 🙂

https://www.pinterest.com/pin/2603712269545288/

2 ACTIVITIES THAT SHOWCASE DIFFERENT LEADERSHIP STYLES

There are three different 'leadership styles.' These are: **autocratic** (also known as authoritarian), **delegative** (also called 'free reign)' and **democratic** (which is also called participative) (Clark, 2015; Johnson-Gerard, 2017).

An ***autocratic leader*** makes decisions without first consulting others, while a ***delegative leader*** allows the staff to make the decisions (Johnson-Gerard, 2017). Finally, a ***democratic leader*** consults with the staff in making workplace decisions (Johnson-Gerard, 2017). Here is an excellent resource for exploring different leadership styles. The workbook also provides some helpful worksheets. The following two activities help participants think more deeply about styles of leadership. The group should be divided into small groups of 3 – 4 participants. The participants work in groups for the first activity, and then they work individually on the second activity.

ACTIVITY ONE (Clark, 2015)
Facilitator/Mentor shares the following scenario: *"A new supervisor has just been put in charge of the production line. He immediately starts by telling the crew what change needs to be made. When some suggestions are made, he tells them he does not have time to consider them."* Instruct the group to work together and figure out which leadership style is used in this scenario. Discuss whether it is effective, or if a different style could work better.

Encourage participants to think about themselves in a similar situation and their reaction to the leadership style discussed.

ACTIVITY TWO (Clark, 2015)
Facilitator/Mentor shares the following statement *'consider a time when you, or another leader, used the authoritarian (autocratic), participative (democratic) or delegative (free reign) style of leadership.'* Have participants to answer the following questions:

a. Was it effective?
b. Would a different leadership style have worked better?
c. What were the employees' experiences?
d. What did they learn from the leadership style?
e. What did they learn?
f. Which style is easiest to use (and why)?

Alternatively, nominate the style which the participant prefers (and why).

DISCUSSION: Have the participants to discuss as a group what they learned about the three styles of leadership.

https://positivepsychology.com/leadership-activities/#examples

Pillar: Legacy

7 KEYS TO CREATIVE COLLABORATION

Instructions: How it can the following be used in your life and in business:

1. **Ownership**: Members need to be empowered from the start.

2. **Dependability**: Creative collaboration requires members to hit their deadlines and develop creative endurance.

3. **Trust**: When members trust one another, they work interdependently and genuinely listen to one another and assume the best in each other. Over time, they become transparent and even vulnerable.

4. **Structure**: The structure should be loose and flexible. But you need to have structure in creative collaboration.

5. **A Shared Vision**: This isn't conducive to a vision statement. It's more like of a sense of direction. A shared desire, a goal you are aiming for, and picture of what you will produce.

6. **Fun**: The best collaborative groups are the ones where you want to be together, laugh and work towards a shared vision. It boosts both convergent thinking and divergent thinking.

7. **Candor**: It's the idea that groups need to be honest about what's working and failing. This honesty allows you to adjust and iterate and ultimately create something awesome.

8. **Propose a scenario** What if you were working on a group project, and you were the only person that did any work, how would you respond? Allow your creativity to inspire you to come up with workable scenarios.

(https://www.youtube.com/watch?v=VmQVNE-MbKI)

PILLAR: LEGACY

PILLAR: LEGACY

"Living your legacy is one of the best ways to feel happy while you journey through life."

– Shyam Ramanathan

In the previous pillars, you have discovered the importance of living, loving, learning, laughing, and leading. All of which are necessary for you to live the legacy you want to leave the world NOW. Benjamin Franklin once said, *"Don't put off until tomorrow what you can do today."* Living your legacy is one of the greatest gifts you can give to yourself, your family, the community, and the world all at the same time. I know what you may think, *how can I do that?* The information in this pillar will hopefully help you begin your journey of living the legacy you desire to leave the world. Yep, it begins with understanding, accepting, and believing what legacy is. Legacy is a living reflection of who you are. It is your story, unfolding in real time, and inspired by what makes life fulfilling.

Understanding what living your legacy entails begins with learning what is legacy life, eulogy and resume values are. This basic understanding will begin the journey you are now on even though you haven't decided to live a life of legacy. As Maya Angelo said, *"…when you know better, do better."*

- **Legacy Life**: is a life that has a positive impact on someone else; makes conscious decisions each day; consciously focuses on the NOW moments that occur in life; happily, shares their time, attention, and essence with the ones they love and encounter daily; and spends time developing and completing their legacy life goals.

- **Eulogy Values**: are what makes you stand for your highest values and by your deepest convictions; gives you the big picture of your life and gives you the impetus to create the life you desire. It is the virtues that show your inner light and inner character.

- **Resume Values**: are the results of a life lived for external achievement. They are the skills and strategies you need for career success and build an external career that results in you living with an unconscious boredom, separated from the deepest meaning of life and highest moral joys.

BE ENTHUSIASTIC:

Get excited about your life! This is your opportunity to experience this world as it is. Genuine happiness draws others to you and allows you to build trusting and long-lasting relationships. Enthusiasm unlocks a life of substance and cheer; and be enthusiastic about life despite the obstacles each one faces.

BE GRATEFUL

Your attitude towards everything in life plays a greater role in how you like life and the opportunities you go after. Develop coping skills to view the world through a prism of abundance. Your attitude is the accurate barometer of how you experience your life. Your attitude sets the temperature for how other people see, relate, trust, and treat you. It can attract abundance and joy. When you're grateful your life has the ability to bring joy. The joy you experience while living your legacy is not based upon your outer success but your internal happiness. His/Her gratefulness is developed one small appreciative moment at a time. So, savor them and revere life.

ACCEPT YOURSELF

In the pillar on living, we talked about discovering what you like, what you are passionate about. Identify those things you believe will bring you happiness and/or the drive you use to live your best life now. By doing so, this will help you live "*…thriving, vibrant, happy 'lives'*." This gives you permission to live life well by doing things today that help you flourish in the moment, and in every day thereafter. Because this isn't something that is taught in the school or in some cultures, where it is socially acceptable. It must be introduced as an acceptable part of life for people to explore its necessity in their life.

Remember, your life is a gift! Accept the gift you have been given as the greatest present you have ever received. Live it by honoring it in the ways you talk about you, the love you lavish on it daily and the respect you freely give and receive. You are unique, no one else is equipped to be you. When you were created, the mold was broken. In an interview, Oprah Winfrey did in 2015, she shares "*What Mispronouncing 'Canada' on TV*" taught her. It taught her to always be who she is and show the essence of her truth. Otherwise, you will not be seen as being genuine. Accept the uniqueness that is you and live the legacy you want to leave your family, community, and world. Activate your gifts and talents and tap into your amazing strengths. If you don't do it, it will never be done. In the same way, you are not equipped to be anyone else.

"Legacy is every life you've touched." – Maya Angelou

Pillar: Legacy

CHARACTER: is the mental and moral qualities distinctive to an individual; strength and originality in a person's nature; a person's excellent reputation.

CHARACTER

Live your life according to your core values. Think about it this way: keep the end in mind and align all your activities to your highest values. Align your actions to what you want your life to stand for to ensure you live your legacy.

INSPIRE OTHERS

The way to inspire others is by being an influencer. One of the side effects of being a leader is inspiring others to tap into the best version of themselves and LIVE! In most cases, simply showing up as your authentic self enables, inspires, and empowers others to do the same.

ALWAYS RESPECT OTHERS

Live your life with one undeniable truth: respect is inherent! It shows that you value others as much as you value the gift that you are to the world. With that as a core value, always respect others. It frees you to continue living your best life while silently giving others permission to do the same.

DESERVING SUCCESS

Take positive action to overcome whatever fears you have developed over the years. It speaks to your self-love, acceptance, and the respect you have for yourself. Living your legacy means taking advantage of the opportunities available to you with the mindset that you are deserving of success. This is a tool to help you experience the success you desire. Believing in yourself means you believe you deserve success, and by acting out that belief daily, you put yourself in alignment with experiencing the success you want and deserve.

In the article, *Enlist In Your Purpose: Live Your Legacy Now*, the author, Heather Burgett, suggests each person seeking to live their legacy now to:

- ✓ Thrive through uncertain times.
- ✓ Stop making everything about YOU.
- ✓ Tap into your signature gifts.
- ✓ Recognize your sole reason to connect, interact, engage and be here for others – leads to unexpected opportunities for success.
- ✓ Be cognizant of this core belief: how I do one thing is how I do everything.
- ✓ Be a visionary who implements steps to create and effect change.
- ✓ Use life altering moments to fuel and/or energize you.
- ✓ Stretch, grow and move through challenges and unimaginable circumstances.
- ✓ Recognize the beauty in knowing YOU have the power to connect and support others.

Pillar: Legacy

LESSON TITLE:

Understanding Legacy

LEVEL: Youth   **WEEKS 41-42**

PACING: 55 minutes

OBJECTIVE(S): What will Participants know, understand, and be able to do?

Students will understand the importance of leaving a legacy behind for others to know, use, and build upon.

KEY VOCABULARY: What key terms will my Participants need to understand?

Acceptance: the action or process of being received as adequate or suitable, typically to be admitted into a group.

Memory: something remembered from the past; a recollection.

Impact: The effect or influence of one person, thing, or action, on another.

Life Map: a visual timeline that traces key moments in your life from the time you were born until the present day.

WEEK 41

LESSON CYCLE:

1. Engage and Connect (15 min)

Start by introducing the topic of "Legacy" to the mentees.

a. Ask participants to share what they think is a "Legacy".
b. Ask them would they consider themselves able to leave a legacy within their family, community and/or the world.
c. What does it mean to be a legacy? Explain.
d. What is the legacy journey? Explain.
e. Ask them to name one person who has a legacy. Someone in their family that has or has left a legacy.
f. What would be a legacy that the mentee could work to leave behind?

2. Lead Guided and Independent Practice (30 min)

Activity: Show the participants this video on *Leaving a Legacy* and discuss afterwards.
https://www.youtube.com/watch?v=H1t50ZefD8A

3. Close the Lesson and Assess Mastery (10 min)

Facilitator/Mentor share with the participants what a legacy is and how to build on their name. Being a leader doesn't make anyone not human. Leaving a legacy helps mark your existence and your contribution to your family, school, community, and the world.

Additional thought: Knowing the legacy you want to leave behind helps you stay focused on what you're doing in the present so that your goals are in line with that legacy. It offers a concrete sense of purpose in choosing what you are giving your energy to. And the whole concept of legacy can be a deeply powerful way of connecting with others. Looking at your roots, ancestral, blood family, cultural, spiritual, or whatever avenue you choose to explore, connects you to those who have gone before you. Planning the legacy, you are leaving behind connects you to those whose lives you touch, and that touch yours. Take some time and really look at the things you carry from past generations. See what you need to leave behind, as well as, what you want to carry forward. (https://tinybuddha.com/blog/living-your-legacy-what-will-give-the-world/)

LOGISTICS: What materials, resources, and technology will I need to prepare and engage?

Computer
Microsoft teams
Pen
Paper or notebook

Pillar: Legacy

LESSON VOCABULARY WORDS

INSTRUCTIONS: Review vocabulary words listed below with the participants to ensure they have a good understanding of each before starting any of the activities.

1. **Acceptance**: the action or process of being received as adequate or suitable, typically to be admitted into a group.

2. **Memory:** something remembered from the past; a recollection.

3. **Impact:** The effect or influence of one person, thing, or action, on another.

4. **Life Map:** a visual timeline that traces key moments in your life from the time you were born until the present day.

UNDERSTANDING LEGACY WORKSHEET

INSTRUCTIONS: Answer the following questions.

a. What is a "Legacy"?

_____
_____
_____

b. Are you working to leave a legacy within your family, community and/or the world?

_____
_____
_____

c. What does it mean to be a legacy? Explain your answer.

_____
_____
_____

d. What is the journey of a legacy? Explain your answer.

_____
_____
_____

e. Name one person who has a legacy. It must be someone in their family who left a legacy.

_____
_____
_____

f. What legacy can you leave behind?

_____
_____
_____

Pillar: Legacy

LESSON TITLE:

Legacy

LEVEL: Employee or Community Citizen

WEEKS 41-42

PACING: 55 minutes

OBJECTIVE(S): What will Participants know, understand, and be able to do?

Participants will understand the importance of leaving a legacy behind for others to know, use, and build upon.

KEY VOCABULARY: What key terms will my Participants need to understand?

Acceptance: the action or process of being received as adequate or suitable, typically to be admitted into a group.

Memory: something remembered from the past; a recollection.

Impact: The effect or influence of one person, thing, or action, on another.

Life Map: a visual timeline that traces key moments in your life from the time you were born until the present day.

WEEK 41

LESSON CYCLE:

1. Engage and Connect (10 min)

Start by introducing the topic of "Leaving A Legacy" to the mentees.

a. Ask participants to share what they think is a "Legacy".
b. Ask them would they consider themselves able to leave a legacy in their community.
c. What does it mean to be a legacy? Explain
d. What is the journey of a legacy? Explain
e. Ask them to name one person who has a legacy. Someone in their family that has or has left a legacy.
f. What would be a legacy that the mentee could work to leave behind?

2. Lead Guided and Independent Practice (35 min)

Activity: Show participants this video on Leaving A Legacy and discuss afterwards.

https://www.youtube.com/watch?v=H1t50ZefD8A

3. Close the Lesson and Assess Mastery (10 min)

Facilitator/Mentor will share with the participants what legacy is and how to build your name. Being a leader doesn't make anyone unhuman. Leaving a legacy helps mark your existence and your contribution to your family, school, community, and the world.

LOGISTICS: What materials, resources, and technology will I need to prepare and engage?

Computer
Pen
Paper or notebook

Pillar: Legacy

WEEK 42

LESSON CYCLE:

1. Engage and Connect (15 min)

Recap thoughts and themes from last week on the lesson on Legacy with the participants.

2. Lead Guided and Independent Practice (30 min)

Activity: Show participants this video on Legacy and discuss afterwards.

https://www.youtube.com/watch?v=iW29aevuQYQ

3. Close the Lesson and Assess Mastery (10 min)

Ask participants why they think it's important to work towards leaving a legacy.

LOGISTICS: What materials, resources, and technology will I need to prepare and engage?

Computer
Microsoft teams
Understanding Legacy Worksheet
Journal Pages
Pen/Markers/Crayons

LESSON VOCABULARY WORDS

INSTRUCTIONS: Review vocabulary words listed below with the participants to ensure they have a good understanding of each before starting any of the activities.

1. **Acceptance**: the action or process of being received as adequate or suitable, typically to be admitted into a group.

2. **Memory**: something remembered from the past; a recollection.

3. **Impact**: The effect or influence of one person, thing, or action, on another.

4. **Life Map:** a visual timeline that traces key moments in your life from the time you were born until the present day.

Pillar: Legacy

UNDERSTANDING LEGACY WORKSHEET

INSTRUCTIONS: Answer the following questions.

a. What is a "Legacy"?

_____
_____
_____

b. Are you working to leave a legacy within your family, community and/or the world?

_____
_____
_____

c. What does it mean to be a legacy? Explain your answer.

_____
_____
_____

d. What is the journey of a legacy? Explain your answer.

_____
_____
_____

e. Name one person who has a legacy. It must be someone in their family who left a legacy.

_____
_____
_____

f. What legacy can you leave behind?

_____
_____
_____

LESSON TITLE:

Living your Legacy

LEVEL: Youth

WEEKS 43-44

PACING: 55 minutes

OBJECTIVE(S): What will Participants know, understand, and be able to do?

Participants will be able to understand the importance of living the legacy they want to gift the world.

KEY VOCABULARY: What key terms will my Participants need to understand?

Acceptance: the action or process of being received as adequate or suitable, typically to be admitted into a group.

Memory: something remembered from the past; a recollection.

Impact: The effect or influence of one person, thing, or action, on another.

Life Map: a visual timeline that traces key moments in your life from the time you were born until the present day.

WEEK 43

LESSON CYCLE:

1. Engage and Connect (10 min)

Introduce the activity: Creating a Life Map to the participants. Explain that a life map is a visual timeline. It traces the key moments in your life from the time you were born until the present day. The events and experiences you draw in your life map can make great starting points for writing topics, particularly for personal writing. Show participants the "Create a Map of Your Life" video clip: https://www.youtube.com/watch?v=e2n8n_8K4V0&t=40s

2. Lead Guided and Independent Practice (35 min)

Activity: Creating your Life Map. A life map tracks your journey through life and marks out important events along the way. Remember, an important event doesn't have to be exciting or memorable for others, the map is all about showing what is important to you.

a. Gather the materials you will use to create your Life Map (i.e. colored markers, pen, pencil, crayons, paper, etc.).
b. Start your life map with the day you were born. Include stories you have heard about your birth.
c. Record the dates of key moments in your life in time order. Your earliest childhood memory (describe in detail). Your most vivid childhood experiences. Your school years.
d. Draw each event to help you remember it.

Pillar: Legacy

e. End your life map with the present day.

3. *Close the Lesson and Assess Mastery* **(10 min)**

Ask the participants how are they with the creation of their Life Map? Allow a few of the participants to share their thoughts and where they are in their process of creating the Life Map.

LOGISTICS: What materials, resources and technology will I need to prepare and engage?

Computer
Pen/Paper
Notebook/Journal Pages
Life Map Activity

Life Map Instructions: What should your map include?

- [ ] A symbol or picture that represents each selected event. The picture should give an indication of how you felt about the event.
- [ ] A label which identifies and roughly dates the event. You can be creative and poetic with these labels e.g. the road to happiness on my new skateboard.
- [ ] Connectors between events which help the viewer understand the order in which they happened. The connectors can also indicate how the road between one event and another event are connected. What important lesson or understanding did you come to during this period of time?
  - Some people use arrows, some people draw roads, some people draw a bunch of islands and draw little boats travelling between each; it is up to you how you see your map. Does your life map have a road map, a diagram, a geographical map, a maze, a swirling circle or a game of snakes and ladders?

Sample list to motivate your life map drawing:

- [ ] Day you were born
- [ ] Stories you have heard about your birth
- [ ] Your earliest childhood memory (describe in detail)
- [ ] Your most vivid childhood experiences
- [ ] Your school years
- [ ] A special trip you have taken
- [ ] A favorite meaningful thing/object you received from someone special
- [ ] The first time you gave a speech
- [ ] The first time you wrote an essay
- [ ] A time you hurt yourself
- [ ] A very funny event
- [ ] A time when you cried
- [ ] Your first bike ride
- [ ] A memorable/favorite book
- [ ] A hospital stay
- [ ] Your first plane flight
- [ ] A day you met someone famous
- [ ] A death in the family
- [ ] Your First love
- [ ] The Day You Realized the Purpose for Life or for Your Life

Reflection of My Life...

When your Life Map is complete, answer the following questions:

- [ ] Imagine your life-map belongs to someone else. How do you feel about that person when you look at the life map?
- [ ] What values do you notice reflected in the important events?
- [ ] What would you change about your life-map if you could? Why?
- [ ] Where are you going in the future?
- [ ] List and describe 3 things you can do in your life stage now to make future life stages happen the way you'd like them to?

(https://www.iroquoiscsd.org/cms/lib/NY19000365/Centricity/Domain/79/Creating-a-life-map.ppt; https://www.edrawmind.com/how-to-create-a-life-map-with-examples.html)

Pillar: Legacy

WEEK 44

LESSON CYCLE:

1. Engage and Connect (10 min)

Have participants finish their Life Map activity from the previous week.

2. Lead Guided and Independent Practice (30 min)

Once they have completed their Life Map activity, have them complete the *'Reflection of My Life'* questions.

3. Close the Lesson and Assess Mastery (15 min)

Discuss the Quote: *"Life is a journey and only you hold the map."*

LOGISTICS: What materials, resources, and technology will I need to prepare and engage?

Computer
Microsoft teams
Pen
Paper or notebook
Life Map Activity

LESSON VOCABULARY WORDS

Instructions: Review vocabulary words listed below with the participants to ensure they have a good understanding of each before starting any of the activities.

1. **Acceptance**: the action or process of being received as adequate or suitable, typically to be admitted into a group.

2. **Memory:** something remembered from the past; a recollection.

3. **Impact**: The effect or influence of one person, thing, or action, on another.

4. **Life Map:** a visual timeline that traces key moments in your life from the time you were born until the present day.

Drawing a Life Map

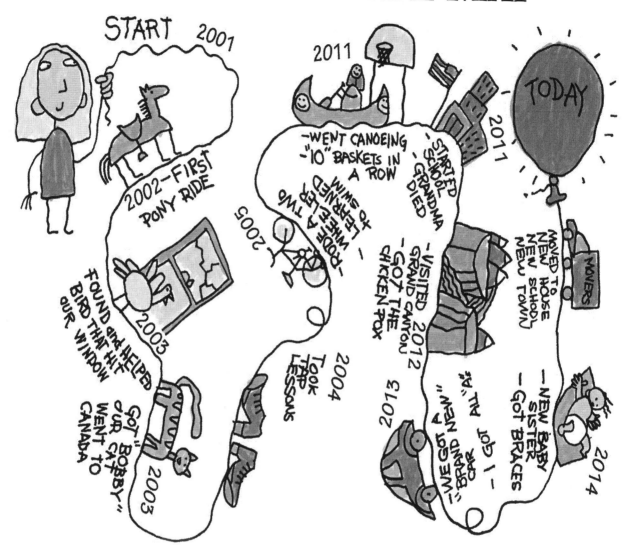

LESSON TITLE:

Living your Legacy

LEVEL: Employee or Community Citizen

WEEKS 43-44

PACING: 55 minutes

OBJECTIVE(S): What will Participants know, understand, and be able to do?

Participants will be able to understand the importance of leading by example.

KEY VOCABULARY: What key terms will my Participants need to understand?

Acceptance: the action or process of being received as adequate or suitable, typically to be admitted into a group.

Memory: something remembered from the past; a recollection.

Impact: The effect or influence of one person, thing, or action, on another.

Life Map: a visual timeline that traces key moments in your life from the time you were born until the present day.

WEEK 43

LESSON CYCLE:

1. Engage and Connect (10 min)

Introduce the activity: Creating a Life Map to the participants. Explain that a life map is a visual timeline. It traces the key moments in your life from the time you were born until the present day. The events and experiences you draw in your life map can make great starting points for writing topics, particularly for personal writing. Show participants the "Create a Map of Your Life" video clip: https://www.youtube.com/watch?v=e2n8n_8K4V0&t=40s

2. Lead Guided and Independent Practice (25 min)

Activity: Creating your Life Map. A life map tracks your journey through life and marks out important events along the way. Remember, an important event doesn't have to be exciting or memorable for others, the map is all about showing what is important to you.

a. Gather the materials you will use to create your Life Map (i.e. colored markers, pen, pencil, crayons, paper, etc.).
b. Start your life map with the day you were born. Include stories you have heard about your birth.
c. Record the dates of key moments in your life in time order. Your earliest childhood memory (describe in detail). Your most vivid childhood experiences. Your school years.
d. Draw each event to help you remember it.
e. End your life map with the present day.

Pillar: Legacy

3. Close the Lesson and Assess Mastery **(15 min)**

When your Life Map is complete, answer the following questions:

- Imagine your life-map belongs to someone else. How do you feel about that person when you look at the life map?
- What values do you notice reflected in the important events?
- What would you change about your life-map if you could? Why?
- Where are you going in the future?
- List and describe 3 things you can do in your life stage now to make future life stages happen the way you'd like them to?

What should your map include?

- ☐ A symbol or picture that represents each selected event. The picture should give an indication of how you felt about the event.
- ☐ A label which identifies and roughly dates the event. You can be creative and poetic with these labels e.g., the road to happiness on my new skateboard.
- ☐ Connectors between events which help the viewer understand the order in which they happened. The connectors can also indicate how the road between one event and another event are connected. What important lesson or understanding did you come to during this period of time?
  - ■ Some people use arrows, some people draw roads, some people draw a bunch of islands and draw little boats travelling between each; it is up to you how you see your map. Does your life map have a road map, a diagram, a geographical map, a maze, a swirling circle or a game of snakes and ladders?

Sample list to motivate your life map drawing:

- ☐ Day you were born
- ☐ Stories you have heard about your birth
- ☐ Your earliest childhood memory (describe in detail)
- ☐ Your most vivid childhood experiences
- ☐ Your school years
- ☐ A special trip you have taken
- ☐ A favorite meaningful thing/object you received from someone special
- ☐ The first time you gave a speech
- ☐ The first time you wrote an essay
- ☐ A time you hurt yourself
- ☐ A very funny event
- ☐ A time when you cried
- ☐ Your first bike ride
- ☐ A memorable/favorite book
- ☐ A hospital stay
- ☐ Your first plane flight
- ☐ A day you met someone famous
- ☐ A death in the family
- ☐ Your First love
- ☐ The Day You Realized the Purpose for Life or for Your Life

Reflection of My Life…

When your Life Map is complete, answer the following questions:

- ☐ Imagine your life-map belongs to someone else. How do you feel about that person when you look at the life map?
- ☐ What values do you notice reflected in the important events?
- ☐ What would you change about your life-map if you could? Why?
- ☐ Where are you going in the future?
- ☐ List and describe 3 things you can do in your life stage now to make future life stages happen the way you'd like them to? (https://www.iroquoiscsd.org/cms/lib/NY19000365/Centricity/Domain/79/Creating-a-life-map.ppt; https://www.edrawmind.com/how-to-create-a-life-map-with-examples.html)

WEEK 44

LESSON CYCLE:

1. Engage and Connect (10 min)

Have participants finish their Life Map activity from the previous week.

2. Lead Guided and Independent Practice (30 min)

Activity: Once they have completed their Life Map activity, have them complete the 'Reflection of My Life' questions.

Reflection of My Life…

When your Life Map is complete, answer the following questions:

- ☐ Imagine your life-map belongs to someone else. How do you feel about that person when you look at the life map?
- ☐ What values do you notice reflected in the important events?
- ☐ What would you change about your life-map if you could? Why?
- ☐ Where are you going in the future?
- ☐ List and describe 3 things you can do in your life stage now to make future life stages happen the way you'd like them to?

3. Close the Lesson and Assess Mastery (15 min)

Discuss the Quote: *"Life is a journey and only you hold the map."*

LOGISTICS: What materials, resources, and technology will I need to prepare and engage?

Computer
Microsoft teams
Pen
Paper or notebook

Pillar: Legacy

LESSON VOCABULARY WORDS

INSTRUCTIONS: Review vocabulary words listed below with the participants to ensure they have a good understanding of each before starting any of the activities.

1. **Acceptance**: the action or process of being received as adequate or suitable, typically to be admitted into a group.

2. **Memory:** something remembered from the past; a recollection.

3. **Impact**: The effect or influence of one person, thing, or action, on another.

4. **Life Map:** a visual timeline that traces key moments in your life from the time you were born until the present day.

Creating a Life Map

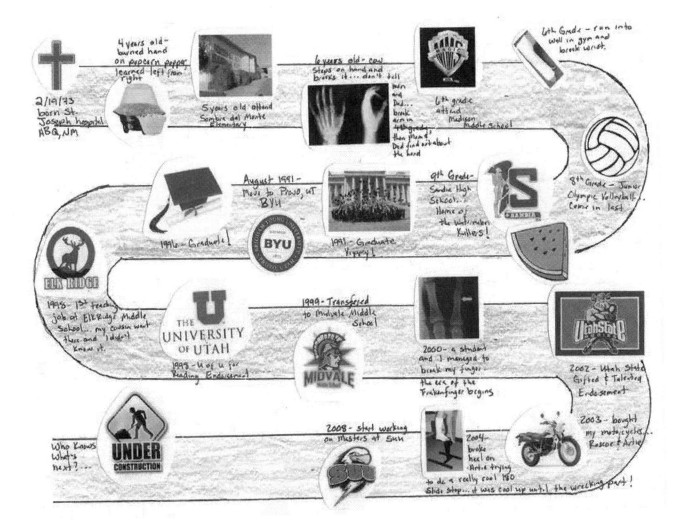

Pillar: Legacy

REFLECTION OF MY LIFE WORKSHEET

Instructions: Once they have completed their Life Map activity, complete the 'Reflection of My Life' questions.

1. Exchange your life-map with another participant in your group or with your mentor, after reviewing their life-map share how you feel about the person whose life-map you have reviewed.

   _____
   _____
   _____
   _____

2. What values do you notice reflected in the important events?

   _____
   _____
   _____
   _____

3. What would you change about your life-map if you could? Why?

   _____
   _____
   _____
   _____

4. Where are you going in the future?

   _____
   _____
   _____
   _____

5. List and describe 3 things you can do in your life stage now to make future life stages happen the way you'd like them to.

_____
_____
_____
_____

Pillar: Legacy

LESSON TITLE:

Creating a Legacy

LEVEL: Youth **WEEKS 45-46**

PACING: 55 minutes

OBJECTIVE(S): What will Participants know, understand, and be able to do?

Participants will be able to understand the importance of creating the legacy they want to leave by honoring loved one now.

KEY VOCABULARY: What key terms will my Participants need to understand?

Acceptance: the action or process of being received as adequate or suitable, typically to be admitted into a group.

Gratitude: the quality of being thankful; readiness to show appreciation for and to return kindness.

Legacy Letter: a written document of your values, experiences, and hard-earned life lessons.

WEEK 45

LESSON CYCLE:

1. Engage and Connect (15 min)

Many people desire to know where they come from, but a sense of belonging is especially important for children and youth. Some knowledge about their family history gives children of all ages a sense of their place in the world. It can also give young people something to live up to—a legacy to respect. Family history also provides an opportunity for children and teenagers to make a meaningful contribution to something bigger than themselves. Discuss with the youth what they know about their family and those family members who have died.

2. Lead Guided and Independent Practice (30 min)

Activity: Encourage participants to talk to their living relatives, especially the older ones. Hearing stories about what life was like in the past helps young people connect to the past. This connection brings generations together and establishes strong family bonds. Have the youth to ask the following interview questions and record their answers on their cell phones:

a. Where did you grow up?
b. What were your parents like? Your siblings?
c. What do you remember about your grandparents?
d. Who were your friends?
e. What was school like for you?
f. What did you do for fun when you were a child? when you were a teenager?
g. What movies and songs did you like when you were young?
h. How did you meet your spouse?

i. What important lessons have you learned in your life?

Have youth encourage their family members to tell the whole story about their life and the lives of their ancestors. Ask for the facts, dates, heirlooms, photographs, dates, etc. They need the facts and dates packaged in interesting, meaningful, and memorable ways. It is the best way to create an interesting video of their family history told by the people who experienced it. Have them fill their stories with interesting information, humorous details, and unusual facts that will capture a person's imagination. This doesn't have to be a big event. Make it a common occurrence around the dinner table, in the car, or at bedtime. Have the youth to schedule a time to show their video clip and discuss the video afterwards.

(htttps://www.familysearch.org/en/wiki/img_auth.php/6/65/Lesson_3_How_To_Involve_Children_In_Family_History.pdf)

3. *Close the Lesson and Assess Mastery* **(10 min)**

Have participants share one story that was shared with them by a loved one about a family member. Ask them what the story says about that person and how they now feel about him/her since the revelation.

LOGISTICS: What materials, resources, and technology will I need to prepare and engage?

Computer
Microsoft teams
Magazines
Pen/Crayons/Markers
Paper or notebook

Pillar: Legacy

WEEK 46

LESSON CYCLE:

1. Engage and Connect (10 min)

Recap activity from last week. Ask participants to talk about the videos they have already completed and how they feel about the activity.

2. Lead Guided and Independent Practice (30 min)

Creating your family tree.

Activity: From the video recordings and the conversations, have them create a family tree to track the family members they have talked to and those they have heard stories about. Have participants look those members up on the computer to see if they can find additional information about their family members that wasn't shared in their Genealogy videos. This will help them to keep track of the family members and their placement in the family tree. Provide the youth with the construction paper, crayons, markers, magazines, etc. they will need to create their family tree.

3. Close the Lesson and Assess Mastery (15 min)

Ask the participants to describe their experience. Did they learn things about their family members that they did not know? Did they hear any funny stories that taught them more information about their deceased and living family members?

LOGISTICS: What materials, resources, and technology will I need to prepare and engage?

Computer
Magazines/Glue/Pen/Crayons/Markers
Journal Pages
Family Tree Activity

LESSON VOCABULARY WORDS

INSTRUCTIONS: Study the vocabulary words listed below for a good understanding of each one.

1. **Acceptance**: the action or process of being received as adequate or suitable, typically to be admitted into a group.

2. **Gratitude:** the quality of being thankful; readiness to show appreciation for and to return kindness.

3. **Legacy Letter:** a written document of your values, experiences, and hard-earned life lessons.

Intentional Mentoring Mentor's Guide

LESSON TITLE:

Creating a Legacy

LEVEL: Employee
Community Citizen

WEEKS 45-46

PACING: 55 minutes

OBJECTIVE(S): What will Participants know, understand, and be able to do?

Participants will be able to understand the importance of creating the legacy they want to leave by honoring loved one now.

KEY VOCABULARY: What key terms will my Participants need to understand?

Acceptance: the action or process of being received as adequate or suitable, typically to be admitted into a group.

Gratitude: the quality of being thankful; readiness to show appreciation for and to return kindness.

Legacy Letter: a written document of your values, experiences, and hard-earned life lessons.

WEEK 45

LESSON CYCLE:

1. Engage and Connect **(15 min)**

So long as we breathe, there is an opportunity for each of us to live the legacy we want to leave. Part of preparing and living your legacy could include telling your stories to those who matter most to you. We all want to be remembered. Yes, you may have written your will and got all the legal stuff out of the way. But what about writing a personal letter to your family and friends to share with them about the importance they have played in your life. To thank them, remind them of your values, what you have learned from life, and perhaps the role they played in making your life richer and more precious. Show participants this video clip and discuss afterwards: https://www.youtube.com/watch?v=_LSqqbZj-Q8

2. Lead Guided and Independent Practice **(25 min)**

Activity: 15 Minutes and 5 Steps to Write Your Legacy Letter. Ask participants how important is working with others and collaborating?

a. **Who is this letter for**: Could be addressed to family in general, or a specific friend or relative.
b. **Thank you**: Write what you appreciate, what you're grateful for about this person(s).
c. **3 things life taught me**: Next list your life lessons. (You might just list one initially and later add others.)
d. **What matters most – your values**: Say what's really important to you. Start with at least one of your values and add more later.
e. **In closing...**: Finally, end your letter and sign off, possibly adding a special saying or poem you like.

Pillar: Legacy

Process/Instructions:

a. Use a letter format.
   1. Be clear on your context. Provide a snapshot of the times and circumstances surrounding the event
   2. Tell your story. Be open and honest in your writings.
   3. Learned wisdom. What wisdom have you gleaned for the experiences you are sharing.
   4. The closer. A blessing that flows from your story and learning to the interested recipients of your letter.
b. Time Yourself and write for 15 minutes and no more.
c. Present the letter to the individual to honor them for their impact on your life. (htttps://sixtyandme.com/write-legacy-letter/)

3. Close the Lesson and Assess Mastery (15 min)

After writing your legacy letter, write your reflections about your experience. Write for no more than 5-7 minutes. Keep your reflections with a copy of your letter in your personal legacy file. These 'process notes' are the mental complement to your heartfelt letter. They provide you with a different perspective about the experience of writing a legacy letter. It is an invaluable reflection – an opportunity to learn more about yourself and the values that matter most to you. (https://www.drweil.com/blog/spontaneous-happiness/legacy-writing-what-it-is-and-how-to-get-started/)

WEEK 46

LESSON CYCLE:

1. Engage and Connect   **(15 min)**

Recap activity from last week. Ask participants to write for five minutes on what they took away from the experience of writing their legacy letter.

2. Lead Guided and Independent Practice   **(30 min)**

Show participants this video clip: https://www.youtube.com/watch?v=WqOxDax2zpE&t=91s

Activity: Ask the participants to share either their reflections or their legacy letter. Each participant will have 5 minutes to share. Once each participant has shared their legacy letter/reflections, talk about the experience and if they will write legacy letters to other loved ones? You can even record the letter and provide the recipient with a digital copy and handwritten copy of the legacy letter.

3. Close the Lesson and Assess Mastery   **(15 min)**

Your legacy letter is a piece of your legacy and is also an opportunity for you to share your thoughts, appreciation, and thanks with loved ones. Consider keeping your copy of the legacy letter and reflections in a legacy box. Something that can be passed down from one generation to another like the family recipes. Take time to design your legacy box (provide participants with empty shoe boxes, construction paper, crayons, and markers). Begin during today's session and finish on your own time.

LOGISTICS: What materials, resources, and technology will I need to prepare and engage?

Computer
Pen
Journal Pages
Legacy Box Activity
5-Steps to Write Your Legacy Letter Activity

Pillar: Legacy

LESSON VOCABULARY WORDS

INSTRUCTIONS: Review vocabulary words listed below with the participants to ensure they have a good understanding of each before starting any of the activities.

1. **Acceptance**: the action or process of being received as adequate or suitable, typically to be admitted into a group.
2. **Gratitude**: the quality of being thankful; readiness to show appreciation for and to return kindness.
3. **Legacy Letter**: a written document of your values, experiences, and hard-earned life lessons.

5 STEPS TO WRITE YOUR LEGACY LETTER

A 15-Minute Activity using the following 5 Steps to Write Your Legacy Letter instructions.

a. **Who is this letter for**: Could be addressed to family in general, or a specific friend or relative.
b. **Thank you**: Write what you appreciate, what you're grateful for about this person(s).
c. **3 things life taught me**: Next list your life lessons. (You might just list one initially and later add others.)
d. **What matters most – your values**: Say what's really important to you. Start with at least one of your values and add more later.
e. **In closing…**: Finally, end your letter and sign off, possibly adding a special saying or poem you like.

Process/Instructions:

a. Use a letter format.
   1. Be clear on your context. Provide a snapshot of the times and circumstances surrounding the event
   2. Tell your story. Be open and honest in your writings.
   3. Learned wisdom. What wisdom have you gleaned for the experiences you are sharing.
   4. The closer. A blessing that flows from your story and learning to the interested recipients of your letter.
b. Time Yourself and write for 15 minutes and no more.
c. Present the letter to the individual to honor them for their impact on your life.

(https://sixtyandme.com/write-legacy-letter/)

Pillar: Legacy

LESSON TITLE:

A Living Legacy

LEVEL: Youth

WEEKS 47-48

PACING: 55 minutes

OBJECTIVE(S): What will Participants know, understand, and be able to do?

Participants will be able to identify the characteristics of a hero and how to become the hero in their own story.

KEY VOCABULARY: What key terms will my Participants need to understand?

Heroism: someone who shows great courage and valor through their words and/or actions.

Characteristics: a special quality or trait that makes a person, thing, or group different from others.

Social Responsibility: involves an individual who is accountable for fulfilling their civic duty and that benefits the whole of society.

WEEK 47

LESSON CYCLE:

1. Engage and Connect (15 min)

Have participants think about the individuals they consider as heroes and/or who they believe have superpowers. The people who inspire, encourage, and uplift them or who they want to be like when they grow up. In addition to treating people with dignity and respect, your heroes also stand because of their beliefs, skills and/or talents. Ask them what they see in the individual that makes them see themselves as a hero or someone with superpowers and why. On a whiteboard write down the values, talents and/or skills that are shared during the discussion. Look for a common theme and share it with the participants.

2. Lead Guided and Independent Practice (25 min)

What are personal heroes? Personal heroes are people who, in the opinion of others, has special achievements, abilities, or personal qualities and is regarded as a role model. A true hero is someone who does something heroic for the benefit of others. Their deed, act, performance, or accomplishment is not for their benefit alone.

Activity: Ask participants to make a list of their personal heroes. Their list should contain family members, celebrities, athletes, etc. People who display values and behaviors they want to emulate. Their list cannot be based upon the amount of money the person has but based on who they are as a person. (i.e., if they select a basketball/football/soccer/tennis player, who are they off the court/field, when they are on the court do they display great sportsmanship.)

3. *Close the Lesson and Assess Mastery* (15 min)

Ask the participants if it is hard for them to admit their mistakes? Why or Why not?

Share with the participants that real life heroes change the world.

LOGISTICS: What materials, resources, and technology will I need to prepare and engage?

Computer
Pen/Journal Pages
Hero Diagram Worksheet
Characteristics of a Hero Worksheet

Pillar: Legacy

WEEK 48

LESSON CYCLE:

1. Engage and Connect (10 min)

Recap thoughts, and themes from last week about *a Living Legacy* with your participants.

2. Lead Guided and Independent Practice (30 min)

Show participants this video clip and discuss afterwards. https://www.youtube.com/watch?v=4a5DyupH9rM or https://www.youtube.com/watch?v=1g82D68N-ys

Activity: Have the participants to complete the *Hero Diagram Form* provided with this lesson plan. Once they have finished the form, conduct a group discussion on what they learned about the hero and them being a living legacy.

INSTRUCTIONS: Show participants the video, have them identify the hero in the story, and write down the five things he/she did that identifies him/her as a hero. Have the participants share their list of characteristics of the hero from the video clip with the group during the discussion period.

Characteristics of a hero

1. Bravery
2. Conviction
3. Courage
4. Determination
5. Helpful
6. Honesty
7. Inspirational
8. Moral integrity
9. Protective
10. Self-sacrifice
11. Selflessness
12. Strength

(https://www.verywellmind.com/characteristics-of-heroism-2795943#toc-12-characteristics-of-heroism)

3. Close the Lesson and Assess Mastery (15 min)

Share that people who engage in acts of heroism have concern and care for the people around them, have a desire to inspire, empower and enable them to step up for what they believe in and be the hero in their own story. Ask what this statement means to them.

LOGISTICS: What materials, resources, and technology will I need to prepare and engage?

Computer
Pen/Journal Pages
Hero Diagram Worksheet
Characteristics of a Hero Worksheet

Pillar: Legacy

LESSON VOCABULARY WORDS

INSTRUCTIONS: Review vocabulary words listed below with the participants to ensure they have a good understanding of each before starting any of the activities.

1. **Heroism:** someone who shows great courage and valor through their words and/or actions.

2. **Characteristics:** a special quality or trait that makes a person, thing, or group different from others.

3. **Social Responsibility:** involves an individual who is accountable for fulfilling their civic duty and that benefits the whole of society.

CHARACTERISTICS OF A HERO

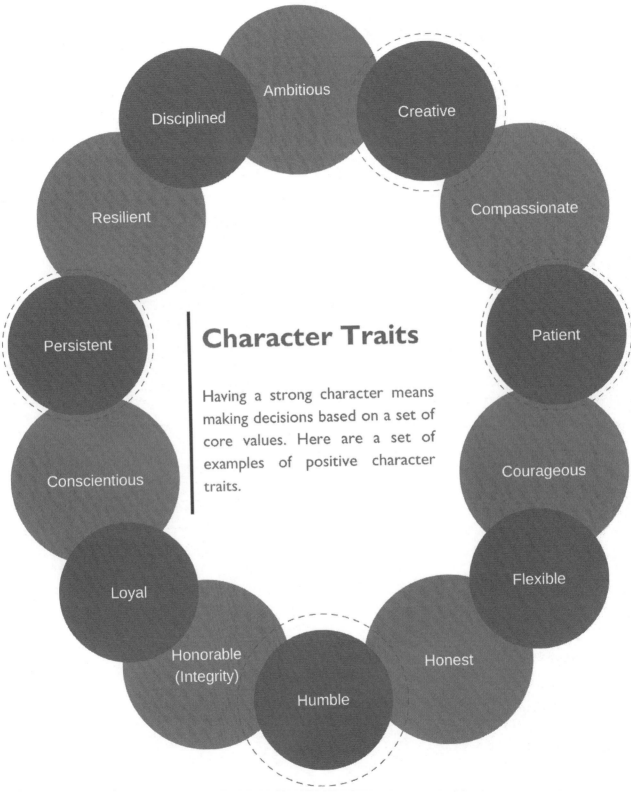

Character Traits

Having a strong character means making decisions based on a set of core values. Here are a set of examples of positive character traits.

Pillar: Legacy

HERO DIAGRAM WORKSHEET

For sections #1-5, write evidence or ideas that describe a hero from the video clip.

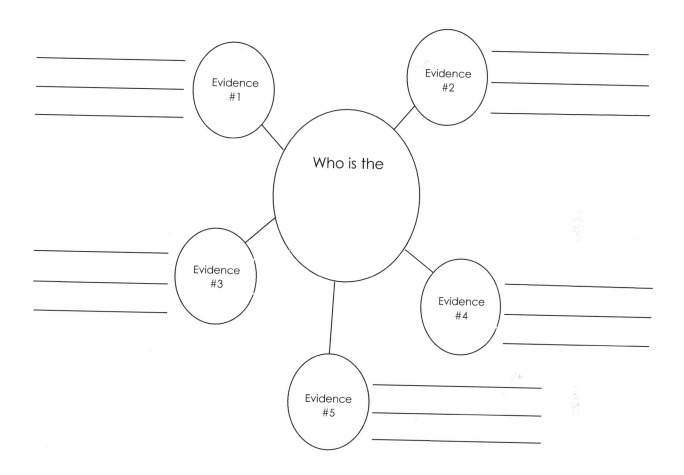

367 | Page

LESSON TITLE:

A Living Legacy

LEVEL: Employee or Community Citizen

WEEKS 47-48

PACING: 55 minutes

OBJECTIVE(S): What will Participants know, understand, and be able to do?

Participants will be able to identify the characteristics of a hero and how to become the hero in their own story.

KEY VOCABULARY: What key terms will my Participants need to understand?

Heroism: someone who shows great courage and valor through their words and/or actions.

Characteristics: a special quality or trait that makes a person, thing, or group different from others.

Social Responsibility: involves an individual who is accountable for fulfilling their civic duty and that benefits the whole of society.

WEEK 47

LESSON CYCLE:

1. Engage and Connect **(15 min)**

In the last lesson we talked about creating a legacy. In this lesson we are going to continue that thought by using what we have learned to live a lasting legacy. Think about the following quote and discuss ways in which you can live a lasting legacy.

"The greatest legacy anyone can leave behind is to positively impact the lives of others. Whenever you add value to other people's lives, you are unknowingly leaving footprints on the sands of time that live on, even after your demise." – Emeasoba George

2. Lead Guided and Independent Practice **(25 min)**

Living a legacy means putting a stamp on the future and contributing to future generations. (*Ask participants how they can put their stamp on the future?*) Facilitator/Mentor continues sharing: People want to leave a legacy because they want to feel that their life mattered. Legacy is more about sharing what you have learned, not just what you have earned, and bequeathing values over valuables, as material wealth is only a small fraction of your legacy. A more holistic definition of legacy is when you are genuinely grounded in offering yourself and making a meaningful, lasting, and energizing contribution to humanity by serving a cause greater than your own. The requirements of a legacy are that you embrace your uniqueness, passionately immersing your whole self into life so that your gift will be to all and that you take responsibility to ensure that it will have a life beyond that of you, its creator, outliving and outlasting your time on earth (*Ask participants what is unique about them and what talent, skill or ability do they have that can be used to live the legacy they desire to leave?*). (https://meridianlifedesign.com/about-legacy/what-is-legacy/)

Activity: Create a relationship with the future and live into it before it appears! Choose one of the following activities to begin living the legacy you want to leave. Create a plan of action on how you can complete the activity you have chosen.

a. Become committed to writing down your thoughts and memories daily in a Journal.
b. Create a recipe journal with family stories attached to each recipe.
c. Research and select a cause or non-profit that supports your family's beliefs. Donate your time and finances as a means of support. Keep pictures and videos of your interactions with the cause or non-profit to share with your family and friends.
d. Create a plan to plant a tree to honor the birth of each child born in the family on family land or in a park your family visits often.
e. Plan a family gathering to honor your family's elders and set aside time for them to share their hopes, dreams, and wisdom with the family. Record it and make copies for each family to have one.

3. Close the Lesson and Assess Mastery **(15 min)**

Ask the participants what they believe the author was trying to say with the following quote: "*Carve your name on hearts, not tombstones. A legacy is etched into the minds of others and the stories they share about you.*" – Shannon L. Adler.

WEEK 48

LESSON CYCLE:

1. Engage and Connect **(15 min)**

Recap thoughts, and themes from last week about *A Living Legacy* with your participants. Ask about the activity they selected and where they are in their planning stages.

2. Lead Guided and Independent Practice **(30 min)**

Show participants this video clip and discuss afterwards. https://www.youtube.com/watch?v=DwKBxabn4QY

Discussion: Facilitator/Mentor lead the participants in a discussion from the first questions asked in the video clip:

   a. Why does anyone need a coach/mentor?
   b. Do you have any goals? What are your aspirations?
   c. Does this poem mean anything to you?
   d. What are you afraid of?
   e. How did he tell Akeelah to show up?

3. Close the Lesson and Assess Mastery **(10 min)**

Discuss the Quote and tell how it applies to today's session: "*Your story is the greatest legacy that you will leave to your friends, family and loved ones. It's the longest lasting legacy you will leave to your heirs.*" – Steve Saint

LOGISTICS: What materials, resources, and technology will I need to prepare and engage?

Computer
Legacy Planner
Pen
Journal Pages

Pillar: Legacy

LESSON VOCABULARY WORDS

INSTRUCTIONS: Review vocabulary words listed below with the participants to ensure they have a good understanding of each before starting any of the activities.

1. **Heroism**: someone who shows great courage and valor through their words and/or actions.

2. **Characteristics**: a special quality or trait that makes a person, thing, or group different from others.

3. **Social Responsibility**: involves an individual who is accountable for fulfilling their civic duty and that benefits the whole of society.

what is my legacy?

LEGACY #1:

WHAT AM I DOING TO CULTIVATE & GROW HEALTHY ROOTS IN THIS AREA?

LEGACY #2

LEGACY #3

kristagilbert.com

Pillar: Legacy

What will your legacy be? Fill these steppingstones with things you want people to remember about you.

Build your legacy!

Leave a Legacy...

"no legacy is so rich as honesty."

WILLIAM SHAKESPEARE

ABOUT THE AUTHOR

Dr. Kenneth D. Davis, Ph.D.

Dr. Kenneth D. Davis recently retired from the Houston Independent School District as their Executive Director of Equity and Outreach. Prior to this role, he was the Area Superintendent of the South Region, Assistant Superintendent of Equity and Outreach, Principal at Jack Yates High School, School Support Officer (principal supervisor), and Principal at Dowling (now Lawson) Middle School. He has had many titles and positions in the past 31 years, which began in the classroom molding and educating young minds.

Dr. Davis has a lengthy and successful track record in the business of education. Starting from the classroom he rose from classroom teacher to being selected as the campus teacher of the year, but the accolades were far from over. Dr. Davis became an assistant principal after his assistant superintendent noticed his flare and magic with teaching and 'encouraged' him to pursue a master's degree in educational administration. In doing so, he learned the role well and became a principal in the Lamar Consolidated Independent Schools within four years.

In the Lamar Consolidated Independent Schools, Dr. Davis moved the school from low performing to an Exemplary status with the support of an open-minded and hardworking staff. After two consecutive years, Dr. Davis was assigned to open a new elementary campus, McNeill, and that school also experienced Exemplary Campus performance. Dr. Davis had been nominated and selected as the Houston Area Alliance of Black School Educator's Teacher of the year, Principal of the Year twice) and awarded the National Distinguished Principal (NDP) for Texas Award, the highest honor an educator can receive.

Dr. Davis continues to share his knowledge and experience in supporting students by creating and developing districtwide mentoring programs like the Ascending To Men (ATM) and Resilient Outstanding Sisters Exemplifying Success (ROSES) that support students in need of mentorship as they matriculate through the educational system successfully and on to a career, college, and/or the military. He continues to be a positive and supportive force in education.

Dr. Davis credits his long-lasting career in education to building relationships, honoring education for all students, growing and developing teachers, and working to build strong instructional and visionary leaders. He works countless hours teaching at the University of Houston to guide instructional leaders to build reading skills for students that struggle and teaching the Equity in The Classroom course. Dr. Davis speaks and presents to future leaders across the country and has worked with several organizations to build and support future administrators through Columbia University and Birmingham City Schools. He mentors current principals, deans, assistant principals, instructional specialists, and teachers.

Made in the USA
Columbia, SC
28 October 2022